# GRIFFRI

## CHRISTOPHER MEREDITH

SEREN BOOKS

SEREN BOOKS is the book imprint of
**Poetry Wales Press Ltd**
Andmar House, Tondu Road, Bridgend, Mid Glamorgan


© Christopher Meredith, 1991


ISBN   1-85411-059-4

Printed in Plantin by WBC Print Ltd, Bridgend

Also by Christopher Meredith

*Poetry*
This
Snaring Heaven

*Novel*
Shifts

# Contents

## NOTE

One piece of Griffri's poetry is a loose translation of a medieval fragment. Other pieces are sometimes modelled on early or medieval Welsh poems though none is a translation.

The story Griffri tells in The Second Hearth draws on tales from a number of countries, principally North America.

All of the people in this story are fictional, including the ones who really existed.

# The First Hearth

# 1

Listen, Idnerth. I've been called a paid arselicker and I'm proud enough of my job to consider that a kind of compliment. After all, who with any sense would do such a thing if they weren't getting paid? For a meal and the high regard of your household I can give your ancestry back to Brutus, obscurely sing your praises, fix with my craft your greatness, your generosity, your et cetera, and do it with words strong enough to make quiver the chin of your most cruel soldier. You will welcome me to your feast, set a high place for me, only a little below your distain and your meadbearer, let me in among your women to entertain them privately — though that I'll admit is a little below my professional status — and you will love me and respect me because I am he who has sung before a dozen princes, who's not above telling the odd story as a lucrative hobble, who's sung to the teulu drawn in battle order, who is the keeper of memory, the lister of the dead, and I am he who affirms the road you choose, or, since god allows even princes only a little freedom, the road that chooses you.

(All right. So you're not a prince, I know. You Cistercians get so literal.)

There's a saying that truth is the best song. Quite a few poets, even I, would go along with this, and when I turn to make my deathbed song, which may be shortly the way things are going, I'll be a true penitent and utter only truth. In the meantime, though, praise for the mighty pays nicely.

All this sounds, perhaps, a little spineless, but you know well enough that my job's not without commitment. I've only got to think of Gwrgant to remind myself of that. You don't know about him? He's one for this great book of yours. Lister of the dead did I say? How can we put what we are into items on a list? Your chronicle and my recitation of genealogies are so much dust. That's where song of either tongue or instrument can do something real, once in a while anyway. It can tell us what we are. But not too often or the clients get put off.

Gwrgant ap Rhys was my master in poetry. I was saying it's not all arselicking. My own prince, Iorwerth of Gwynllwg and his family have taken risks once in a while. Iorwerth will make war when he has to and raids when he has the opportunity, and you've seen yourself he's not a young man. Older than your Arglwydd Rhys. He must be pushing fifty.

You know there are enough Frenchmen hereabouts who'd have me hacked to bits if they had a chance, and a few Welshmen too. All right, we've been together in the recent wars, more or less. But my own master in poetry, Gwrgant ap Rhys, who was — although I'm not impartial I say this unblushingly — the greatest poet that ever sang, was butchered by a most accomplished thug who happened not to be French. That's what comes of being in the teulu of a prince who loses.

I'll tell you about that later. There's plenty of time from now to your Night Office or whatever you call it. There's enough wood and you people don't work hard enough to need to sleep. You want to know about my country and how I came to learn my trade, you say.

Listen.

## 2

My career was broached by the death of my father.

Although he was only a poor man and living in an out of the way enough place not to have to bother himself with arms, he distinguished himself in battle in the service of Owain Wan, the father of Iorwerth, who was then more or less ruling Gwynllwg. Owain was an old man and at this time gradually yielding power to another of his sons, Morgan.

The nature of my father's distinction is obscure, though I'm told it was to do with killing a man and giving his fine horse to this Morgan. Whatever it was, when my father died gloriously and in agony of his wounds following some skirmish or other, I was about nine years old. Owain himself had recently died — of old age I'm ashamed to say — and Morgan decided to reward us in memory of his father. His reward to our hearth, which was poor and not within a day's walking of any court the prince kept, was to take this child from his mother and put him to an apprenticeship in poetry.

Apparently my father had boasted to Owain and in the presence of Morgan in that doting sort of way that fathers often have more than mothers when it comes to children — I think it comes of the fact that we don't have to clean up the shit after them — anyway, he'd boasted that his youngest loved to sing. This had lodged without particular reason in Morgan's mind. So we're shaped by the tides that run in important heads.

How can I tell you what I was then? Remembering can be a constant sorting out, a putting of things into lists, even. Now is a kind of chaos, a brink we teeter on endlessly. So when in remembering we sort things out, we miss the point of what it was actually like.

Our house on the treeline I remember best because we lived there in the summer. If I smell wormwood I remember the place. My mother hung withered bunches of it, and white wormwood, everywhere to keep the flies away. There were a few pigs among the trees and on the pasture were the goats who seemed to carry their lives on regardless of us, except when we caught one to milk or kill.

The house was high on the east side of the valley, in a southward angled curve of pasture just below the heathery mountain back. The curve sharpened down the mountain into a deep cleft thick with trees that ran south at first and then turned westward as it opened out near the valley floor, where there were a few clearings for oats and meadowland and the house where we spent most of the winter.

We knew every tree and rock in that cleft and every stony handbreadth of the stream that ran in it. Although my mother would warn us about the boar when she wanted us at home she'd send us out into the trees if she wanted, say, angelica gathered at the end of summer, against the winter colds.

I knew the best places for it and one I kept secret, where a big tree grew sideways out of the steep mountain. I thought that fallen tree was a miracle or the work of people from under the ground to build a bridge across to the other mountain. The angelica grew in a lush churning of wet earth where the roots had wrenched and skewed in some old storm. Through the tangle of stems there was a dark opening that frightened me, so of course it drew me as foxgloves draw bees. When the sun shone, I liked to sit there in the wood's light-splashes by the oozing ferny entrance into the mud and at the end of the bridge that led into the air.

The place held its own silence which terrified me and excited me. Now I can think it was just I who was being quiet for a change and perhaps it was my own inaction frightened me. That and the fact that it was sheltered from the wind and that there was no stream of any consequence nearby and so no sound of water.

I will never know any other place so well. It was an intimacy that never came back to me after I was taken away. Yet in another sense I didn't know it. I didn't know where or how it was. The world extended first to as far as I could crawl outside the door, then to a few bowshots, and then to as far as we'd dare walk in half a day.

One day in spring my father took me up on the mountain. He pointed what must have been north to where a far mountain spread two peaks in the sun.

'That's Cadair Arthur' he said, 'in another country.'

And then he raised his other arm southward. I think he looked something like me, with darkish hair, a wide mouth, wide set eyes and a small nose. He didn't keep his moustache so trim as I do, though, nor did he shave his chin so often.

'And that' he said, 'that tiny piece of something that glints like a wet blade turned in firelight is Môr Hafren. The sea.'

He stood with his arms outstretched and fingers spread smiling down at me.

I asked what 'the sea' was and he dropped his arms and tried to explain, but I wouldn't believe him.

My mother explained to me how the mountains were made in a much more credible way. Once in a blizzard Gogrfran Oer the giant came from the north to hunt the great boar and in their struggle the frozen spikes of Gogrfran's beard and the jabs of his javelin scored the valleys in the earth. The cleft of hill we lived above in summer was gouged by his porridge finger when he scrambled to his feet in some part of the battle.

Of course, when I did my apprenticeship with Gwrgant I learnt the variants on this story but I still use that old version for the children sometimes. When I think about the shape of those mountains I'm half inclined to believe it.

I think she must have told us the story in winter to try to keep us out of danger. When you're young and there's a storm you get excited and enjoy it. You go and run round in it. When you're a bit older you sit there miserable and worry about the rooftree. I used to get out and try to go up to the top house in winter, especially if there was snow up there, which there sometimes would be even if there was none on the valley floor. My brothers or somebody generally caught me before I got very far and gave me a good thump. But if I got away I'd spend whatever daylight there was at the hafod and on the frozen moor.

It was in winter too that I remember us going to church. It was a long way. To a child it was the edge of the earth. I dimly remember my father on the mountain — perhaps it was the time he spread his arms to try to say the extent of things, I don't know' but I remember him pointing westward to Twyn yr Hyddod and the deer were moving there in nervous groups and then swinging his arm left, southward, where the mountain across the valley swelled and then pointing, making the shape of a polecat's back with his arm to show that he meant the other side of the highest place and saying,

'That's where Sannan's church is, where you've been once for god and the angels to name you Griffri ap Berddig.'

I must have been very young not to have been there since. There were no more namings after my time because I was the last and my mother's days for giving birth were finished. So I suppose we most often made the long journey to the church in winter when one of us died.

It was as it is everywhere. In summer occasionally someone would die after a chronic slackness of the bowels. In winter we would suffocate from the inside, or just freeze. My mother would say sometimes that god was hurting us for the time when Caradog had led the men to fight on the side of the French, and that was the first time I heard of Frenchmen. I remember thinking, in that way that children have of questioning what's assumed and fundamental in the world, that it was odd to suffer every year for things that had happened before we were born.

One of my sisters, in fact my favourite sister, Mallt, had a baby girl that died, and my mother took her distaff and beat one of my brothers nearly senseless. My brother shouted something that made my mother stop and she stared at him, but then Mallt, who was dying too, said that it had been her cousin, a taeog tied to the churchlands over the mountain, whom she'd met at a funeral the year before. This made my mother even more angry and she went out into the snow and cried.

There was a terrible freeze and there were scooped heaps of snow on the meadow that reminded me of the shape of Cadair Arthur. My father was away — serving Morgan I think — and I stood next to my mother, not understanding why she was crying.

There was no way to the church. My mother hugged her daughter and her granddaughter and in the end she buried them both at the edge of the meadow, breaking the frozen ground to start with using the sledded axe that we kept for slaughtering cows.

Of course, ordinarily we would have kept the corpses until after a thaw, when the ways would be less difficult and the river Gwedog might be fordable, but I think she couldn't bear the thought of watching time ruin what was left of her children.

I don't remember what my father's reaction to all this was. Perhaps this was at the time he was wounded. Nor do I remember what the priest said, if he ever found out. I remember my mother praying at a muddy heap of clods at the edge of the clearing among a spatter of spring flowers in sunlight and it must have been then that she talked about making a pilgrimage to one of Dyfrig's shrines in Erging. She had a childhood memory of having been there once and I think dreamed of asking him to intercede for the baby's soul, as well as Mallt's and her own. I don't know whether she ever knew that Dyfrig's bones had been moved from Enlli to Caerdyf years before. As I say, it was an out of the way place. News of that sort would never come through, especially if you didn't get to church much.

Perhaps I've made it sound as though we were well to do, but the land wasn't much good. The winters were quite bad, relatively, though I didn't realize that at the time. We had a handful of cattle but I believe they had a habit of dying at inconvenient moments. I may have invented this, but I think I remember my father and eldest brother making bows and going out one evening with serious faces and coming back in the dark with a couple of new cows. We had what peace we did because the place was too poor for people to choose to live there and it wasn't on the way to anywhere else. Even huntsmen were very rare, though I once saw the priest and his wife on horseback picking their way over Twyn yr Hyddod and he had a hawk on his hand.

My brothers would hunt sometimes, or lift trout from the Gwedog while the others worked. I'd trail behind with a halfsized bow and any twig I could find for an arrow and upset the rest by asking loud and irrelevant questions at the crucial moment when they had their weapons poised. Sometimes I'd extemporize one of those great compositions of which my father had boasted— badgers, hedgehogs and soup, I seem to remember, were the major motifs of my work at that time — just as someone's fingers were about to close in the belly of a trout. This, you can imagine, didn't greatly increase my popularity with those tree kings and river princes, my brothers, so I was often banished to the top or bottom house, depending on the time of year, where my art could be better used to torture the pigs or my sisters.

At reaping time I'd stumble about among the oats picking them by hand one panicle at a time until my fingers were raw and I felt sorry for myself. The world, you see, is either miraculous or hellish, or both. The first oathead was a tree, a blond, handsized willow, a piece of whiskery sun that spoke marvels in its rays and branches. The last was a prickly old demon who spat fire on my hands and lacerated me with terrible satires.

I think this must be half invented. It seems bright in my mind, but that's nothing to go on. I'm not sure whether I remember my sense of my own importance then or I'm creating that out of what I've observed in my own children since. But let's say I did have a sense of how important I was then, though I suppose my family viewed me other ways. When the time came for me to be taken away I was just coming to an age when I could be genuinely useful about the place, so I've never known whether they watched me leave that day with sadness or gratitude.

### 3

I have some impressions from around that time. The stronger the memory the harder it is to sort it into a neat place. Sequence and reason don't came into it.

I remember Gwrgant's face as it was then. Smooth, thinnish, young. He had black hair. He shaved his upper lip as well as his chin which made me think at first he was a priest.

He smiles and shows me where I must sleep. I stand for hours watching him at work or eating. He lets me follow like an orphaned lamb. He keeps his harps away from the damp, but not close to the fire. He has a candle and a smooth table and parchment — the first time I've seen these outside a church — so I decide he must be a priest.

I ask him to hear my confession and he laughs.

'When I sing, you'll hear my confession' he says.

And he sings a few lines of his boastsong, which I can't understand because of the long words and their disjointed manner, and I'm frightened because I think there are devils in him. He stops suddenly and looks at me in silence.

I remember from an earlier time being pulled onto a horse by man wearing leather shoes. He smells strange and is thinner than my father. The man sings songs which I can't understand and gives me strips of dry meat from a pouch. He has two spears and lets me hold the smaller of these until my arm gets tired. As we ride, the dark wattle house on the edge of the trees where my mother and the four cows are goes away in to the distance behind us and my sisters are watching and my brothers are waving, but my mother has gone into the trees. He rides up onto the mountain where my father took me and we go south through the heather for a long time. And there is a man with sunken cheeks and carefully trimmed red moustache. It's indoors, the biggest room I've ever seen, and smoky and men are laughing. The red man wears a torc of twisted iron and he's close to my face, smiling. I'm trying to sing. I've been asked to sing. I falter and there are sympathetic laughing noises and I'm ashamed and look at my feet.

I look up and there's another man who looks just like the red man except that his hair is darker. He stands with his weight one foot, his head turned to one side, looking at me and the red man.

And another time — I don't know if it's the first time I go to my master Gwrgant — there's a small boy, a little smaller than I am and he's Gwrgant's son, Cadwallon. He has dark hair but his skin is very white. He has some fluffy yellow stuff in his hand which he says is bread, but I don't believe him because it's nothing like the bread we occasionally had in my home. Still, I take it from him because he's smaller than I am and it tastes all right. Cadi says nothing to Gwrgant, though his brown eyes speak their hurt .

Cadi and I and Gwrgant and his wife Non and their little daughter Mair and an unidentified two year old with a vicious bite share a mattress, but Gwrgant is often away at Morgan's court and it isn't so warm so I snuggle to the master's wife. When she's asleep I examine her because she's not like my mother, more like Mallt was, with squashy white skin and big breasts that through her offwhite shift feel as hot as and softer than a sow's dugs. But sometimes I call Non 'mam' by mistake and this makes me blush. When I've finished this inspection I try to climb over her to be nearer to the fire.

There's a river wider than any I've ever seen and I'm amazed at the flatness of the land along its banks and at so large an area low down yet clear of trees. I recognise oats and there are beehives on meadowland and other stuff that I've seen in other places, small areas of it, when I was on the horse with the leather shoe man. Wheat, Cadi says.

Cadi shows me how to catch trout with my hands as I've seen my brothers do. He tells me names for the colours on a fish and names for trees. We make up verses. Well, he makes up verses and I try to. Another time I'm better at it and we make up verses answering one another. He gets me to warble the words like Gwrgant. We play games repeating sounds.

The unidentified biter is with us sometimes when we play and he irritates me. Cadi is very patient with him and even seems to like him. Cadi tickles him so that his body draws together like the mouth of a purse and he laughs and goes a dangerous shade of red, as though the blood is going to burst from his face. Cadi keeps this up until the unidentified is no longer amused and contrives a position, drawn in as he is, from which he can exercise his art on the knee of the poet's son with such precision and enthusiasm that two crescents of red wounds open there.

Cadi hops away, preferring not to comment on this turn of events, while the unidentified lies quietly where he's been left, his head to one side, smiling coyly.

Sometimes when Cadi and I play, the unidentified stands between us facing Cadi to break the game. When we play a rivalry of verses he shouts loudly when it's my turn. He shouts such pieces of information as: 'Milk in the cow' and 'Hedgehog in the water.'

I begin to like him at this point. He is as I was. I am as my brothers were.

Gwrgant teaches us in the mornings. Non and Mair abduct the un-

identified at these times in the name of education. We chant genea-
logies. Gwrgant raps a ruler on the table. When Cadi falters Gwrgant
is harsh but when I falter he is not so harsh. Morgan ab Owain Wan
ap Caradog ap Gruffudd ap Cetera has, it seems to me, an unreason-
able number of ancestors. Cadi and I agree he should have made do
with half a dozen like the rest of us.

One day I get right through from Morgan to Adda without hesitat-
ing or making anyone the grandson of their own son or suchlike.
Gwrgant and Cadi, who have been smiling unnaturally and nodding
at every name and leaning forward with their hands raised all through
my recitation, suddenly relax as if they've just thrown down some
terrible burden after carrying it up the mountain, and for the rest of
the day we practise archery.

Other days we learn law triads and grave verses. We sing them
without understanding, though I recognise many of the names from
the genealogies.

> Whose grave is this in Gwent Iscoed?
> Oak door of Glywys, maker of strewmeat,
> Tewdrig Sant in winding sheet.

> Whose is this grave on Gwy's green bank?
> Tewdrig Cleftskull, English he scattered,
> For Glywys in his dotage martyred.

> Who's buried here at Nant Pencarn?
> Caradog ap Gruffudd, king of men.
> At Mynydd Carn ravens made his crown.

Gwrgant says to me, 'We'll make a verse for your father, Griffri.
He was a brave man and for years people will sing his name.'

He looks at me then. Something about the way I look makes him
quiet. He puts his cupped hand to the side of my head and holds it
there a moment.

'Not yet, eh? Sometimes no song is best.'

Gwrgant tells us stories. Sometimes they have singing in them and
sometimes I enjoy them, though they're not as good as the funny
stories Non tells me at night. Gwrgant's stories often make me tired
and have words I don't understand. He makes us learn them by
heart, a piece at a time. We learn the singing first and then the spoken

parts that aren't poetry. Cadi already knows some of these and tries to whisper them to me when I forget. When Gwrgant notices he is angry with Cadi, not with me.

In the big smoky room Cadi tunes his father's harp. The shutters are back and the afternoon light makes the fire look dull, the smoke solid. People carry big dishes. The red man and the man who looks like him sit together and a small boy is with them, younger than I am. I ask Cadi who the red man is. He looks up.

'Don't point. That's Morgan ab Owain your own patron, stupid.'

It's quiet while we eat and while a priest says a prayer. Then there's a lot of talking and Gwrgant sings. I don't understand much of what he sings, but I hear Morgan and god mentioned. The people call out requests and he does some verses where people join in sometimes, and some of them are grave verses and I join in too and Cadi does some verses on his own and then there's a lot of shouting and people smile and then Gwrgant turns to me and smiles his unnatural smile and motions me forward and I sing a verse on my own and then there's a shout so loud it frightens me. I feel a burst of uncontrollable pride.

Afterwards Gwrgant takes us to a room where there are a lot of women. Gwrgant says a lot of things I don't understand except that he often uses the names of men in the court. He sings some poems quietly and tells a story. One of the women is young and very beautiful. She wears footless stockings as Mallt did, with a tongue covering the upper part of her foot and a cord at its point tied around her second toe. She has on her hand a silver ring mounted with a large square stone the colour of campion. The edge of the sky turns that colour sometimes in the evenings in this place. I've noticed this because it's different from the sky around my home and I think perhaps there is a different sun here. I'm surprised when the unidentified rushes in and with him another child, a little older, with reddish hair, and the young woman embraces them and plays with them. Her name is Angharad.

I dream. Sometimes when Cadi coughs in the night I wake and snatch at the tail of the dream. Cadi goes to what's left of the fire and squats on his haunches. He rakes air into his throat and spits on the embers, then blows making a bubbling sound in his windpipe. In the dream I'm travelling very fast and without effort high over the ground as if I'm a bird flying. There's the trackless mass of trees and strips of mountain ridges and the thread of river like sour milk. The sky is dark blue and red like bruises. I swoop down and then up to miss smashing into the crowns of the trees and I see the bruised air and the black horizon. I come to a figure standing on the heather. He stands with his arms flung out, the fingers spread, like branches. I come close to his face, to his untidy red moustache and his head has been split by an appalling wound.

He whispers, 'I am Terddig the martyr, stupid.'

He goes small into the distance very quickly and I turn and swoop down into the trees. The air's dark as if there'll be a storm. At the edge of the clearing an old woman is lying face down on the grass.

Cadi coughs. He dries his lips on his sleeve.


## 4

Slowly I learnt the shape of this new world.

Gwrgant's house was big and long to me then. There was a byre separate from the house and a stable and a small house where a family of taeogion lived, all this at the edge of the meadow, and a couple of apple trees. It's in a sheltered place and it's there that I first remember seeing martins build their nests, taking mud from the rivers and the places where the cattle trod. I called them 'little magpies' at first when I talked to Cadi about them because of their colouring, which amused him greatly and gave him another point about which he could feel superior. He told his father about this name in our next lesson. Gwrgant was quiet a moment and put his fingers to his lips.

'Griffri' he said at last, 'that's very good. We'll use that in a poem somewhere. Remind me if you hear a likely place for it. Like people birds take bits of mud from the world and weave them into places where they can be alive. We do the same thing with words.'

I don't remember if I exchanged a look with Cadi then, but I imagine I did and I can imagine how it was.

The house was a short distance from the court. There was a stretch of woods between the edge of Gwrgant's meadow and the court land but a track was beaten through it and it was — still is — easily passable when it's not too wet. It seemed to me a populous area with homes fitted in wherever there was a piece of pasture and quite a few houses of taeogion. In a day's walking there was a good chance that you'd meet at least one person.

I say the court — in fact it was Iorwerth's home then, and one of the places Morgan used, not the main one either. Not that I understood much of that. It was built on a cliff of split and plated rock that seemed to me then immense. Some large trees somehow clung near the top so that when they were in leaf the palisade along the cliff's edge was almost invisible. At the foot of the rocks the trees were cleared and there was a rolling meadow almost to the river — not the big river I mentioned, I'll come to that — and then trees impassably dense south and eastward except to those familiar with the way. The only ways to the court are a long incline through trees from the west — the way we always came — or from the low mountain that backed it to the north. But that was closely treed right over the ridge. The palisade enclosed a modest beili, though I thought it magnificent then. Water was plentiful and pure, running straight from the low mountain. In the palisade the hall stood on a grassy plinth of rock. At that time it was about four spears long and two wide and — this amazed me — the lower part of its wall was made of stone and whitened on the outside. There were always men with spears and bows around there, sometimes even with swords. These soldiers often hung around the smithy having jobs done on their weaponry.

'If the French come again' Cadi told me, 'we all have to come here and the teulu kill them and then there's a big party. If too many of the teulu get killed we have to go over the mountain and up the valley you came from, in the trees.'

'To my house?' I said.

'I think that's too far for us to go, and hard. My mother told me it's always winter there. I'd rather have the French chop me up than freeze to death.'

He rubbed his mouth with the palm of his hand.

'It isn't *always* winter' I said. 'But it is a lot of the time, and at the hafod there's mists that last for years. Your sun here makes the sky gentler colours. But you've got the same stars as us. Do they really chop you up?'

'They chopped your.' He stopped and watched Angharad and her maid Cristin, who was about our age, as they crossed from the gate to the mound. They were danced around by the unidentified, who would periodically stop, stick his head on the grass, and look through his legs. This view of the world caused him such excitement that he occasionally flipped onto his back and right over onto his feet again, at which point he'd realize his victims were making their escape and run after them. 'Yes they do. They chop you up. And if they don't chop you up, then you've got to watch out. They make you work for them and then when they go after somebody else you have to be a soldier for them and then somebody else chops you up.' We watched the unidentified catch up with Angharad and embrace her about her thighs so that she almost fell face down in the grass. 'It's called politics. My dad told me about it.'

Cadi's knowledge of things seemed to me to be stupendous, though I never told him that.

'And another thing' he said. 'About women. Did you know —'

We watched Cristin hitch her skirt as she followed Angharad up the wooden steps of the mound '— if they don't have a baby —'

'They always have babies' I said. 'Except if they get old.'

'Not always' he said. 'My mother's not going to have more babies and she's only a bit old yet.'

'What about them then?'

He watched Cristin go into the hall, wiped his lips with his fingertips and then looked at his hand as if he expected to see something.

'If they don't get babies' he said, 'all blood comes out of them.'

I looked at the closed door of the hall with a new interest and then up at the mud bird-palaces hanging at the eaves as I considered this.

'What for?' I said.

'I don't know.'

'Where from?'

'What?'

'Where does the blood come from?'

Cadi went on looking at his fingertips as if he was inwardly debating whether I really deserved to have this knowledge. At last he looked at me as if he'd decided, but without much conviction, that I did.

'Their mouth' he said. And as an afterthought, 'Sometimes their nose.'

'What? Just the once?'

'Yes.'

'What happens after?'

'Nothing.'

'They're all right then?'

'Well, yes. Except they don't have babies.'

I looked at my toes, the palisade, the treed ridge. They went on being themselves despite this news.

'What about men?' I said.

'Men don't have bables.'

I knew that. Cadi knew I knew it. I knew Cadi knew I knew it.

We looked at one another.

'They start them off' I said.

'So what?'

My mind slipped, like a skewed cartwheel, into a different rut. I thought of Mallt, pale and bad tempered.

'Is it like a monthwound?' I said.

I think Cadi's eyebrows drew together.

'A monthwound?' he said.

'My sister used to have them a lot' I said. 'She'd be useless for days then. Lie around moaning. But she stopped having it then and then she died. Mind, she had a baby so it couldn't be.'

'Oh, a *month*wound' Cadi said. He gave out a laugh composed of a single 'Ha', then made his mouth small and shook his head judiciously. 'No, it's nothing to do with a monthwound.'

'So can a man get it then?' The wheel had slipped back into the other rut.

'What?'

'Can a man get it. This bleeding.'

'Men don't have bables.'

'They start them off though.'

Cadi's face went tense. It was too much. He crouched, brandishing his fists and made a kind of restrained growl in his throat. Then he launched himself at me and hit me over.

We had many conversations like that and for a long time the sight of a woman with a nosebleed aroused in me feelings of intense pity.

On this particular occasion, after his urge to murder me had spent itself, we sat up on the grass, I with cowshit on my chin, which was nothing new, and Cadi with blood on his. It was coming out of his mouth.

# 5

I remember that as if in sunlight. I seem to remember our eyes reduced to slits by the glare, the using of hands for shades. The grass was daisystrewn where we sat. I notice, seeing them in memory, how some have white petals and in others the petals are white where they joint with the bud but stain to something like campion, or the colour of the horizon as it is at dusk sometimes, at their tips. I think I remember thinking how curious is the variety and sameness of things, how people are all alike, have the same parts, feelings, yet each is different. Good stuff for a meditation for one of your lot. Don't laugh at the inadequacy of my theology — in my line you have to know a little about these things, but I don't claim any expertise. Take two daisies of the same kind and they're utterly distinct, yet describe them and they are in everything the same. Is it infinitesimal discrepancies distinguish us one from another, or are we somehow utterly different?

But I surely didn't think such things then. Perhaps there was no sun that day.

Angharad ferch Uchdryd was beautiful then, with fair hair and a long nose and a broad forehead. But just thin the fairness a little thicken the nose by half a fingersbreadth, make faint lines, fainter than the oldest manuscript, and the beauty's gone and there's an ageing face. Tiny variations change things utterly.

Poor old Meilyr, whom you know, is *nearly* an ordinary man, and yet — well, you know him. I'll tell you how I came to meet him later.

I'm no expert on these things. Still it's spring, and sunny in my memory. The picture's stubborn.

At a time when it was raining — it must have been autumn because I remember the mash of leaves plastering our thatch — when Gwrgant was trying to teach me how to read, the man who looked like Morgan the prince came to see us.

Gwrgant wasn't much of a teacher when it came to letters. Cadi could already read quite a bit and I learnt more from him than I ever did from his father.

'You're too old to start' Gwrgant would say. 'Too old for poetry. Good god, boy, you must be ten years old.'

I apologised politely sometimes, but that seemed not to help. He was only like this in the darkest moments when it looked as if I'd never get my p's the right way round. He wasn't much use with a pen and had no Latin to speak of. He'd learnt to read late himself and like most of the older fashioned poets preferred voice and memory. I agree with him in fact, though I sometimes use parchment when composing. Too many poems are getting written down these days. It's spoiling the business. Anyway, it gets too easy for people to pinch your material.

We sat on stools at the table, Cadi and I on bundles of rushes to make us higher. The first time I wrote with a pen was over the faded old lineage of a family of Ystrad Gul whom the French had destroyed. I didn't know then where Ystrad Gul was, of course, but I found out soon enough. I remember noticing how the line at some point became the same as Morgan's, which I had off by heart by then, though it was difficult to make out some of the old fashioned writing. My mother and Mallt used to tell me that reading was a kind of miracle that made words come out of your head, when we saw the priest with the book at Sannan's church, but I discovered that it's just a thousand small irritations clustering together to give the impression of being something else.

It couldn't have been a cold day. The door was standing open and the shutters were off the windows, though the fire was smouldering, looking ashy in the light from the door. On the far side of the fire a young taeog called Lleucu was showing Mair how to use the loom. Non was trying to keep the unidentified busy by means of a battery of strategies involving an apple, wooden counters, and a thin, anxious looking black kitten.

Cadi and I scratched at our pages sometimes. But mostly I looked out through the doorframe at the dripping eaves, the prospect of the fringe of almost leafless trees fading into the grey of torrential drizzle. I looked back to my page and then up at Gwrgant's face. His brows like Cadi's were drawn together as he wrote.

He never composed this way. He would work his poems out aloud a few phrases at a time, usually with the harp, going back over the whole thing again and again, singing and resinging and changing the odd word. He'd rock back and fore on his stool muttering irrelevant comments in his ordinary speaking voice here and there among all the fragments of song. To watch him you'd think he was madder than Meilyr. In fact most people, even Non, kept away from him when he was composing. They really thought something had got into him. I get the same treatment sometimes, though because I use the page and write it down as I go along people can see, or think they can see, how in control I am. But as I began to see how carefully and accurately Gwrgant was working I lost my fear and would sit quietly on the rushes and watch and learn.

But at this moment, in our writing lesson, Gwrgant was sitting with his eyes cast down on his page. Studiously and with great labour he was sketching the crude shape of what could have been a cow or a horned chicken with broken wings.

There was a shout from the door.

'Hywel!'

Gwrgant turned his page face down on the table, jumping as if he'd been stabbed.

A man was standing in the doorway. His blue cloak was wrapped round his head and he was very wet. He was crouching, turned to face where Non and the unidentified were playing and his arms were spread wide. One hand was open. In the other he held a scabbarded sword. The metalled tip of the cloth scabbard gleamed with rain.

The unidentified dropped the kitten, which he'd been asphixiating with the apple, and hurled himself into the man's arms. The man managed to place his sword against the doorpost and then held his son in the air. He threw him up three or four times to see how high he'd fly, though to our disappointment he always caught him.

While this was going on Gwrgant rose, lifted his hands forward and bid the man god's welcome.

'Oh, hello, Gwrgant' the man said. 'And how's the son of Iorwerth?'

He turned the boy upside down in his arms and tickled him. Hywel ab Iorwerth, no longer unidentified, slid down Iorwerth's body, laughing and feigning resistance as he went, until his head touched the floor and he folded in a fat heap among the rushes.

This Iorwerth was the man from my smoky memory, with sunken cheeks like Morgan, only this man's hair was darker. They had all shouted encouragement when I sang a verse and Morgan and Iorwerth sat with a small boy.

Lleucu brought the bowl for him to wash his feet but he waved it away saying he wasn't staying long. He stepped closer, shaking his cloak fully onto his shoulders, took up a cloth that was draped near the fire and started to dry his head, arms and legs.

The smoky boy himself next appeared in the doorway, and with him two soldiers whom I recognised from the Court. Gwrgant motioned them in. Cadi and I sat on the floor so that the men could have the stools. Non fetched some bowls and a jug.

'Here' Gwrgant said, 'Mair will play some music.'

He raised a hand to his daughter. She exchanged a look with Non, which Iorwerth observed.

'No, thanks very much' he said. 'That's all right.'

He roughed the hair of the smoky boy, who stood uncertainly near where Cadi and I sat.

Gwrgant gathered the pages and looked dismayed at the tabletop, presumably at the smudgily reversed image of his cow or chicken.

I'd seen the boy around the court several times, sometimes with Angharad. I'd seen Iorwerth there occasionally too, but he was always with a crowd of soldiers and on his way somewhere. The boy knelt with us and plucked at the rushes. He had a fat face and he was smaller than I was so I said,

'Who're you then?'

Cadi made a sharp upward movement of his head and tutted. The boy knelt with his face screwed to one side and one eye shut, for no particular reason.

'My great grandfather was a king' he said. He turned his open eye in the direction of Hywel the identified, who was being retrieved from his rushnest against his will by Mair and Non.

'That thing over there' the king's great grandson said, 'is my cousin. Iorwerth is my uncle but my foster father too.' He paused, then added, as if his own authority wasn't enough, 'My dad told me. Like the poet Gwrgant is Hywel's foster father.'

'He's his foster father too, sort of' Cadi said, pointing at me.

'Have you only got one eye?' I said.

Cadi put his hands to his head and said, 'This is Owain. He's Morgan's son. His great grandfather was Caradog. *At Mynydd Carn ravens made his crown.*'

Owain opened the eye, at the same time closing the other. 'Yes' he said. 'Only the one, so I have to keep swapping sides.'

27

We all thought that this was the funniest thing since Hywel had bitten the priest on the arse when he was bowing before the altar and we made a lot of appreciative noise.

'Owain one eye' we sang.

'Quiet now, boys' Gwrgant said, completely without effect.

Non and Mair brought Hywel to us and we sat in a circle. Hywel decided to sit on Owain's lap so that he could observe the eye swapping close up and occasionally snatch at a closing lid.

Gwrgant and the soldiers talked a great deal about politics as Cadi had defined it.

'You're in a good place — a bad place — to get raided here' Iorwerth said.

Gwrgant glanced round at us and motioned Iorwerth to speak more quietly.

Iorwerth drew his fingers down his moustache.

'I've heard' he said, 'that Ifor of Senghenydd may have designs this way. It's less than a day over the river to his nearest court. I think he might be keeping watch. Looking for a time when the teulu is away.' Iorwerth looked hard at Gwrgant, as if judging the effect of what he'd said. 'Morgan needs me a lot. In Caerllion and along the Wysg. It's difficult, you know. We're stretched.' He shrugged. 'You know what it's like. Without princes the men of Ystrad Gul have ended up fighting for the French, under their law, for Iarll Caerloyw. He wouldn't use them against us — he knows what would happen. But they're in a difficult position. If we lose ground in the south east we could end up like them, fighting for the French in other countries, without hearths, depending totally on spoils.' He looked again at Gwrgant and then away. 'You're a poet' he said. 'You know there's nothing to praise in that.'

Gwrgant said that he was surprised to hear about Ifor's intentions, that he'd heard nothing, but that, come to think of it, it was in keeping with Ifor's character. He was sure that a few men, a few of the younger ones perhaps, would be enough to keep an eye on things while Iorwerth and the teulu were away. A regular group with spears and bows going through the trees, a few riding along a ridge, just to be seen.

While they talked one of the soldiers, a young man with fair hair, would look across and make faces at us. He had pale eyes and a big chin. He bared his teeth at us in a mock snarl, which we might have found frightening, except that his front teeth were missing. Cadi and I tried to muffle our laughs.

'We're going over into Senghenydd today' Iorwerth said. 'Just to see how things are. I've sent out a couple of other groups of three at other points, just to see whatever they'll see. If there's a chance to talk with Ifor or his men I'll take it. Even he'll see that making a chance to help the French come here would be bad news for him. They'll do more than just pinch his cattle.'

'Perhaps' Gwrgant said, 'Ifor thinks he can handle Gwynllwg as wisely as your brother does. The French would seem more like an opportunity than an obstacle then.'

The toothless soldier crossed his eyes and waggled his head.

'Toothless ap Meatmouth' Cadi said, quietly.

I watched Iorwerth, whose hand was over his mouth. I didn't understand what Gwrgant had said, but it seemed to me a wise thing that somehow turned Iorwerth's ideas inside out. So I expected the prince's brother to look thoughtful. But his eyes became bright and this hollow cheeks filled, rounded. When he took his hand away there was a big smile.

'Ifor couldn't do it of course' he said, 'but that won't stop him from thinking that he could. Your patrol idea's a good one. That's really what we're doing today. When Morgan comes to my court next we'll see if he'll tour the border himself. You suggest it. Perhaps they could talk then.'

The pale eyed soldier sipped from his bowl and went on pulling faces. The fourth man, who was darkhaired, very young, without hair on his face, was listening carefully to everything that was said.

Gwrgant and Iorwerth talked on in this way, with a sense of quiet inevitability about them. Perhaps I'm inventing what they said, but I remember the talk of Ifor Fychan ap Meurig and the four figures around the table, the friendly soldier making Cadi laugh, the quiet one listening, the other two sitting forward facing one another, their hands on the table.

At last we became restless and went outside. Cadi and I sneaked the soldiers' spears away from where they'd left them by the door. Mair restrained Hywel from taking one of the bows and in the end bribed him with a stick which she said was a spear. After we'd examined the three horses tied in the lee of the byre and decided not to involve them in our play, Cadi decided that a cow which was unlucky enough to be half a bowshot away lying in the shelter of a bush would be Ifor's men, or the French, or the English, or anyway *them*.

We charged, uttering the obligatory fierce noises and hurled our javelins. The cow stopped chewing momentarily and in a detached way watched the spears splut into the mud and then droop at crazy angles just over a spear's length from their throwers. Hywel tore around terrorizing the cat, which must have thought till then it had escaped. Owain One Eye threatened to tell his uncle and foster father on us, but didn't.

Mair took one of the spears and we shouted all kinds of derision. We pointed at the way she held the shaft and roared. She ran and threw and naturally the spear made a perfect arc and hit the ground an arm's length from the cow's streaming muzzle.

There was a moment's quiet.

'You stupid girl' Cadi said. 'That was very dangerous.'

'Anyway' I said, 'they aren't only meant for throwing.'

Owain agreed with me and expanded on this point.

So the three of us generously explained some of the rudiments of warfare to Cadi's young sister. She wasn't impressed and went to rescue the cat.

The three men left shortly after, refusing Gwrgant's offer to go with them, and leaving Owain with us for the rest of the day. We watched the horses go. I expected them to gallop but they ambled off. The funny soldier wore a helmet — the first time I remember seeing one — which made him look even funnier, and the youngest man's horse was hung about with supplies, including a stoppered jug.

That afternoon, after we'd eaten, we played at making verses with Gwrgant. Some of them were good, most of them were awful. Cadi sang

> Three things to terrify the world:
> A toothless soldier when he smiled,
> Penteulu's son
> Who bites your bum,
> Christ's mother who a spear hurled.

Which Non objected to as blasphemous until the allusion was explained, when she looked at her daughter with a mixture of disapproval and pride.

Mair answered Cadi

The three worst soldiers you could meet:
Hywel racer after cat,
Useless Griffri,
Coughing Cadi,
Who throw their spears at their feet.

Which supplied in venom what it wanted in elegance.

Lleucu and her husband, who looked after Gwrgant's animals, brought firewood in and sat with us as dusk came. It came early because the drizzle turned to rain and the clouds closed on the mountains. Hywel slept red cheeked, which meant the cat could relax too, almost singeing itself at the fire. The firelight was beginning to take over from daylight, turning the shadows upside down and making dark places for sprites to crawl into.

This I remember very well because it was in the crackling quiet that Non heard the horses walking back and a note was sounded on a horn and we gathered to the doorway to see.

Iorwerth, on horseback, his cloak wrapped on his head, came towards us from the trees. Behind him, with mud on his face, walked the funny soldier, leading the other two horses. On one of these were the bags, the neck of a smashed jug hanging by a cord from the pommel.

'They thought I was Morgan' Iorwerth said. His face was wet with rain. 'I heard them shouting. Eneas's horse started and cut across my track.'

The first I noticed of the young soldier was his bare feet pointing to the ground, hanging at one flank of the third horse.

Gwrgant walked to the horse's other flank and pulled the young man's cloak up. The ringlets of his dark hair were rainplastered on his neck. His skin was the colour of a mistletoe berry, except where a black thread of blood ran down to his ear. I followed the thread up to where the snapped arrow angled out of one side of the nape of his neck.

'You're very alike' Gwrgant said.

There was a confusion of subdued voices and awkward movement. The grownups didn't seem to know what to do. There was a firm hand on my hand and Non was pushing my fingers to my chest, my

*31*

forehead, my shoulders each in turn.

'They were good, they were true shots' the funny soldier said, anxious to explain. 'The back first and then the neck as he fell.'

I saw the other arrowstump sticking from a dark island in the man's tunic at the base of his back, the other side of his spine from the neck arrow.

Gwrgant stepped back and rested a hand on the quiver hung from the saddle. He looked up at Iorwerth.

'He was a good man' Gwrgant said. 'An intelligent soldier.'

Iorwerth's gaze shifted and he said, 'He'll lie in court tonight. Even though he was a taeog, make a poem for him.'

## 6

We were scared for a long time after that. Gwrgant kept his spear at his feet at night and groups of soldiers from the court called in often before travelling north and west along the river that bordered Senghenydd. I looked at spearpoints and arrowheads again and saw them in a different way.

Cadi and I went running in the woods between our house and the court, where it was safe to play, and we climbed trees and tried to ambush squirrels and courting couples — though in the case of courting couples our planned offensives often melted into mere spying missions of a particularly intense kind. Owain ap Morgan would join us too and was very adept and fit though he was several years younger than we were. He often outstripped Cadi, whom we would sometimes leave shivering and out of breath under a tree as a rearguard.

At home, I observed Gwrgant working on his poem for the dead soldier. It seemed a terrible, frustrating struggle for him and he was often bored and moody. Even so, when he sang at the funeral feast you'd swear Eneas had been his own son. I couldn't yet understand the language of these big poems very well but still I felt my throat go tight and my breathing labour, I can't explain why, when the image of an outstretched tree glorying in leaves and daylight spread in my mind through the phrasing of the end of the poem.

I looked around at the others in the silence after that. The teulu and the rest showed no signs of being moved. Looking down, Gwrgant stepped back from the hearth.

The soldier's mother came before the place where Iorwerth sat and said that if there was galanas she'd prefer her portion to be in goods rather than another death because the family was poor. Could the lord put this to his brother the prince so that, if there was any chance of it being done this way, the legal process could start?

The skin of Iorwerth's face tightened. He looked down, then back at the woman, who was very straight and dignified, as if he was annoyed that she wasn't collapsed in tears. He muttered something about the time and the cost. But then he said he'd mention it to the prince, or the woman could put it to him herself at his next court there.

Afterwards, at home, Gwrgant said, 'I'm glad that lot's over. I managed to reshape a marwnad I did for an uchelwr in Erging, years ago. A bit rough round the edges but I think it held together?'

He said this as a question and I realised, surprised, that he was asking our opinion.

We nodded.

'If he wants a poem for every man that dies the poets'll have to levy reinforcements.'

Non dragged the mattress closer to the fire.

'Don't worry' she said. 'Poems are too expensive for that. He wanted to whip up feelings a bit I think.'

Gwrgant, who'd been swigging some of the mead he'd been paid for the poem, looked round at her.

'Or a kind of expiation' he said. He swigged again.

She paused in pulling on the coverlet. 'What?'

'I mean that he.' Gwrgant stopped and looked at me and Cadi and Mair. 'The arrows were meant for him.' He smiled. 'That's what I mean. Yes.' He looked back to his wife. 'He was imagining his own death. The spring of praise for dead soldiers is the guilt that you've survived.'

He finished his jug and we all watched his adam's apple riding in his throat. Before the rest of us could get onto the mattress he was fast asleep, flat on his back, the voice that had made the tree that moved me turned to a rhythmic pigsnort.

## 7

The crisis kept Gwrgant at home enough for our apprenticeship to develop with fewer interruptions. My head was crammed with poems and stories and, yes, lists too, Idnerth, that I could spout with my eyes shut. Sometimes the chanting filled me with pleasures that are impossible to describe, like the smell of green wood on the fire, or the taste of an apple. Often the words streamed out uncomprehended and my mind would be on some other thing, on Eneas dead, or on an owl's nest we'd found.

Gwrgant knew well enough how we felt — he often felt the same way — and broke the learning with work among the animals and walking and archery and, if we misbehaved, the odd half day at the quern.

Non warned us that the trees on the border side were full of spirits and she never went into them, not even into the fringe for a piss, though it meant she had to walk three bowshots to some other place. But we'd already peopled the trees with our own fears. Any heavy noise in a bramble was an enemy. Every scuffling was a ghost. Cadi thought that Eneas's soul could have gone into a bird, like Lleu in the story.

'See' he said, 'with all those branches it'd be easy for his soul to get tangled somewhere on its way up.'

We looked at one another wide eyed.

'In fact' he said, and I knew that he was going to speak my thoughts, 'he could have gone into a tree.'

We looked at the trees again. They were leafless by this time and the twigs clickclicked against one another in a stir of wind. There was a grove of immense beech trees nearby. There had been no beech trees at my old home and these, when I'd first seen them, had astonished me. The trunk of the largest of them now became shaped and fleshy as a man's back. Horrified and fascinated we walked around it. Looking up to where the branches started, I saw countless fragments of people — noses, cheeks, and especially bare heels, blending one greygreen part into the next. As we moved I looked at the trunk again and I felt that I was always seeing the back of someone who slowly kept turning away.

There was a high scream. Cadi ran past me very fast, making obscure noises like someone trying to be sick. I copied this action quite accurately without bothering to look in the direction he'd run from and I drew level with him as we reached the clearing. Cadi slowed as he ran out of breath and fear at the same time. We slid on the wet ground and fell together. I was ready to scramble up and run again but Cadi pulled at my shirt.

'The owl' he said. 'I saw him.'

'I didn't see the owl.'

'He went right over my head. Missed me by a handbreadth.'

I looked back into the trees and then down at my foster brother. His skin was whiter than his teeth.

'I didn't see him.'

I helped him up.

'A corpse bird' he said. 'Worse if you didn't.'

I shrugged. 'There's always owls.'

As our terror ebbed further Cadi's breath came back and with it excitement. We debated whether a man's soul could go into a tree or bird. Cadi was quiet sometimes and I knew he was thinking about the owl so I kept talking. At first we thought the bird was plausible but the tree wasn't, because birds like people have limbs and eyes and can move. But then we thought of Christ in the bread and wine and the evidence of the strange tree, and we were unsure.

We decided to appeal to Non on the matter, as she had more patience with us than Gwrgant concerning such things. It took a long time before we could make our story and the drift of our thinking clear to her, mainly because we both spoke at once and used a lot of pronouns without saying what they referred to until she crossexamined us.

She put her hand on Cadi's forehead and watched him while he talked.

'An owl?' she said.

'So can men's souls go into these things?' I said.

'No' she said with great sureness, smiling as if the question was silly, and she looked uncertainly towards the trees.

## 8

I remember in another winter standing with Mair, Cadi and little Hywel near the byre and we were breaking the thin sheets of ice on the puddles made by the cattle's feet and the grass was blue as smoke with the frost and the trees were greenblack and the air was the strange grey it sometimes is when the world is frozen. Colour shrinks into the core of things at those times and if the sun is hidden you have to coax colour out with fire, or with rubbing your fingers and cheeks.

Cadi was wearing shoes which Lleucu had made for him, but Mair and I had got tired of making fun of them.

The four of us stared at the two apple trees, black and stark, which an age before — I suppose it must have been a few weeks before — had been bent in lovely bows by the weight of fruit. We and the crows between us had carried off all of that and it was nearly Christmas and the time for salted meat and long sleeping, and the war had never happened.

A few cattle had disappeared from other holdings, but that was always happening. The soldiers had given up patrolling the woods. We were to go with Gwrgant and Iorwerth to Caerllion to Morgan's Christmas feast and leave Non and Mair with only Lleucu, who was pregnant, and her man. And in the house Gwrgant had a guest called Rhys Ddu who was a storyteller and a poet, but mainly a storyteller, and he was coming to Caerllion too, with two of his men.

'You know who he is don't you?' Cadi said. He coughed and rubbed his mouth.

'Who?' Mair said.

'He's the storyteller of Ifor of Senghenydd.'

'What do they want *him* to come for?'

'I don't know. Probably it's like a peace sign. Morgan and Iorwerth love peace' Cadi said. 'My father told me. If we keep peace with Ifor we can keep the French away. But he's only a storyteller.' He sniffed and paused as if that alone told us how insignificant Rhys Ddu was, but then he explained, 'Storytellers are always cadging things. There was even one that learnt French so he could go and tell stories to them. My father used to know him.'

I thought about this.

'Didn't they chop him up?' I said.

'Don't think so.'

'Why didn't they?'

Cadi shrugged.

'He wanted to cadge things off them too I suppose' he said.

He told us in a pointed sort of way that the French wore shoes all the time, even more than the English, and that they wore shirts made of woven chains.

Mair and I looked at one another with pursed lips, then at Cadi. We weren't willing to believe this and argued that they must take their shoes off when they went to bed. But even so little Cadi would not allow.

'You ought to be a priest you did' Mair said.

The thought pleased Cadi. He allowed himself to smile at his sister and asked her why.

'Because when you explain things' she said, 'they get harder to understand.'

'Understanding?' Cadi said, not smiling any more. 'What's the odds of that?' I recognised one of Gwrgant's speeches from our lessons. 'Nobody looks at a mountain and asks what it *means*. I'll be pencerdd one day. All that matters is the shape of the song and how it feels.'

He rubbed his nose, coughed and spat. A dazzling flower of blood spread its petals on one of the little sheets of ice.


# 9


Caerllion, I discovered, was the place where I'd seen the huge river and a lot of flat land and a lot of land without trees even though there wasn't a mountaintop.

Standing with Gwrgant and Owain ap Morgan on the river bank, I was startled and terrified to see a horse in a rowing boat. I'd never seen a wooden boat before, let alone one carrying a horse. Gwrgant laughed when I ran behind him and he explained the ferry.

'Not far away, across that side' he said, 'the French are very strong. They use French forest law and blind you if you try to hunt the animals. But Morgan still collects dues there and the people come to him for law and protection. In my great grandfather's time a famous poet lived there called Berddig, your father's name. I sing some of his stuff occasionally.'

He spread his arms, pointed northward, inland with his left and south with his right.

'And there and there the French are strong, but we're here, where Morgan's family had a palace even in the age of giants. Over there' he pointed across the river again, eastward and south 'Iarll Caerloyw has a huge fortress made of rock at Ystrad Gul and you must never go there because he'll chop you up and put you in one of his overcooked stews. That's why the French and English are overweight and have such rotten teeth — they eat too much bread and overcook their meat.'

I looked into the bristling mass of bare trees on the far bank and then down at the expanses of pale grey slurry that edged the water. Could the river ever be bigger than it was now? And why then was it low in winter?

After a pause Gwrgant laughed and cuffed our heads. We watched two men coax the horse out of the boat and up the slope from the jetty.

I asked Gwrgant about the river and whether it was high or low. He told me about the moon and the sea swelling and shrinking and pushing and sucking the water up and down the river. I thought of how my father had told me about the sea and what it could do, and how I hadn't believed him. The world was getting bigger and stranger and more worrying.

\* \* \*

Cadi had become too ill to come with us, which had made him very sullen. Gwrgant told him that he should guard the others while we were away, which made him a little happier.

We travelled to Caerllion on horseback with Iorwerth and Angharad his wife, Cristin her maid, and Owain as well as Rhys Ddu and his two men. I was surprised at how many of Iorwerth's teulu accompanied us — half a dozen on horseback with spears and another six on foot with bows and knives. Our cavalry made a cordon round us when the terrain permitted, but mostly we had to saunter nose to tail or in pairs.

I listened to Rhys and Gwrgant talking about work. They talked of Gwalchmai the poet and Gwrgant acknowledged his debt to him in his own development. Rhys talked of the influence of old Bledri on his own storytelling but bemoaned the master's selling out to the French. As if, Rhys said, he'd been a mere clergyman.

'I can understand a forced submission' Rhys said. 'He had skill, he was clever. People loved to listen to him. In his way he was a great man. But I can't forgive him.'

'I'm sure he'd be upset at that' Gwrgant said.

'The greatness of all his stories becomes sentimentality without a real commitment under it.'

'There are Bledris in every country' Gwrgant said. 'There'll be more. Sometimes they're well intentioned. Wrong, but well intentioned.'

Rhys spoke in a sharp, emphatic way. He wasn't a pencerdd and never would be, having specialized in storytelling. Gwrgant somehow asserted his higher rank by speaking more quietly and slowly. As I rode along behind their horses I wondered if Rhys and his companions had been among the men who had killed Eneas.

We stopped to rest briefly at a small river, Nant Pencarn, at a ford, but not for long because it was too cold. Owain and I dismounted and ran in the woods. When we came back to the rest of the group there was a scene that stuck in my memory.

Gwrgant was some way off, among the horses and the soldiers. Nearby, Angharad was sitting on a stone over which a blanket had been spread. Cristin was kneeling in front of her, rubbing the lady's feet to warm them. Close by them Iorwerth and Rhys Ddu stood, talking. As Owain and I approached, Rhys glanced at us and then continued speaking, more loudly, it seemed to me.

'— yes, it must be boring sitting through all those court cases. I enjoy following a nice juicy rape though. Or divorces can be interesting, too. There was a woman divorced her husband in Ifor's court the other day because of his halitosis. But these interminable disputes about boundary ditches and borders leave me cold.'

'Yes' Iorwerth said. 'I avoid them if I can.'

On Christmas Eve more animals and fowl were slaughtered than I'd ever seen together before. In the brief daylight in the large beili around Morgan's hall at Caerllion every other person seemed to be a butcher and there were a lot of important people, the various officials, claiming their allotted haunches and innards and so on of the prince's Christmas meat.

Gwrgant had shown me the remains of the old city from the age of giants. He said it was older even than the time when Macsen and Cynan from the north had marched on Rome. I saw walls of rock and great cracked slabs. There were modern houses built among the stones and some of Morgan's soldiers had tents pitched in sheltered places along the southern fringes. The edges of the town were regularly patrolled and Iorwerth and Morgan themselves often did the rounds.

'The French think that Arthur lived here' Gwrgant said. 'Let them think. It's a pretty enough story.'

Rhys said that he was thinking of moving Arthur to Caerllion in future in his stories.

Listening to all their talk and seeing water that could swell and boats that could carry horses and a city of giants, I felt that the world teemed\with|puzzles.

Even in the beili among the slaughtered animals I still felt lost. The sheer amount of activity meant that the sight of the split carcasses, the snow of plucked feathers, couldn't cheer me.

An old woman sat on a block of wood. She was skinning hares. For each pelt that she peeled off with a shucking noise she sent up a mechanical prayer to Saint Melangell. She slung the pelts in this dish, the carcasses in that, where they looked like a pile of newborn human babies. The old woman's eyes bulged larger than the hares', and\they looked deader.

A small hand picked up a couple of the skins and held them up to me. Sharp eyes and a sharp nose, but chubby cheeks. Cristin smiled at me.

'I get the pick of these this year' she said. 'Want one? It'd make a nice hood before the snow comes.'

I declined, as politely as I could.

We looked around the yard because we didn't know what to say. Iorwerth and Angharad and a young man and a pregnant young woman were sauntering from one little scene of bloodletting to the next, inspecting the meat.

'Come on' Cristin said. She held out her free hand to me so that I could escort her as her mistress and the other woman were escorted. 'You're a bit young but you'll have to do.'

She made great play of examining the antlers on the severed head of a stag.

'I come of age next spring' she said. 'I'm twelve in May. When's your birthday?'

'I don't know' I said. 'Gwrgant thinks I'm about twelve. Ish.'

She looked at me as if grudgingly interested.

'Do you know what Cadi asked me to do?' she said, looking at the tines of the antlers again.

'No' I said.

'He's too young anyway. I asked Angharad. Anyway, I'm not really sure how to. I mean, I've got a fair idea, but I can't really see how it's possible.'

'What?'

'Not yet, anyway. Can you?'

'Er, suppose not.'

'I mean, I've heard Iorwerth and Angharad of course. It sounds like constipation to me.'

Dimly I thought of my expeditions wlth Cadi and Owain and of the couples in the trees.

'Do you think Cadi will be a poet?' she said. 'Of course, it's a while yet before he comes of age.'

'What did he ask you then?'

'Your master would be pleased if I got married quick. The pencerdd gets a share of the virgin fee.'

I recalled this vaguely from some law we'd learnt by heart, but I had no idea what it meant. My hand was sweating where she held it, and where she held it was up, so that everybody could see our connection. In her other hand were the bloody hare pelts. Her due. I looked at her face. Her nose was straight but not long. Her hair, where it showed under her hood, was fairish but not as fair as Angharad's. Her sharp eyes and her sharp nose made her — particular. Infinitesimally different from all other people, utterly different perhaps. I realized that I had been in love with Angharad, but here was something more practical. So I would give up being in love with Angharad and be in love

*41*

with Cristin instead.

We stood and watched three soldiers come in through the gate. They talked with Iorwerth, then one of them went up the mound to the hall.

'I'm going to be a poet' I said.

'I know. Who's paying the fees?'

'Fees?'

'You're supposed to pay the pencerdd.'

'Oh. Morgan's my — my pattern.'

'Patron?'

'Patron.'

Cristin smiled more. She had beautiful small teeth.

'What's more' I said impressively, 'I saw a horse in a rowing boat yesterday.'

Cristin squeezed my hand. She had seen Morgan and Rhagnell his wife come out of the hall and follow the soldier down the wooden steps.

I looked round the yard, elated and confused. The place was stranger then ever. Although it was overcast and grey, all the colours glared as in some powerful torchlight.

'That's Dyddgu' Cristin said.

I realized that I was looking at the pregnant young woman and that Cristin was following the line of my gaze.

'Morgan and Iorwerth's youngest sister' she said. 'The handsome man's the baby's father, Seisyll. He's a prince. But his father's had a lot of trouble with the French' — she waved her hare hand vaguely north — 'up that way somewhere.'

She turned to me and was looking closely into my eyes, squinting.

'Grey' she said. 'Not even any green. Cadi's are brown. Cadi's are lovely. Like an owl almost.'

The owl flitted across my mind, cast a shadow. The colours in the yard darkened momentarily. I looked at, without seeing, Morgan on horseback going out through the gate, the three soldiers, carrying bows, running with him, one ahead of the horse and one at either flank.

'He spits blood' I said.

Cristin's eyes' close to mine, widened slightly. It seemed to me that her eyelashes were extraordinarily beautiful acts of god.

I suppose I must have had erections many times before that, but it's the first occasion I actually remember getting one.

'That explains it then' she said.

'What?'

'Why you're training. Why he asked me.'

'Asked what?'

'Poor old Cadi.' She looked down. 'Perhaps I should have let him. Not that I can see how.' Her grip tightened again and she looked up at me. She became calm and dignified. 'Come on' she said. 'We owe this to Cadwallon ap Gwrgant.'

She led me away. The glaring red of blood and the different reds of fur and the glaze of dead eyes hailed us as we walked towards the hall and people stared as we passed. Inside she took me to a partitioned room and we lay by a post where a strange triangular shield of a kind I'd never seen before was hanging. We lifted back one another's skirt and spent a long time in intense looking. Her skin in the half gloom was mistletoe white and smooth, but not as squashy as Non's, and she smelt milky. She had nippleless little buds for breasts — not much bigger than mine — and in the loin, a sparse light down where there were strange tight folds. She passed her fingers through my few scratchy black pubic threads.

'I still don't really see how' she said. 'But I haven't bled yet mind.'

Curious things were happening to me. I felt hot and cold at the same time and as if my body, all of it, was growing and changing shape inside my skin. She was the same person. There was the fine nose and the shrewd eyes — but I felt I was seeing someone completely new. She inclined her head and where the hood fell away I saw a sculpted whorl with a lipped edge. Sorry if I'm getting a bit poetic. Her ear, I mean. But I couldn't have said the word for it. The word wouldn't have been it.

'Hm' she said, still staring. 'It's a bit like Dyfrig's thighbone in the reliquary. Only smaller of course. The split bit at the end. Poor old Cadi.'

Then —

Look, I know you Cistercians disapprove of this sort of thing, officially anyway. This modern habit of celibacy worries me a bit. I'm glad to see that most of the Welsh clergy have got the sense not to have anything to do with it, though I know you lot are a little more particular. You're still the best order, mind. Better than those Benedictine bastards anyway. Isn't there a kind of self love, though, in guilt and scourging? I remember Meilyr telling me about the time your Abbot Cynan had himself whipped for wanking. But then, perhaps he enjoyed. No, surely not. But listen, our being there was a kind of ceremony. It's fanciful, perhaps, to see the threesided shield as a trinity over us, but there was the truest kind of devotion between us. Don't be offended, please. There could have been nothing more innocent for a Christmas Eve.

Anyway, there was a bustling in the hall and two small boys burst into the room, playing swords with a couple of sticks. They flailed and kicked up the rushes until the taller boy, who was Owain ap Morgan, saw me and Cristin.

'Look at that' he said.

The smaller boy, who had reddish hair, stopped and stared at us.

Cristin was sitting up. Her dress was in its proper place and she demurely embraced her own knees.

Her narrow eyes slid to one side and she quoted the law at me, 'It is right that there should be *six* columns in the king's hall.'

I sat up and covered my lap.

'What were you doing pointing that at the roof?' the smaller boy said.

'Who's he?' I said to Owain.

'My great grandfather was a king' the smaller boy said.

'He's Owain' Owain said.

'Owain who?'

'Iorwerth's son. We both got named after our grandfather. Iorwerth and my dad, Morgan, swapped us for the fosterage.'

Owain ab Iorwerth smiled and bobbed up and down in excitement.

'It saveded them having to learn a new name for us.' He thought this was very funny and laughed for a long time.

'He's Hywel's older brother' Owain ap Morgan said. 'So watch out.'

I remembered a redhaired boy with Hywel, rushing into a room where Gwrgant was singing to Angharad and a lot of the other women.

'And' Owain ap Morgan said 'The French are here.'

'The French! The French!' the smaller Owain said. He gritted his teeth and brandished his stick. 'Ha! Ha! Ha!' He sliced the air before him and danced fighting nothing round the room.

*44*

'The French?' I said.

Cristin was getting to her feet.

'Let's go and have a look' she said. She looked down at me.

'I—'

Her eyes became even narrower. Owain and Owain looked at me. I got up, slowly. Because of my erection, which I did not want to attract further comment, I crouched as I made towards the door, pretending that this posture was part of my stealth.

There was a certain amount of shuffling backwards by the two cousins at this point and little Owain decided that he had an acute stomach ache. Cristin and I became concerned and parental and coaxed him out into the hall and towards the big door.

When we opened this we saw the backs of two soldiers — one of them was Toothless ap Meatmouth. He was hanging on his spear and stood with one foot on top of the other to keep a little warmer.

Between and around the two men I saw fragments of the scene in the yard below. I felt my breathing stop a moment as I saw a broad bloodsmeared knife hanging in a man's hand. It was one of the butchers standing by the hanging ox carcass. Around the yard everyone had stopped working and was looking towards the gate. The harewoman was gone. A short man was standing on her block to get a better view.

I could stand up straight now without digging anybody in the leg or stomach. On tiptoe, between the men's backs, I could see Morgan's reddish head, and Iorwerth next to him. They were both wearing swords. Behind them, nearer to us, were Angharad and her sister-in-law Rhagnell. It was quiet except for one voice. In front of Morgan two men were standing. They were both tall and both were wearing helmets, a bit like the one Toothless wore, except that there were flanges that came down over the nose. One of them wore a loose white gown over his other clothes and a silver cross hung over the front of that. He was holding a sheet of parchment and something small was hanging from it. The other man stood with one hand on the hilt of a big sword. He was the one who talked. It was a peculiar articulated kind of barking, yet everybody listened.

Behind these two, other Frenchmen were standing, half a dozen perhaps, in the gateway. I had an impression of helmeted heads, breath forming on the air, a spear with a flag hanging on it, and beyond all that, through the gate, large horses wearing masks. The men

45

were standing in a few very straight lines. I wondered why they did that.

To my right the young woman Dyddgu was standing near a fire, one hand stretched across her belly. Behind her was the man Seisyll, I recognised his curly hair, holding a spear.

The speaker stopped. There was a strained pause. I noticed that little Owain was holding hands with Cristin. Then the man in the white gown started to speak. He read from the parchment and I recognised it was Latin, though he had a foreign accent. The sheet quivered a little in his hand and the hanging thing swung.

All the time, it was the gleaming of the swordman's tunic that drew my attention. There were sharp spikes on his heels, and his body was covered in an intricate coiling glitter which despite its intricacy was organized in straight lines like some strange script illuminated in bluish silver.

At last the reading stopped and the robed man fumbled at rolling the fluttering parchment. Morgan's old priest stepped forward and started to speak, at last in Welsh, but this time he spoke too quietly for me to follow, though I could tell that he was talking to Morgan. At one point he hesitated, conferred with the robed man in Latin for a moment, and then continued.

'When are they going to start the politics?' I whispered.

'What?' Cristin said.

Toothless looked round, saw us and raised a finger to his lips. At the same time Angharad looked round and pulled Rhagnell's sleeve. The two women came up the steps towards us. The two soldiers moved aside. Angharad and Rhagnell pushed us back. In the closing gap of the door I glimpsed Rhys Ddu and Gwrgant near Morgan's priest, listening hard, the pails of blood, the swordman glancing at us, the coiling gleam of the tunic.

Rhagnell was annoyed because there was no fire in the hall.

She and Angharad and Cristin and the two Owains talked. Each Owain sat in his mother's lap and I saw Angharad exchange a look with Rhagnell when Cristin sat next to me. The princess soothed her son.

'Was that Gwilym Iarll Caerloyw?' Cristin said.

'No' Rhagnell said. 'He was just his servant. Don't worry. He's just been sent to ask my husband for Christmas presents — not that he'll get any.'

She talked on about how sometimes it was right to send presents but that just now they could not afford to.

I didn't know what she was on about, though I wanted to believe her that there was no danger as I listened to her western accent. It seemed inside out, to have to be able to afford not to send gifts, a puzzle at the birth celebration.

The air was tense. I felt that if I moved it would twang like a bow-string. Perhaps Morgan could make the silver men go away in the end, but he had been standing and listening, even when I knew he couldn't understand. And the men in straight rows and the sword-man were all wearing shoes and there was the intricate shingled gleam of their tunics made of woven chains.

## 10

Why this is all so clear in my memory I don't know. I could pick out all sorts of reasons and play variations on them. For instance, I could say that I remember our pubescent rite because of the arrival of the French, or that I remember the arrival of the French because of our rite. Or there was something in the coincidence of the two — subtly different this one, and therefore utterly different — something beyond the mere fact of coincidence, and so the scene stuck. And so on. In one life, you can talk about strong feelings, physical sensations. I expect you remember the first time you got really drunk, but you'll have forgotten some of the others. But when it's a whole people, what then? Did we all feel that twanging of the air? Perhaps only I did. I don't know if *we* remember things because they're significant, or if they're significant because we happen to remember them. And there's a crucial difference between these.

What Morgan remembered, or chose to remember, when he spoke at the dinner on Christmas day is interesting.

I sat between Gwrgant and one of Rhys Ddu's men. My mind was full of tunics and bloodflowers and the unexplored fleshfolds, but the prince spoke of other things and didn't directly mention the previous day's unexpected visit. He wore the iron torc and spoke before the

47

prayer, first of all listing his obligatory gifts of meat and clothes and so on to the officials.

After a pause he went on,

'Fifteen years ago I killed with my own hand Ricert ap Gilbert at Coed Grwyne and my brother and the teulu that was with me then witnessed this. Some of them are here now, and some of their sons.' He looked at me. 'That day a fire spread across the south. Today, after food, Gwrgant will sing of the action at Bryn Buga that came after that, that began the winning back of our land, our inheritance from Wysg to Rhymni, when the enemy was driven out and the people freed. And this was possible because god had punished Henri ap Gwilym Bastart with death for the long winter of his reign.'

Gwrgant was wearing his unnatural smile. Morgan's stilted attempt at grandeur was hurting his ear, though I'm sure the master had helped the prince to prepare the words.

'And in the confusion wrought in England in the early days of Estefyn of Blaes, we struck.' He paused. 'In the days of my grandfather there were bloody wars among the Welsh, but what was sought was to make Glywysing one kingdom and to restore it to the greatness of the days of Tewdrig Sant. Caradog my grandfather tried to do this, and failed.'

Rhys's man next to me murmured from behind his hand, 'Even though he was fighting with the French on his side.'

'Now' Morgan said, 'god's welcome to Rhys Ddu of Senghenydd who will entertain us later, and whom I license to visit our court, should he wish, at any of the three feasts. In these tense but, for the most part, less bloody times, it may be that our borders can be opened less painfully, and we may move in a more careful way towards one Glywysing.'

A few men nodded and muttered approving noises, but most did nothing. I couldn't see Rhys's face. His man next to me had his hand clapped tightly over his own mouth. Iorwerth, sitting near Gwrgant as is customary, was looking at his brother, his head turned to one side.

There was subdued quiet and Morgan stood looking puzzled, as if he hadn't understood what he'd said himself.

Gwrgant trained me many times in ways of performing through awkward gaps like these, which could be the ruin of an otherwise skilled poet. I felt a kind of darkness pushing into the hall in the moment's silence, and Morgan was supposed to send all that away, as he'd sent the French away the day before. The craft is to let the darkness that falls between words seem purposeful. Morgan was no poet, of course. But the moment was short. Even as I felt that something was sliding away from us, the prince retrieved it and called the priest for the prayer.

You've got to understand that this was the biggest feast I'd ever seen to that time, and I'd never eaten at a table before. I'd never seen such a large fire, nor so many candles, nor such meat. Gwrgant would slosh some mead out of his horn into a little bowl for me every now and then and Rhys's man on my other side would top it up out of his. The music and the voices became distant and echoing and faces shone as if polished. Women were bustling the smaller children away to sleep. Men were putting their arms around their wives, or one another, or somebody else's wife. Then a man with a pole was calling for quiet and Iorwerth was ceremoniously handing Gwrgant the harp and Gwrgant was singing the action of Bryn Buga, which starts

> I glory in Tewdrig's line that day
> When dawn cleaved red the eastern sky —
> Skull of air cleft in saint king's memory —
> Three hundred horse rode under Morgan's thigh
> And spearclash echoing in valley —

Noise and pictures flickered through my mind as he sang. I realized, and then rerealized, if you understand me, with a new excitement that I was following the poem. Out of a few hundred words the battle suggested itself to me. The pictures were richer than the real fire and the shining faces. And the darkness that had pushed into Morgan's silence, the darkness of the stranger's articulated barking in the yard, the owlshadow, were all gone. I felt that I could snatch up a spear myself and storm the rock fortresses on my own.

In other words I was pissed.

Well, no. Because I really did feel, begin to hear the song there. Had I understood what the sickly mead was doing to me I would have regretted it. It was actually hindering, clogging, I don't know what word I need, the elation of the poem.

Gwrgant finished and sang a song to Christ, but the first poem so dinned in my head that I didn't hear the second piece. When he came back to his seat I wanted to clap him on the back and shout approval, but he was unhappy and complaining.

'What a stupid choice for a Christmas. I ask you. The action of Bryn Buga.'

'It was good' I said.

I wanted to explain his own song to him, felt that he couldn't have been listening. I think I tried to say something, but I'm sure it didn't make sense. He looked at me and patted my shoulder.

'Perhaps you're right' he said, though I don't know what I said to be right about. 'Convenient remembering. Old glory in a new deadlock.'

Later Rhys Ddu told the story of Caswallon and Fflur. I thought of Cadi as Caswallon and Cristin as Fflur and it made me feel sad, though I couldn't tell why. I looked around for Cristin. The last time I'd been close to her had been when we'd stood together to sing the plygain in Cadog's church that morning.

But she was gone. The celebration fragmented into small groups of dancers and staggering singers who seemed to get no further than endlessly repeated broken phrases of slurred song.

I was tired. Through the cracks of all this fragmentation the warm certainties of the evening bled away.


## 11


It must have been at that Christmas court that my status was resolved.

I have a memory of being with Gwrgant, his hand on my shoulder, brought before Morgan, and Morgan's legal adviser is there. A thin, cleanshaven man who could be a monk, but I'm not sure. I can't see the top of his head and he's wearing some sort of furry gown.

I confuse this with my memory of the smoky time when I was first called on to sing, but I'm sure it is another occasion.

Gwrgant talks and the lawyer talks and then Morgan and it goes on a long time. What I remember must surely be reconstructed from what I've learnt since, from other events that this time has a bearing on, so it's not a complete, true memory. But there are fragments of it hung on a kind of smoking darkness.

Gwrgant says, 'I'd like to ask that the prince's wishes, following Owain ap Caradog's broad wishes, for this boy should be made into firm decisions so that his status shall be known for all purposes of law and inheritance and so that we shall in future all know truly who he is.'

I'm surprised he talks like this, so formally, like Morgan at the feast. I've heard him and the prince talk as old friends, standing at the doorway of Rhun the smith's forge, talking about horses.

The lawyer speaks quietly. There are a lot of words I don't understand. The lawyer says I'm still technically a taeog, the church owning the land my brothers keep, that taeogion are forbidden apprenticeships in poetry. Morgan murmurs something. The lawyer takes the book from his sleeve and consults it for a long time. Then he nods and says, 'Except when there is the express permission of the king.'

His mouth turns into a thin line and he looks at me.

Morgan nods and waves his hand.

Gwrgant whispers to me, 'They always say *king* in the book.' Aloud, 'The boy doesn't know his birthday. Can I suggest we agree on one here so that he will have a fixed date for reaching adulthood and its rights and responsibilities?'

Morgan looks at the lawyer, who nods.

Gwrgant suggests Saint Gwynllyw's day and they agree. Cadi's birthday. The lawyer gets up and walks around me and says I'm to be twelve. This makes me thirteen next spring. Just over a year of boyhood left.

Gwrgant agrees and then talks about parenthood, leans towards Morgan and says something quietly. I think I hear him say the name 'Berddig'.

Morgan looks into Gwrgant's face, turns his head to one side, still looking, and says, 'How's the boy?'

Gwrgant looks down. His fingers tighten on my shoulder.

The lawyer objects, talks about complications. Gwrgant offers to go north to see my mother. The lawyer's quiet, then talks about the fee. The apprentice or parent must pay the fee to the pencerdd. The prince would be released from his obligations as patron if the pencerdd were to become legal guardian.

The prince turns in his seat and looks angry, starts saying something about god's eyes, but Gwrgant speaks up, says he'll agree to that. Morgan is stopped by this. He looks at Gwrgant again, scowls at the lawyer, looks at Gwrgant a third time, more thoughtfully, then sits back and waves his hand again. 'I don't know why we have to go through all this rigmarole' he says.

Gwrgant takes me away.

We're by the ford where Cristin rubbed Angharad's feet and the men of the teulu are letting the horses drink. Gwrgant walks with me into the trees. He says he'll be glad to get home. We talk about animals and he speaks verses about the boar and the wolf and the mountain in winter. There's thawed frost and cold pale sunlight that dazzles because the sun is so low and meshed in the branches.

'Listen, Griffri' he says. 'Would you like to call me father?'

I stop walking and I can't look at him. He puts his palm on my head and I turn and run away towards the horses and the people.


## 12

How should I feel when I tell you that it was out of Cadi's death that I made my first real poem?

In performance, of course, there would be the sense of confidence and inevitability. Destiny knocking at the gate and hearts plucked along with the strings. But the question, believe me, isn't rhetorical.

It's interesting to talk to amateurs. Angharad is quite a talented poet, and she and Cristin are both good storytellers. To them, I think, the craft is a kind of acrobatic move that you hold for a few moments before you topple. They may be right. But if I were to look at it that way my poem of Cadi would best be forgotten. It would merely use him, it would be opportunistic.

With a commission it's different. You just get on with it and assume the purity of the client's motives, pile the standard phrases together in some way that seems artful, appropriate — good, in the craftsmanlike sense. Just starting, though, I hadn't thought of these things, or about anything much. The poem arose out of a need, I suppose, and out of the fact that I was trained, or half trained. I was fourteen, a man, and Cadi had been dead over a year. Remember what you were like. You weren't always so saintly. The world is either miraculous, or hellish, or both, full of strangeness, full of moments when you feel you're in a competition.

I wasn't a calculating sort of man, and I think I never have been, but it does trouble me to think that the marwnad I made for Cadi was kind of proving, a handstand made of words performed before an audience made weakheaded with grief, something to do with the uncontrollable burst of pride I felt when I first sang a learnt verse in front of the prince.

But when you live through the craft, as well as by it, all this changes and the words arise out of something more than the mere need to perform. They fulfil something and they lead somewhere. They make spaces for the spirit. Put half a dozen poets together and they'll talk about performance, about the gymnastics. What's just under that is pride, jealousy, the sense of competing. I need hardly explain the futility of that to a Cistercian. Still the pride's important, perhaps as a starting point, or a grubby underside to what matters. The craft makes places where you realize you're alive, where a totality is harmonized, so that the gaps between words are shaped and have a sense of being purposeful.

Unlike the way I'm drivelling on at the moment. It can also be a kind of prostitution. I do it for payment, provide satiety and the release of strong emotions, help my clients to affirm themselves. Because that's what we want. That's what Morgan wanted when he called for the action at Bryn Buga at the Christmas feast. To be told that he was who he thought he was and that that was all right. I don't despise this, it can be very helpful. Nor can you divines, though you may affect to.

But I'm running away from myself. I think, at best, when I made my imperfect little marwnad for Cadi I was trying to make space for a spirit other than my own. I sang it for Gwrgant.

At best. I'm beginning to realize even as I say this that I must sound as if I care more about the craft than I do about either Cadi or Gwrgant. But it's false to think of them, song and the people, as com-

53

peting for my regard, so long as I hold to the thought of living through the|craft.

It's too late for this kind of talk. What happens is easier to say than why.

In the spring after my Christmas, my first Christmas, at Morgan's court there was some skirmishing along the border with Senghenydd to the north of where we lived. The princes and Iorwerth weren't involved and it was more a matter of cattleraiding than gaining territory. Although it was so minor and nobody was killed so far as I can remember, I heard Iorwerth and Gwrgant talking often about the impossibility of the kind of peace Morgan had seemed to want. Gwrgant hoped that it might be so, but the prince's brother always spoke of the dangers.

The dispute went on, always seeming to be somewhere else, but not far away, just out of sight in the trees. Men of the teulu, Iorwerth with them sometimes, would often cross the end of our meadow. Non's stories about the creatures that lived in the trees became more frequent and frightening. She took special care to tell these to little Hywel, who was coming to the time in his boyhood when language floods the world and any story spoken in the right tone of voice is utterly believed and lived in every muscle. He developed a terror of the trees to the west and north.

I meanwhile, acquired the sophistication of a Cadi or a Cristin, admired the artifice of Non's technique, watched Hywel's open mouth and widening eyes with an adolescent mixture of contempt and condescension. Still, I avoided the beech grove at dusk.

Gwrgant argued with Non about these stories, said it wasn't right to instill fear into a boy who'd be very important one day. Non answered that that was righter than letting him get killed before he had the chance to get important. They argued about other things, too, though rarely in front of Cadi.

So my first official birthday came at a time when Cadi's illness, the last heavy stages of Lleucu's pregnancy and the constant possibility of war all chafed at us, made all the ordinary business of life strained and difficult.

That day, Saint Gwynllyw's day, Gwrgant took me to Dyfrig's shrine in Llandâf and Angharad and Cristin, together with a couple of members of the teulu, came with us. I think it must have been Gwrgant's intention to bring Cadi too but Non insisted that he wasn't well enough. Although she didn't say anything in front of Angharad, I could see her anger at Gwrgant's leaving her with Cadi, and Lleucu so near her time. Still, it was for Cadi that Gwrgant wanted to touch Dyfrig's bones. As we rode he discussed the efficacy of this pilgrimage with Angharad.

'Your love will tell itself to the saint' she said. 'It's one of the most effective relics there is. That's why my father sent a knucklebone from it as a gift to Iorwerth's father when we got married.'

She was riding astride her horse and Cristin and I rode behind. I looked at Angharad's bare heels. Though it was quite cold she wasn't wearing her stockings and on her lower leg, exposed where her skirt was caught up on the horse's flank, I could see the small bumps of flesh raised by the wind and the tiny, fine, fair hairs.

'The law' she said, 'has been well administered since that happened. The oaths made on it are almost always sound.'

Gwrgant said nothing.

'And of course the shrine isn't diminished by the loss of a knucklebone. Some superstitious idiots thought that it would be when my father gave the present. But a saint's love can't be diminished, only made greater or more useful.'

I looked down sideways at Cristin's foot. Then I looked up and saw she was watching me.

'I'm —' I said. And stopped, because I wasn't sure what I was. Then I remembered something of myself, my official self. 'I'm thirteen today.'

'Oh' she said. 'And have you seen any horses?'

'What?'

'In rowing boats.' Her eyes smiled but she held her mouth in a straight line, just.

I felt thwarted in some obscure way, and excited. I smiled at her tentatively and then, with a feeling that my head was very large and awkward, looked once more at Angharad. Had I been able to take my eyes from her legs and concentrated well enough to see as well as look, I would have been surprised that she was holding a book and reading aloud in Latin. Gwrgant said 'Amen' at the end, though I knew he hadn't understood a word, and she shut the book.

'Cristin will pray to Teilo' she said, 'and Griffri can pray to Euddogwy.'

The first time I remember seeing the sea was on that journey. It looked a tame enough blade of grey under the overcast sky, the colour of the tidal mud at Morgan's court, away below us beyond treed plain. We were quite high up, making our way down through the trees, looking down on the backs of magpies and hawks wheeling, shreds of smoke occasionally marking a house. It was the image of peace, but I thought of Gwrgant's talk of how strong the French were there, and my father's words about the sea, and Ifor's men somewhere at our right hand.

I was determined that my amazement at Llandâf wouldn't show. Cristin had been there before and so had the others. I felt them occasionally looking at me to see if I was impressed, so I pretended to glance around nonchalantly.

In fact, I was terrified.

There were a lot of people, some of them strange in speech and dress, some very tall, some with hair fairer than the fairest hair I'd seen. Angharad's hair looked dark next to theirs. There were monks and priests, the usual beggars. That was the first place I saw money changing hands. The enormous stone building — I know it's not that huge, but this was as it looked to me then — the enormous building, longer than a bowshot and roofed with impossibly neat thatch, was either miraculous or the opposite.

On some scaffolding a gang of men were carving the stonework of an arch over a door. They had dark hair and pieces of gold fixed to their ears, and they wore rings on their fingers. One of them was standing shouting down to a priest. He barked like the man in woven chains on Christmas Eve so I couldn't understand, but I felt he was treating the priest with contempt. In one hand he held an axe with its head on sideways and he waggled this occasionally as he talked to emphasise some point or other.

Another priest in beautiful robes came to us, a servant with him, and Angharad dismounted, ran, and embraced him. He looked old and had a fat face, a great split ball of fat at the end of his nose. We all had to dismount and bow and kiss his hand. He wore a silver ring like Angharad's, but grander, with a smooth stone the colour of a gentle sky at dusk. he smiled at us and cocked his head forward in the imitation of benevolent concern that priests are so good at and talked and smiled and nodded all at the same time. He looked like an overweight fox in a skirt.

From where I stood, the unfinished arch made a frame around him as he turned smiling from Gwrgant to Angharad at either hand as they talked. His speech was opaque in places with phrases of Latin, which is what you'd expect. But I was surprised when Angharad answered him in similar style, and in a completely relaxed way. She even, in one anecdote, caught the priest's forearm in both her hands. The demure servant, a young priest himself, moved his eyebrows the merest fraction. Angharad carried on, words pouring from her as if they'd been stored in a growing pile, waiting for this moment.

The professional mask of the bishop — I guessed by this time that this creature was a bishop — seemed to me not to move at all, though Angharad's accustomed self control which I found so seductive had vanished. She even called the fat fox Uncle Nicol.

The bishop gave a croaky laugh which didn't convince me and said, 'Your father Uchdryd would have loved to see you like this in the flower of your days.'

Gwrgant's eyes flickered downward, reacting to the stock phrase. But I thought the words were beautiful. When you're a child, adults seem fixed, changeless. You suppose that like rivers or mountains they were always there before you. But Angharad must have been fairly young then, perhaps twenty-three.

Through the wooden scaffolding in the distance behind the bishop I saw the emerging detail of the carved stone. A kind of arched zigzag. A mouth stretching wide with chevronned inward pointing fangs.

'Uchdryd was a great bishop' the fat fox said. 'Saintly, loved by all, especially the Welsh. You were the dearest child of his later years and god rewarded his goodness by gathering him to the heavenly kingdom in the perfection of his old age. I've commanded that to be written.'

He stood in the open jaw where the French masons were at work carving more teeth. Like the open mouth of a wolf, I thought, though I'd never bothered to get close enough to a wolf to be sure of my comparison. I wondered how god could live in such a place. And if he did, what kind of god then?

Gwrgant was looking towards the doorway too. Bishop Nicol noticed this and glanced over his shoulder.

'Yes' he said. 'The, um, improvements would have had Uchdryd's blessing I'm sure. Indeed, they started when we were both young men. He had a grasp of the practicalities and was a good administrator. I don't care much for the modern architecture myself. But if we are to serve god, we must survive. If we are to survive, we must learn to — to accommodate ourselves to the, um, needs, of the age.'

He smiled. One set of jaws inside another.

The priest who'd been arguing with the mason was walking away, his hands clasped in front. The mason, on the scaffolding above, waved his strange axe after him and blew a short sharp fart.

The bishop, I discovered, had a great house and his own teulu. After we'd washed our feet there and eaten a little, we went to pray.

Walking into the wolf's mouth horrified me. Cristin held my hand and she actually had to pull me in over the threshold.

All the paraphenalia that's so familiar now, the numberless candles, the bright paintwork, the endless song and so on was astonishing. Clusters of candles and daylight splaying from the windows illuminated parts of the place in yellow and grey, but it was difficult for me to hold the idea of the whole in my mind. Inside, it seemed even larger than it had looked from the outside, the gloom patched with these stray, lit scenes suggesting an unending random sequence of chambers.

'Needs of the age indeed' Cristin whispered.

'What?'

She put a finger to her lips, went on, 'The French don't like their bishops to have wives.'

'Why not?'

She shrugged. 'Anyway, they don't. There'd be no Angharads for you to stare at then. That's the way things are going.'

In that place, which seemed at that moment the opposite of a place for god and the angels, with its intense cold and flames flaring before walls painted with blazing colours, Cristin became to me full of subtle understanding, as able to read me as Angharad was to read her Latin book. I gripped her hand tighter.

Angharad put a coin into a bowl proffered by a monk. We came to a little catafalque on which stood a box. In the front of this there was a metal grille. Some candles were positioned to throw light into the box.

Gwrgant and Angharad knelt. While the monk watched they each poked a finger through the grille and then prayed. Presently, Angharad moved away and motioned for me and Cristin to take her place.

On our knees we looked into the box prison. It was shingled with the smashed yellow bones of the saint who had lived ages before, perhaps in the time of giants, when Morgan's ancestors had lived in a great palace. To one side in the box was a small, crazed dome, in it two darknesses where the saint's eyes had been. What attracted our eyes most, though, was the place near the middle where, out of all the fragments, the long gentle curve of femur erected its knobbed end.

I looked to Cristin, who was already looking at me, biting her lip, and we made snorting and choking noises as we tried to hold back the laugh. When at last that had passed I could still hear a low voice.

Beyond Cristin I saw Gwrgant, his closed hand to his forehead and his eyes shut, murmuring a short, endlessly repeated prayer.

## 13

You already know that it didn't work.

We stayed that night at the bishop's great hall and the following day came home. I was relieved that, distracted as he was, Gwrgant remembered to pay the courtesy of escorting Angharad and Cristin, with their two soldiers, to the gate of Iorwerth's court. I looked manfully ahead as he and I rode away from the Court down the westward incline. At the last moment just as we turned onto our track through the tame woodland I looked back, but she hadn't waited.

Our meadow, when we got to it, was empty of people. There was nobody outside the house. We crossed the mud from the stable to the door in silence. Gwrgant stopped. I waited too. The door was shut but I could smell human shit and vomit stronger than the smell of the cows. In a story something would have happened. There would have been an animal, a pig loose, something to talk about, a bird would fly up from the roof. But it was cold March, too early for the martins. The mud nests hung empty. There was nothing except stillness and what we would make happen. The scene behind the door would be some slight variation on what we were already imagining.

The door opened as if on its own and as we walked in I felt as if I was falling slowly. The corpse was on the mattress, covered by Lleucu's husband's cloak except for the head and feet. Non was on her knees, buckled against her son, the side of her head to his cheek, hand to his neck, and she was rocking with a short quick movement that remembered the nursing of babies. Mair was lying on the floor nearby, her body bunched, her face red with crying, her eyes and lips screwed shut, but she was asleep. Hywel, four or five years old by this time, stood watching Non, his porridge finger stuck deep and unmoving in one of his nostrils.

A hand rested itself on my shoulder. It was Lleucu, the taut dome of her belly pressing against my side. She looked tired and in her other hand she held a stinking, sodden cloth.

I heard a thin, high squeal and looked at Non and then Mair, but it had come from Gwrgant, who staggered across in front of us. In a strangely controlled way he reached back over his shoulder, twitched his cloak over his head and doubled down to the ground. Hywel took his finger out of his nose, put his hand on Gwrgant's back and bent over, looking concerned at the cloak-enveloped head.

My arms had gone round where Lleucu's waist used to be and I was clinging to her, willing her to pick me up, except that I was too big, nearly grown up, and she was too tired, too pregnant.

Hywel said, 'Don't cry, Gwrgant.'

There was a groaning under the cloak and Gwrgant spoke no words.

## 14

No words.

The birth of Lleucu's second child over a year later — unlike the first this one survived — has something to do with the poem I made. That and the peculiar sense of my hands and feet and head almost visibly growing away from one another, the thickening mats of my pubic hair, my testicles completing the transformation from a hard little bud into a scrawny, heavy, hot purse; the increasing frequency of unbearably intense arousals; the need to sleep longer and longer; the growing gluttony; discontent; love of company; love of solitude; the new ability to understand jokes; to make them myself; to throw a spear further than Gwrgant could — all this tumult was part of it.

Though none of it's mentioned. If it was a performance, a proving, a shaky handstand always on the point of toppling, then perhaps it compounded the guilt of which it in part attempted to absolve me.

Cristin and I had talked of these things, in a way, during the summer after the death. She was technically an adult now. I was still an apprentice in every sense.

We walked in the tame wood between the court and Gwrgant's house. Most people were working or practising for war, so it was quiet. In less than a year I'd have my own arms and be with them.

It was dry. We lay on a bank near a dense plait of tree roots.

'They're like the carvings on the old crosses' Cristin said.

'What?'

'Them.' She nodded towards the roots. 'Like the carvings.'

I caught glimpses of her teeth as she talked, saw the lower part of her ear through her hair, its precise shape, the sculpted whorl, an intricate carving. Awkwardly, I moved my gaze to the root tangle. Scaly pipework spilled and looped like the innards on Christmas Eve. The yellow summer light began to have the same unreal brilliance of that time. I looked back to her.

'There was one by the cathedral' she said. 'Probably Dyfrig himself stood by it and spoke once. Did you notice?'

'What?'

'One of the old crosses. Stop saying "what?" All folded in on itself like that.'

'Oh. I did.'

'Did what?'

'Notice.'

I was lying.

I looked back to the roots. They looked as if they might writhe and grow out of their skins. I'd watched waves of grief breaking over Non and Gwrgant, without any understanding at first. There were times when they cried, or were unnaturally silent, or unreachable in thought, and moments later, normal, working at the ordinary business of life. Lleucu, grieving her baby, had tried to explain. She told me that she would have other babies, but Gwrgant and Non would never have another son.

I shifted towards Cristin so that our sides were touching. I turned and placed a hand speculatively on her ribs. Her eyes slid to look at me. She did nothing except articulate her hip so that it rubbed against me, slowly. Then we were pressed together, as though we wanted to push ourselves till we occupied the same space. Her skin smelt of milk and her hair smelt smoky. 'Do you think' she said, 'it made any difference when we laughed?'

'What?'

She pinched my back and then pressed it with her palm.

'Stop saying "what?".'

She drew her tongue along my neck and spent a long time biting my chin, my ears, my eyebrows and, less successfully, the bridge of my nose. Heat and cold. Growing and changing shape. I writhed like the roots, decided to try to kiss her teeth.

'I mean' she said. She pulled her mouth clear of mine so that she could speak. 'I mean in the cathedral. You know.'

My head was in the nest of her shoulder. Through a thicket of hair I could see the root plait. Living lines woven to the glory of god, like the old crosses. I knew.

She went on. 'When we laughed. Do you think it changed anythlng?'

'Changed?'

'For Gwrgant. For his prayer.' We continued our slow writhe as she talked. 'It was sort of an insult to the relic the way we laughed.'

'Would god punish Non and Gwrgant for that?'

'It wouldn't be like that. More like stopping the prayer getting through.'

'It's a terrible punishment just for that.'

'But it wouldn't be like a punishment. You heard. We stood — we knelt in the way of prayer.'

'Sounds like punishment to me.'

I could still see the living knotwork through the strands of hair. Here was the real church. How could god live in the belly of a wolf? The chiselled fangs had yawned us in.

'Perhaps it was a desecration to move Dyfrig from Enlli' I said. 'To take him into that place.'

Each of us placed a hand on the other's thigh, entering the true nave. What kind of god could Gwrgant have prayed to there? Only Dyfrig's thigh bone had gestured some sort of defiance in that place of coldness and lurid colours in flamelight. Here we lay by the true rootwoven cross in the rustling trees. We tugged each other's skirt aside and slid a hand along the nave, approached the chancel.

'You just want' Cristin said. She interrupted herself wlth a little noise that was neither quite a groan nor a gasp. 'You just want to find anything, so you can shift the blame.'

I stopped myself from saying 'what?' and thought back over her words. Concentrating was getting difficult. But I realized somehow that she might be be right and she was clever. She was perfect.

'You're perfect' I said.

'What?' The word tailed off into breath.

'The real church.'

'What?'

My hand in the warm chancel brushed at the altar. Her hand brushed over the hot, heavy.

There was a short time after that for which there are no words, like the smell of green wood on a fire, or the taste of fruit.

Suddenly Cristin was sitting up, clearing her throat, holding her hand with the fingers spread in front of her as if it was a buok. There was a rustling in the tiees behind us. Then she was shaking her hand as if to dry it and saying 'Ych' and turning, looking around, she smeared the sticky stuff onto my shirt.

'What was that noise?' I said.

She smelt her fingers, rubbing them together, made a face. The sticky stuff had spread to all sorts of places. It was drying, making my skin feel brittle and withered. Bits of tree litter were sticking to me. She leant her head towards me and laughed.

'I think we'd better stop' she said.

There was more rustling. Whispers. Cristin saw me look towards the top of the bank.

'It's Hywel' she said, loudly. 'And Owain ap Morgan his cousin. Didn't you see them?'

I dragged my tunic down and stopped myself, just, from shouting some threat. Then, casually, 'Oh, yes. Them.'

Suddenly Owain stuck his head above the top of the bank. Hywel's little hand appeared and covered Owain's eyes.

'Don't look!' Hywel said. 'You'll get a baby into you.'

I jumped to my feet. They ran, stopped at a safe distance and embraced.

'Darling' Hywel said.

'You're perfect' Owain said. 'Let me squeeze your squidgy bits.'

I think I'm not making it up then I say I laughed before I sat back-down. They were the ghosts of Cadi and myself.

I looked at Cristin. The strange light was still filling the air, seeming to come from everywhere. I looked at how she sat. Those shapes. The sticky palm rubbing at her hip. Her eyes cast down and then flicked towards me. Eyes, I thought. The centres. It is either miraculous or hellish. The true. The real.

'You went all silly for a bit then' she said.

Something surged in me. Shall I say again that it was like a wave? We were running and I was shouting bits of Gwrgant's boastsong, jumping at branches, falling, trying, unsuccessfully, to throw Cristin in the air. I must temporarily have cleared a whole district of its wildlife and Cristin was very forbearing of my idiocy.

Safely distant still, Hywel and Owain ap Morgan followed us, mimicking me and waving their wooden swords.

## 15

Waves?

Remember, I'd never seen one, at least not from close at hand, at that time. I had only the words of others to go on. The waves continued to break over Non and Gwrgant, and Mair was much embraced, given endless small gifts. Hywel, too, to his bewilderment, was patted, tweeked, snatched up and carried about arbitrarily, kissed, more than he was even by his true parents when they came to see him.

For my part, I was no longer — if I ever had been — the kind of fluffy little chick that attracts that kind of attention, with my elongating bones, erupting flesh, and the unpredictable switches of the register of my voice. I helped with the cattle and the churning at home, travelled often with Gwrgant to Morgan's main court in Caerllion and to some of the other houses in Gwynllwg where he sang. My apprenticeship proceeded and I think it was at this time that I began to understand it. I began to think of myself as a Poet, though I'd made no poems worth the name, and could imagine myself as nothing else. I have a picture in my memory's eye of a gangly boy, his nostrils held high, a few dark hairs beginning to shadow his jaw just below the ear. He's wearing a solemn mask worthy of a bishop as he rides through the trees carrying a light, yellowshafted spear. The older man, thirty odd, is relaxed, half smiling even, when he looks round at his apprentice.

Yet I could have had no such picture of myself at that time. There's the sorting out of memory. The now I had then, like all nows, was a chaos.

We carried on with my learning, the interminable memorizing, the counting of beats, the strange, archaic vocabulary. The musical jangling began to be penetrated by meaning as my understanding grew of the compound words, the verbless compressions. Like many another, I think I got absorbed in the complexities and lost sight of the whole. My concentration was patchy.

'No no no no no no. Stop. Listen' Gwrgant would say. 'Listen to the note now. Listen to the word. You're not listening to yourself.'

And I'd have to start again and he'd stop me in the middle of a word, trying to mask his irritation with faked patience.

'They'd laugh at you up north' he'd say. 'The fish in the lakes in Gwynedd sing better than you do.'

But I often saw him not listening himself, staring down into the rushes, or watching Non move about the house, or, most unnervingly staring at me.

Early that autumn he went away on tour and refused to take me with him, saying that he was going to Ifor's court at Gelligaer and then north and east to Seisyll's part of Gwent Uwchcoed, which was dangerous because the French were very strong there, and then on into Brycheiniog where they were stronger. He went to sing mainly, as this was the slack time before the preparations for the Christmas court had got going. But Cristin told me that he was going to make inquiries about possible marriage deals for the children of Iorwerth and Morgan. Actually she said the children of Angharad and Rhagnell.

'And' she said, 'I think he's escaping for a bit.'

Angharad was with us.

'Old head' she said. 'All men want to run away. War and poetry are the nearest they come to good excuses.'

I didn't follow this but felt, somehow, that it was perverse and unpleasant, that I was being dismissed.

Cristin wasn't smiling. 'I wouldn't mind doing that myself sometimes' she said. 'Non can't.'

'Neither can he' Angharad said.

He was away no more than a fortnight, and only one member of the teulu with him, which worried me when I thought of his visit to Ifor's court.

I was helping Lleucu to carry water down from the spring the afternoon they came back. I'd thought there were no men about so that I could carry the pails without feeling any embarrassment. The water from that spring is pure and soothes griping guts, provided you drink from no other source, because it was blessed by Saint Cadog. Non thought she should always have used this spring, and I think she connected her not doing so with Cadi's death. Guilt enters at every door.

When I saw the two figures on horseback coming out of the trees at the edge of the meadow, I was caught between excitement and shame at being seen carrying the pails. I ran a few steps, spilt a lot of water, stopped, put the pails down and ran on to meet the two men.

September sun was dusting the bent tops of the yellow grass. It must be hindsight's invention that makes me want to say that the cooling air and the billow of dark green woods at the rim of the meadow were heavy with the sense of the end of summer.

I slowed when I saw a third man walking alongside Gwrgant's horse.

'God's welcome — back' I said, raising my arms.

Gwrgant was wearing a new cloak and there were a number of extra bags slung on both horses. It had been a good trip.

'Well, Griff' Gwrgant said. 'Do you know him?'

I looked at the stranger beside him. He wore a woollen cloak that looked familiar, rough and not dyed. He had a straggly, sparse moustache, untidy hair, a small nose, wideset blue eyes. I was aware of Gwrgant and the soldier looking at me as if to observe my reaction. The stranger stepped forward, smiling, extended a hand. The hand came to my shoulder and I realized, as the fingers fiddled there, that this wasn't a greeting but that the stranger was examining the iron clasp of my cloak.

'Well' the man said quietly, looking from the clasp to my face. 'You've done all right. Fostered out like a real prince.'

Something in my face made the three of them laugh. I felt conscious of my hairless lips, the thin cloak, neatly hemmed, my hair carefully cut around my ears by Non's scissors. The stranger spread his arms wide and smiled at me.

For a moment I felt that the ground had suddenly moved from under me. You know the feeling of waking with a start, the huge momentary confusion. A storm and treetops. A sky of bruises.

Even when he was introduced as my brother Heilyn, I can't say that I remembered him. There were the ghosts of things that had already shaken me — family resemblances, gestures, something in the voice. Of course, he'd grown up since I'd left. That was it, I told myself.

He was ill at ease too. After the soldier had said goodbye and carried on to the court, Heilyn was clumsy washing his feet in the bowl that Mair proffered. He seemed to have trouble looking into people's faces and didn't know to refuse the music Gwrgant offered. So poor Mair picked away half heartedly at an out of tune harp, unable to try on the gown Gwrgant had brought her from Dyddgu at Scisyll's court.

After Gwrgant had greeted his wife — which itself was a subdued scene — and delivered the news of Dyddgu's son born at the end of spring and Dyddgu's illness ever since, we all sat, not talking, at the fireless hearthstone. In the end my brother and I exchanged some stilted conversation. Asking about each brother and sister in turn I began to realize that I couldn't remember all their names. Heilyn helpfully filled in the gaps when I hesitated, glad of the excuse to be able to say something.

'And my mother?' I said.

'That's why I've come' Heilyn said. He looked to the hearth and then up at Gwrgant.

'She's dead' Gwrgant said. His voice disappeared on the word 'dead'. He cleared his throat and repeated the word flatly. 'It was pure chance we passed that way coming back' he said.

Non watched, a closed hand to her chin. I could see that she wanted to do something but she didn't know what. She came beside me uncertainly and put her arm round me. I looked at the ashy hearthstone, tried to get up and make for the door, then sat down pressed against her. The tuneless music had stopped, though I hadn't noticed when. Her other hand came to my neck, then my face, brushed the dry cheek.

67

I thought and thought but could only imagine someone face down at the edge of a clearing. I couldn't remember her face.

## 16

'Stay' Gwrgant said the next day. 'Work here for me and you'll be handy to fight for the prince when the need arises.'

Heilyn wavered. I remembered what Angharad had said. Running away.

'You'll be placed' Gwrgant said, 'to serve as your —' he made the slightest pause, then realized that he couldn't call the words back 'father did.'

Heilyn looked at him, then away, shaking his head. 'No. No. I can't. You know how it is. Thanks anyway, but no.'

His insistence seemed to invite further persuasion, but Gwrgant said nothing.

I was amazed when Heilyn left riding on the back of the gift Gwrgant made to him, a strong young pony he'd accepted from Morgan in place of some accumulated debts. My brother thanked my master in a strangely formal way for the gift, as if in some ceremony, though it went beyond all conventional generosity. As he rode away awkwardly — awkwardly because he clearly wasn't used to riding — I felt relieved.

My fourteenth birthday came. I prayed for Cadi on Saint Gwynllyw's day. I still do, but don't think me a good man for it. Every prayer we make in any cause is secretly a prayer for ourselves. Gwrgant told me in front of the family that I was now a man and was no longer answerable to him but directly to the prince for all my actions. As his son I was free to leave whenever I chose, but as his apprentice I still had a few years to serve, having made a late start.

In the beili of the court, Iorwerth gave me a quiver of a dozen arrows whose heads had been made by Rhun the smith at Caerllion. He dipped one of these in the blood of a lamb and smeared it on each of my cheeks and then on the point of my chin.

'The promise of your beard' he said. He handed me the arrow. 'Come with the teulu when you're called.'

The day was overcast and the trees were restless with a light wind. A few of the teulu were there. I felt them watching, and the taeogion, and Owain ap Morgan and Hywel standing with Non, and all the girls, watching me. Even the whitened hall on its grass plinth stared at me. There couldn't have been more than twenty people there and yet, although I'd seen the rite before a couple of times, I felt they were thousands and I was filled with a sense of newness, an uncontrollable pride, a tingeing of absurdity inside my bloody mask.

Owain would be imagining himself in my place, some of the men remembering their own time, recognizing the emotions in me as something that had been theirs, about which they could be sentimental now, or smug and dismissive.

Iorwerth's thin face was still close to me. Often he gave me the impression of speaking ironically, of using double meanings that never quite came clear, and his habit was to stand with his face to one side as he talked. There was none of that now. He looked straight at me with a solemnity which I felt wasn't merely a performance. He'd said the words many times before, yet he said them as if they were, new, meant, and not an empty form. He seemed alive in a way that I'd never observed in him before. But more words came, outside the custom.

'Be Gwrgant's second' he said. 'And when he can't sing, sing in his place.'

He stepped back and suddenly relaxed, the heightened vitality leaving him.

People began to move and talk, some to pat my arm or back and talk to me. I looked towards Non and her eyes were full of water. The unexpected words echoed in my head. *When he can't sing.* A year and Gwrgant hadn't sung, not the important song anyway. I looked around but couldn't see my master. The blood on my chin. Two boys sitting among daisies, perhaps. Non was imagining Cadi in my place, or seeing me in what should have been his. Things fractionally different. The lips and fingernails of the thirteen year old corpse had been the colour of campion or the stone in Angharad's ring.

How much of my first patchy attempt at song came into being then I don't know. For, I suppose, a couple of months, phrases floated in my head. My life changed as I was no longer expected to help with the menial work, though I still did some, grudgingly, as Lleucu's second time approached.

I went out several nights to watch the border against Senghenydd on foot with a few others and Toothless on horseback in charge. It was exciting, briefly, and then miserable and cold. I slept and the others laughed at me. At home I wandered in the tame woods avoiding Owain and Hywel who wanted to involve me in their children's games. I still wanted to be involved, secretly, but was afraid of being seen by the soldiers, or worse still by any of the dozen or so girls whom I'd inwardly canonized as saints of my true church. I went hunting, too, often on my own. The hunt, though, finding and hitting a mark, hardly mattered. It was being in the bursting dazzle of green that made me entire. I saw Lleucu's new son, when the women let us back into the house, and this too, was some unbearably good breaking forth, full of newness. Idiotic with wonderment and frustrations, I walked among the trees talking to myself, frequently erecting and frantically demolishing fleshy shrines to my new saints in lonely places. And don't think I'd use such a metaphor out of coyness or merely the desire to blaspheme. It has more force than that.

And from all this sense of growing like some strange plant in a hot summer, hardly knowing myself, came an archaic, gloomy bit of pared away verse. Don't ask me to explain.

Gwrgant must have sensed something. He asked me, one day, if I had a piece to sing. We were outside, by the edge of the meadow. It was the end of June and there was sun and clouds that drew overhead quickly, thinning the colours and cooling us for a few moments and then passing. He had been teaching me lists of key rhymes and had seen my eyes wandering up into the fret of branches. There was a towered clump of foxgloves nearby, standing like a city in a story. I watched the bees whirring among them, entering the tapered stacks of drooping mouths.

'Well, yes' I said. 'I have.'

He had been in the middle of explaining some vague old word that nobody used any more that was very handy if you were stuck for a rhyme and I think he was more bored with it than I was and so had interrupted himself.

He paused, said, 'Come on then.'

I did my best to act embarrassed. 'Well, I don't know.'

He'd always been very harsh on the single verses, the exercises I'd carved for him on some set subject or to some formal stricture, and a part of me did genuinely resist him. He played out the etiquette of coaxing and refusal and coaxing with a patience I can admire now. God allows us only a little freedom. Something would snap between us if I didn't give in.

He was sitting on a log, I on the earth. Before he let me start he insisted we change places. All the business of movement, sitting, settling became clumsy.

He glanced to the buildings in the distance across the meadow, then to me, gestured.

'Right. What's it called?'

I took a breath.

'Marwnad Cadwallon ap Gwrgant.'

I was too selfconscious to be looking for his reaction, but I think there was none. Not a muscle in his face moved, not an eyelash.

He gestured again for me to start.

Make the darkness between words speak.

I paused. The bees spoke, quietly. Wind washed the leaves. I spoke the words, without singing:

> When Cadi died
> Gwrgant made no song.
> The flesh was yellow, purple the lips.
>
> When Cadi died
> Gwrgant made no song.
> The strings stilled and the voice choked.
>
> When Cadi died
> Gwrgant made no song.
> The jaw was slack and the eyes rolled up.
>
> When Cadi died
> Gwrgant made no song.
> His heart cracked on the rocks of grief.
>
> When Cadi died
> Gwrgant made no song.
> His twelve years' darling froze his tongue.
>
> When Cadi died
> Gwrgant made no song.
> His boy was yellow, purple the lips.

When Cadi died
His father made no song.
Griffri, not grieving, sings in his place.


For moments after I'd finished, the poem hung about me in the air. Then I heard the bees again, the leaves stirred.

Gwrgant was staring towards the buildings. I glanced round to follow his gaze. Lleucu was walking towards the house. In one arm she held the tight bundle of her new baby. The other carried the big bucket, slopping with milk. Her body was skewed over with the burden and she took small steps.

'Thirteen' Gwrgant said.

'What?'

I turned back to him. He was looking at the ground.

'He was thirteen. Just. Not twelve.' He looked up.

I shrugged.

'It didn't fit' I said.

The speaking silence the poem had made around itself was gone. There was the buzz of our talk. I knew he was something like impressed. Confused feelings flowed through me. Childish — or mannish — pride, remorse, a sense of things having changed, relief. So it had been a kind of wobbly handstand in part, but only in part. I had a sense of arriving somewhere, but I didn't know the place yet, or whether it was good or bad.

'Did Morgan have three hundred horses at Bryn Buga?' I said.

Gwrgant smiled, got to his feet.

'That was an official poem' he said. 'I wasn't even there. They tell me I got the weather right, though. That dawn.' He paused. 'Your song. It's a bit old fashioned. A touch of Llywarch Hen about it, and Berddig.' He saw me looking surprised and laughed. 'Don't worry. People are always reminded of what they know, things that never occur to you when you're composing. It — it —worked.'

He found the last word with difficulty, spoke it quietly.

Suddenly he said, 'Let's eat.'

And he was walking away from me towards the buildings.

Standing by the log and the foxgloves I watched him go. Of course, he meant Berddig the poet. I felt pulled in all directions. In its essence my effort tried, clumsily, to make space for a grief. 'Purple' was all wrong, too slack, but it tried. There was the sea cracking on the rocks, a wave breaking that I'd never seen, though that, somehow, I thought was right. But there was too, obscurely, a sense of wounding. Looking back I can see a naive opportunism, how Gwrgant would be almost as confused as I was, how my words might seem like a bloody arrow brandished in his face.


## 17


I must have been seventeen or so when Meilyr came back from Tyddewi.

There. I promised I'd get round to him.

Henri was king several years by then. In fact Estefyn, the old king, died that year I turned fourteen and Henri went from France into England about the Christmas. I remember being puzzled by the shock it sent through the older people. Morgan even called a meeting with Iorwerth and the chief men of the teulu, Gwrgant among them. It's the first time I remember a message coming to us about English affairs. A priest came from Gwent Uwchcoed with the news that Dyddgu, the pregnant woman I'd seen at the Christmas court, had died after her long illness, and requesting the fosterage of her baby son, Morgan ap Seisyll, with either of his two important uncles — that is Morgan the prince or Iorwerth the penteulu — in Gwynllwg. Then with affected casualness he said that on his way he'd heard from an Englishman at the gate of Abergafenni the news about Estefyn's death and who the new king was. Iorwerth's hand went to his mouth and he pressed his moustache, as if checking that his mask was in place. He murmured that he hoped the new king would turn out to be less of a bastard than his grandfather had been.

But the crowning of the new king seemed to change nothing for a long time. I listened, wearing a serious face as that seemed appropriate, when the older men talked gravely about how it had been in the time of the first Henri: massacres and campaigns and desertions a loss of rich lands; the long retreats and hiding; then the great breaking out under Morgan and Iorwerth and the restoration, almost twenty years before, which my father must have been a part of. I never got any clear picture of this. It seemed to me that the men, casting nets into the past, drew up an intricate, threshing confusion, a heaving plait of creatures that lived in struggle. And the French fought one another too. They weren't one monster that came out of the dark but scores, snapping at one another as they moved among us.

Still at the feasts Gwrgant and I sang, recited Morgan's line back to Brutus and then to Adda, praised god. That continuity, that praise, Gwrgant said, was the thing to hold to, to help make the heaving confusion into a pattern. I don't know what I thought of all this. My thoughts were a chip of wood afloat in my emotions. The sea again —so useful to a poet on an off day. The battlesongs could make me angry, full of horror, want to rush out to the border. The marwnadau could twist me with pity — but whether I was responding to Gwrgant's performances or to the world itself as he channelled it, I'm not sure. Perhaps in the end there's no difference. Though I think there probably is a fractional difference at least. The men in woven chains and the barking captain, the snapped arrow and its thread of blood repeated themselves in my mind unbidden sometimes and all the safenesses of the feast were rocked.

That suited me in a way. At that age, like many another, I ached for something, though I wasn't always sure what it was. Often enough the ache was unambiguous and I walked the woodland or the mountain in a kind of voluptuous torment, my mind filled with whichever of my saints I'd seen last. Guarding the border with Senghenydd on clear night I'd pay more attention to the stars — than to the earth. If you stay awake a long time stars grow brighter and some grow stronger colours. Toothless knew the stars well because of these patrols and taught me many of their names. One night on the hill with him I remember Caer Gwydion seeming more immense than ever like a river across the sky.

Some of these things went into a boastsong I tried to make. It was a confusion of Gwrgant's boastsong and my own feelings and I never finished it —

> Tonight on the hill I saw
> Arthur in his battlecar
> Culhwch knocking at his gate

74

Indeg stretched across the night
Caer Gwydion spilt like semen
Across the dish of heaven

Arad wheeling round Polaris
Endless dark where no star is
Points glittering like raindrops
When wind stirs dripping branchtips

All right. I make no claims for it. But the blaze of things and — the tumult inside went together, or tried to.

Things are either miraculous or the opposite. The following morning, at dawn, we saw three men ford the river below us and emerge from the trees in a clearing where cattle were grazing. I had my first battle. There were four of us.

Toothless deployed us in an arc in the trees, positioned so that we could all see him, and ready to drive Ifor's men back towards the river. The man came across the clearing unaware of us. I had to try twice to put an arrow to my bow because of my hands shaking. I watched them — my hands — as if they were somebody else's. My left shook so much that the bowshaft rattled against ths treetrunk I was leaning against. They must have heard that, I thought. But the men came on as if out for a stroll.

Then I lost all feeling in my right hand and I couldn't grip the fletched end of the arrow. I watched myself, puzzled. Why can't he do this? Finally, somehow, he drew the bow and I was in my own self again, looking along the shaft.

The nearest man was wearing his bow across his shoulder and he carried a stick ready to tap the cattle. The other two came forward more warily, holding their bows. The first man was enjoying his display of casualness, evidently. My arm ached. One of the rear men called something. The first man, smiling, half turned and started to call back to him. Before he'd finished he suddenly crumpled, sat on the earth. He held his shoulders and arms forward as if trying to stay seated, but fell onto his back. Something whipped the earth at my feet. There was a yell. Toothless and the others were running forward screaming. I followed, shouting as I'd been taught. The other two men were already at the far edge of the clearing and still running. I made to fire my arrow but realized it had already gone. Toothless and I stopped by the fallen man. Our other soldiers followed the two who were retreating.

'What did you shoot so early for?' Toothless said.

The man had an arrow in his chest. He was still alive. He had brown eyes which looked in my direction, though I thought he couldn't see me.

'We could've had the lot' Toothless said.

I thought I knew the man. I thought for a moment he was one of Rhys Ddu's men, the one who'd sat next to me at the Christmas feast once and given me mead. But I looked again and saw that it wasn't him, though there was a resemblance.

Toothless stooped over the man and reaching down took the knife from his belt. The man tried to stop him, hanging on to the blade, but Toothless peeled the clinging hand away as if it was a wet leaf sticking to his foot.

I looked at the arrow stuck in his chest and realized it wasn't mine. I felt a mixture of relief and shame. Toothless was waving the hilt end of the knife towards me. I stared at him and then around me at the ground. My arrow had fallen short. I could see its feathers sticking out of the grass and began to understand. My arrow had fallen short and the man's companion had raised the alarm, firing at me. Then Toothless and the others were forced to shoot and give chase.

Toothless was still waving he hilt at me and I was still staring. At last he stopped and looked down.

'All right' he said. He shrugged and made a noise that I think was meant to be a laugh. 'This is for Eneas.'

He knelt and slit the man's throat.


## 18

Sorry.

I've gone off the point. I'll get like those old men — you know the sort — all they want to do is talk about the battles they've been in. They'd cry if you raised your voice.

That day in the clearing, when we stripped the body and shared the goods out while the cows stared, joined Eneas and the woven chains as a recurring, uncontrollable memory.

But I was going to tell you about Meilyr. I met him at Morgan's smithy in Caerllion. I was with a crowd of young men of the teulu and Owain ap Morgan. Owain had come of age by that time I think. This was quite a big event. Morgan and Rhagnell made a big fuss and settled property on him, including some land at Pencarn and a hall where Morgan had sometimes held court to collect dues. And for that reason from then on Owain was called Owain Pencarn. The fatfaced smoky boy who habitually shut one eye was gone, almost. Owain had become lean and sharpeyed. It had dawned on me at some time that one day I would probably be his poet and so I watched him quite closely, seeing echoes of some of my own recent past. Iorwerth had begun, with Morgan's agreement, to give Owain jobs along the Senghenydd border leading a group of men, myself among them sometimes. After the incident I've just told you about all the old enmities returned. Morgan himself rode into Senghenydd with Gwrgant and Owain Pencarn, young as he was, to warn Ifor's men off our cattle. Ifor had the cheek to say that the meadow the cattle were grazing rightly belonged to him and that he was owed galanas for the man he'd lost. Morgan told him this wasn't on of course, and Ifor's answer was inevitable. He felt himself free to claim a life and to raid or make war to reclaim — as he put it — the disputed territory, which was only a couple of hours' walk to the north of Gwrgant's house. The truth was that Ifor was smarting from what Iarll Caerloyw was doing at the southern edge of his land, wittling it away piecemeal, collecting dues from Ifor's poeple and commiting all kinds of barbarity, justifying it by referring to which ever law — Welsh, French, or even English — suited his purpose.

I was beginning, dimly, to grasp some of these things. Owain Pencarn himself, who discussed these affairs with his father and the thinfaced lawyer, taught me much. What must have hurt Ifor most was that it was said the Iarll called him a vassal and kept a running total of how much Senghenydd owed him in the way of tribute.

Owain smiled when he told me how his father had said, 'Don't think you can settle *your* debts to *your* master with *our* cattle' — told me how Ifor's face had frozen, how he'd said, quite quietly, that there were no debts in his life, except what he himself was owed.

Ifor, I'm sure from experience, would have been quite prepared to settle the matter then, except that Morgan had brought too many men with him to make it an attractive thought. So there was a very thin show of cold courtesy and a sort of stand off, the quiet time of preparation that some people mistake for peace.

It's a mistake I would have made myself if I hadn't been close to Pencarn. Perhaps I'm making my own picture of things too clear anyway, putting shape onto the chaos I was living in. I think I saw a lot of people moving around, went where I was told to go. Then in quiet moments when I talked with Owain or Gwrgant, or Cristin even, the pattern in things would come clear — but only momentarily.

Cristin hadn't yet married. Although she was Angharad's maid, her family was neither rich nor important, so no one was particularly interested in making a match with her. Her father had been a taeog in Gwent Iscoed and had been pressed, with others, to fight for Iarll Caerloyw in Estefyn's wars against others of the French in England. He went one day, Cristin told me, so that the roof over her family would be spared, and he never came back. Afraid that her sons might go the same way, Cristin's mother considered running away. One of the sons was threatened with blinding for hunting and they decided to go somewhere where, even if they were poor, they could depend on the pot.

She told me all this one day in the woodland, the dangerous woodland, to the north and west of Gwrgant's house.

Gwrgant had taken me on several tours by that time — the final stages of my training. She and I lay on a dry bank where beeches grow and I told her about singing at Seisyll's court and for Bishop Nicol at Llandâf when some important Frenchmen had been present, which had made the occasion a little strained, how Nicol had tried to translate bits of what we sang for the French clerics.

I told her about tablecloths and red wine, and the absurd, elaborate displays of servility that these great people expected from their inferiors. She already knew a lot of this, of course, and I knew she did. Still she lay quiet and listened, stroking the place where Non carefully clipped my hair behind my ear, or sometimes putting a finger on my moving lips, my adolescent attempt at a moustache.

I think I hardly noticed. I was too busy performing my worldliness. And I went on to my biggest adventure, far to the north to the court of Owain Cyfeiliog with Gwrgant, told how splendid it was, and how that Owain had a man whose sole job it was to look after the prince's hawks, and how Owain raised the great blue meadhorn to us when we sang, and how he himself was a poet and how he sang to us. I think I forgot to mention how often Cyfeiliog allied himself with the French — perhaps then I didn't know about it. His court really was the greatest I'd seen then — it wasn't just out of the need to show off that I told Cristin about these things. I was realising what I had seen by re-membering it in words, particularly the great regard that Gwrgant commanded in every hall he entered.

But I carefully didn't mention the young women of these places, — some of whom would often be, rightly, I used to think, impressed by and interested in a young stranger of a certain standing. I chose not to remember them. Gwrgant, too, had women in some of these places. Curiously, he was a little sheepish with me about them and at first tried to keep them secret from me. Impossible of course. I began to realise he'd had thoughts other than for my safety when he'd refused to take me out of Gwynllwg before my coming of age. Even after we'd established that he could trust my discretion following a half drunk though, as far as I can remember, stilted conversation one night in Cyfeiliog, his sheepishness remained. Which puzzled me a little, and amused me.

So there was an odd reversal, he becoming something like a naughty boy, I affecting a benevolent if cynical worldliness. Though the reversal could never quite be complete. I was for one thing vaguely disgusted at the thought of an old man like him being a prey to the same forces which — of course perfectly rightly — drove me. So my sophistication wasn't merely affected, but duplicit. I was troubled, which perhaps he was aware of.

But Cristin heard nothing about any of that.

She was about seventeen then. Her face had kept its roundness, her eyes and mouth their sharp expressiveness, her nose its straightness. I remember her — this is probably invention — in a thin, pale green dress, loosely belted, sitting up as I tell her about these marvels, hugging her knees. Her hair is drawn back tight and she wears no headdress. Her body has reached its fulness. There's the miraculous mass of folded thigh and hip. I imagine her breasts inside the gown, pressed midway against her thighs. When she moves her toes I see the fan of ridges rise in her foot.

She pursed her lips against her knees, her eyes sliding sideways to look at me. I stopped talking then, lying flat, only my head straining up absurdly, and looked at her. Now I know the memory is right. After lying next to me, preening my fine hair while she told me of her family she'd shifted and closed her body from me after I'd started talking, in this seductive hoop.

'I —' I said.

She laid a cheek on her knee and smiled. 'You.'

There was a long moment of a sort of nakedness that must have been full of birdsong, though I don't remember it. There was instead a speaking silence.

She had preserved her virginity, just. Other men admired her but the fact of my interest — I a teulu member and well to do, who'd taken part in a defensive action and seen the horrors of war, who rode with Toothless and Owain Pencarn — I supposed kept them at a distance. It probably had more to do with Cristin herself, and the fact that Angharad was her mistress. We tormented one another on a series of ecstatic brinks whenever the weather was good enough, and once or twice when it wasn't.

I shifted onto my side, stretched a hand to the green cloth taut over her thigh.

'I talk a lot of shit' I said.

She draped a hand onto my outstretched forearm. I caught her under her leg and pulled her towards me. She fell awkwardly against me and I pushed her onto her back, started to mount her, trying to pull up her dress.

She said, 'No' in a patient sort of way, pushed down on the cloth. 'Don't. How could you? Please.'

I said 'Please' too, many times, moving my face to follow hers, trying to fasten onto her mouth.

'No. What's in you?' she said.

There was a kind of half hearted battle of hands and thighs, as if neither of us really knew what we meant. She caught hold of my penis and steered me away, kissed my face and pulled the flesh snood on and off the head, stopped kissing, pulling, tried to push me away again, restarted the noes.

I caught her back hair with one hand, pulled it back tighter. Her chin went up and she made a small noise of pain, a whine I suppose you'd call it, opened her eyes wide, held her mouth straight and stiff. She stopped moving, held herself very still and so did I. I still held her back hair and she watched me with half closed eyes. There was another long moment, a different kind of nakedness. The eyes. I saw no energy there now. My wise, ironic girl was gone. She'd shown me her frailty, told me about her family, and I'd heard nothing.

As my rage left me I realised that I'd been enraged. My hand relaxed at the back of her head and we were Cristin and Griffri again lying under trees where there was birdsong, wind washing among leaves.

I moved off her and lay, looking down.

'I'm sorry' she said.

I wondered what she meant, but the same words choked in my throat.

'I don't want a baby' she said.

The reason seemed commonplace and inadequate to me. Reasons, I thought, were unnecessary in these matters.

'You're —' I coughed and started again. 'You're plenty old enough.'

The words were all wrong but I couldn't call them back. I meant, I think, that it was time, the season. I reached out and pulled her dress straight. It was the nearest I could come to an apology, but even that was wrong, though I didn't quite know how. We walked without talking, a couple of arms lengths apart, but not homeward.

I've seen a mare kick a stallion away and then watch him circling, but I, in the untame wood, was no tactician, was merely bewildered. Her instincts were better than mine. I had more subtlety at making lovesongs than at making love, as you'll have gathered. I'd looked at something in myself that made the world jangle with discordant colours, frightening shapes. That was all I knew then, and the feeling that I'd ruined things, spat on an altar.

Neither of us knew what to do next, so it was lucky that the soldiers came.

## 19

Cristin froze and spread her arms looking straight ahead. She'd been walking with her forearms folded across her midriff, looking mostly away from me. I turned to try to speak to her, then looked in the direction of her stare and saw a man approaching holding a drawn bow.

I had enough skill at arms by this time to look round for more. Another archer, slightly further off, approached from another angle.

I saw the man sitting down in the meadow, knew the numbness in my hand again, felt that tree against my shoulder. This passed. A series of futures presented themselves to me. Myself sitting, the shafts sticking from me and the galanas paid. Or myself a hostage, if they took long enough to find out who I was. Cattle, Lleucu's children sent as slaves in payment for me. I saw myself at a harp in Ifor's court, then gloriously leading a detachment against Iarll Caerloyw. Or myself mutilated, messengers sent to taunt Morgan. Rhys Ddu knew Morgan's love for Gwrgant, Gwrgant's love for me.

I wanted to run but could do nothing better than a kind of lame hopping on the spot. I wanted to shout; *It wasn't me! My arrow fell short!* but luckily I couldn't manage that either.

I looked at Cristin, then saw her, the green dress, the uncovered head. She might be enough of a diversion for the two archers to allow me to get away, if I could get my legs to work. But no, they'd shoot me first, surely.

She looked at me and her mouth was a thin line, her eyes expressive once more. Contempt. She knew me better than I knew myself.

She turned to face the archer again and I saw her smile. I looked too, and saw both archers lowering their bows and smiling. There was someone laughing, two voices. Iorwerth and Toothless stepped from behind trees. I felt myself smiling stupidly, too late. The archers were familiar now, local men who served the penteulu when the need arose.

'What were you two up to then?' Toothless said.

Cristin looked at me. I don't remember where I looked.

'I was going to say you should have brought your spear' Iorwerth said. 'This is a risky spot. But I expect you've got one hidden somewhere.'

He and his men thought this was very funny. Iorwerth's laugh, though, died when he looked from Cristin to me and back and saw how it was between us, though Cristin herself by this time was suppressing a smile. Then she laughed and he laughed again. I had to do something to stop them.

'Where are you going?' I said.

'Aw' Iorwerth said, as if he was sorry for me, which I think he was. He put an arm round my shoulder and took Cristin under his other arm. I watched how his hand slipped onto her waist.

We walked.

'Hunting' he said. 'Hunting.'

'No dogs? On foot?'

'Well, we might pop up into the disputed territory and have a chat with our friends over the river. Perhaps. See if we can set a few snares.' He smiled down at me. 'I like to combine business with pleasure.'

'Bit risky just the four of you' I said. 'You'd be a rich prize.'

'They'd start a war if they killed me' he said, 'and they can't afford it now, not the way the Iarll's treating them. Neither can we.'

I'd meant a rich prize for ransom. I thought of Eneas dead those years before. They'd tried then. The brink we teetered on.

His fingers worked on Cristin's hip. The brink I'd teetered on minutes before. But Iorwerth's brinks were different, moments of cold assessment, like the moment when the bow's poised and you can see the effortless energy in the eye of the living target. A hidden spear. The metaphor made no sense, or was a kind of blasphemy, more than spitting on an altar, yet I understood it.

Iorwerth was looking at me. He'd said something that I hadn't caught.

'What?'

'I said would you like to come with us?'

There was a pause. No. *I* paused. His arm was heavy on my back, the solid hand clamped on my arm. His face turned to the front but his eyes were still on me. Flinching from looking into the eye, I saw the splay of wrinkles below the temple, the deep line graven in the sunk cheek. The face overhung me like the cliff his court was built on.

Of course he was teasing me, brandishing the arrow in my face. There was only one answer.

'All right' I said, my eyes dropping further. 'Yes.'

'No.' Suddenly he stopped walking and broke his arms from us. 'No, not today. You aren't armed, and you'd be a greater prize. Words are cheap but poetry is rare. You need more training, and as you say, someone should take Cristin back.'

I hadn't said, but I didn't argue.

'Go back now' he said. 'Don't follow us.' Then, as if he felt he needed to explain, 'My wife's too fond of Cristin for her to be set at risk.'

The two archers fanned to left and right ahead of him. Toothless, carrying a spear, dropped a few paces behind. This rearguard turned and smiled at us. He raised the head of his spear between his legs and made slow, thrusting movement with his hips, lifting and twisting the shaft as he did so, so that the flat blade spiralled upward a few inches. At the other end the blue banner coiled round the shaft, which stuck down like a rigid tail. As it turned the banner feathered up dead leaves and dirt.

## 20

I've done it again.

I'm being more successful at suggesting the chaos of my life than I thought I would be. I promised you Meilyr the madman a whole log ago. Put another on and I'll see if I can conjure him this time.

If he were here now he'd see a few more figures around this fire than we can. I used to watch for the sprites to creep into the shadows when the dark came when I was a child, but only a few times did I get an ambiguous glimpse of one. I've seen the empty milkdish many mornings in the byre, but never caught the pwca that drinks it — nor would I want to.

Perhaps you can riddle this. If spirits are spirits and so substanceless, how can Meilyr find them with his human eyes? Most of us, I think, only see them in other guises, when they enter other things, as I thought I saw Gwrgant once — though I was wrong at that time — when he sang bits of his boastsong, or like Cadi's owl. Where hell penetrates the world it becomes flesh for Meilyr, flesh and voices beyond the rest of us. That's the nature of his facility, though no one can explain it.

We were in the smithy at Caerllion, I said. Owain Pencarn, recently come of age I think, was to be given a heavy sword looted from the French, which Rhun the smith was to repair. It needed straightening and some work on the hilt.

Rhun was quite an old man even then. He's one of these people whom you can't imagine ever having been young. He doesn't bother shaving and so has a straggly grey beard, which makes him look even older. Long acquaintance has made him wear his high status very casually. He collects his dues in meat, clothing and rest from the prince at the three feasts, but without any showing off. He never makes the effort to wear his official leather cap even on special occasions so he's often taken by strangers at the court for his own servant, or even a beggar. His inclination is not to embarrass them by saying who he is and I'm told several visitors have left the court having given him a scrap of dry meat out of pity or a belt round the head for insolence without ever having learnt the truth.

He works with infallible skill and in complete silence. It's said that his ability's based on magic though Gwrgant, who was as close to Rhun as anyone could be, told me this was nonsense. Still we all believed that luck would be brought to anyone learning any craft if they saw Rhun at work. So Gwrgant and I took a succession of visiting poets and storytellers to his workshop. I think Gwrgant was particularly anxious, in the early years, that some of the old man's skill with metal should rub off on me as skill with words.

The first time I saw Gwrgant and Rhun together they sat on a bench in the smithy, a jug of springwater between them untouched. Gwrgant sat with his hands on his knees and leaning forward — a habit developed from sitting with the harp. Rhun sat as he always did — straight backed, his arms folded and the fingers of each hand wedged in his armpit, his enormous thumbs pointing upward at the opposite edges of his chest, like this.

'So' Gwrgant said.

Rhun's head tilted a fraction and his eyes dropped a fraction so that he looked at the earth. The bristles on his lower lip possibly stirred, suggesting that he might be pursing his lips.

'Me too' Gwrgant said.

But this was an eloquence the smith rose to only in Gwrgant's presence. His beard seldom moved except when he ate. He spoke so rarely that when he did — when he does — people gather up his words as if they were jewels, though,what he says is generally commonplace and sometimes irrelevant. Once I met him in the woods and almost didn't recognise him outside his own domain. He mumbled something to me which I didn't understand, but with careful thought and a reconstruction of the moment I eventually realized that he'd said, 'Gwrgant's boy.'

Morgan himself and Iorwerth came with Owain Pencarn, me, and other young men to the smithy. It was a rainy autumn day, which made the forge an attraction. Gwrgant was already there with Hywel, who, nine or ten years old then, showing neither interest nor skill in song, had been brought into the magic presence for a cure. It's no insult to Hywel for me to tell you that it never worked.

Rhun looked at the bent, hacked blade, the damaged hilt, and we were all quiet. He looked at his servant, a man as old as himself who acted as interpreter, and mumbled something.

'Next Thursday' the servant said.

'Today' Morgan said.

I expected Rhun to shrug, but he didn't. He peered around us for a while, as though counting to check if this was a record attendance, then he and his servant went to work with bellows and tongs and hammers and whetstones, and without any communication.

I watched Pencarn watching the blackish blade grow red and yellow in the hearth. The flames made a tiny point of light in each of his eyes. We were all, the younger ones, imagining ourselves on horseback, the blade hanging at our hip. Hywel crept to his father's side and looked from Pencarn to the blade and back, then back to the blade, which he watched intently. It must have been about then that we discovered the weakness of Hywel's eyesight. It's not very bad, but enough to make him even fiercer in battle than he might have been, as he moves to a close engagement very quickly.

His brother, Owain ab Iorwerth, came to the open door with his mother, Angharad. She was losing her maidenly figure with bearing children who, apart from a daughter or two, didn't survive. Owain ab Iorwerth was about eleven and beginning to look like Angharad, developing the long nose, the broad forehead, the clear eyes.

I looked from Owain ab Iorwerth, his curly, pale red hair, his fine features, to little Hywel, his face chubby, his eyes blank and dull, to Owain Pencarn, the favourite who had the pick of the female servants, who'd call me to song one day perhaps, hand me the harp. I would call him the expected names. Hawk, dragon, wolf, oak door of Gwynllwg.

At last the tonged sword was steeped in the trough and there was that sound —*tish*— like seared flesh. Rhun lifted it out and inspected it, pointed to a place where more work was needed on the hilt and gestured.

'More time' his interpreter said. 'Another day.'

'It'll do for now' Morgan said.

Rhun should have held the finished blade above his head but he seemed incapable of such performing. Without looking up he offered the hilt to Morgan.

The prince took the sword and chopped the air a few times. Then he jumped forward and swung it crosswise, scattering half dozen uchelwyr of the teulu. The sword spoke with a low note, like the short, blown warning a dog can sound from the back of its gullet.

We all laughed. Morgan handed the sword to his son, who did hold the blade in the air and we cheered. He wasn't standing near the fire, yet the points of light were still in his eyes.

Somebody shouted, 'Stuff them with it, Owain.'

More laughing.

Owain Pencarn stiffened his arm and waggled the point in the air.

'Right up' he said.

Rhun stood near him holding the tongs.

The other, younger Owain watched admiringly and I remembered the mock fight of the two cousins at the Christmas court years before. Over his shoulder I could see Angharad, childruined, framed in the doorway. She observed us all without smiling.

Suddenly she looked up and moved to one side. A stranger, a priest, appeared and spoke with her and she pointed towards us. He turned and came in, leading by the elbow a man whose cloak was swathed around his head.


## 21

Morgan bid the priest god's welcome and asked his blessing on our teulu. The priest pushed back his hood. His name was Cadell. The prince and his brother and Gwrgant and many of the older men knew him, though, like Rhagnell, he spoke with the accent of Penfro. He had one of those wrinkled, sundarkened faces that, having got beyond youth, seem to set like dried mud and become incapable of further change.

Pencarn lowered the sword. Even so young he knew, as I was just beginning to learn, that priests could sometimes choose — or have chosen for them, since god and the French allow even priests only a little freedom — to live within different borders from ours.

But Cadell, stepping forward, took the sword by its wet blade and raising it used the crossed hilt to make his benediction on us. Which was well judged and brought a shout of approval.

Cadell looked at the sword more closely and smiled towards Rhun. 'I can see this has been in the cauldron of regeneration' he said.

I thought I saw one of Rhun's toes move, but I could have been mistaken.

Gwrgant spoke for him, and there was feeling in his voice. 'A pity cauldrons for regenerating men only belong in stories.'

There was a murmur of assent among the older men.

I knew what, whom, my master was thinking of, but Cadell's smile widened. It seemed to me he'd calculated an answer like that as a means to his own repartee.

'Ah' he said. 'The church is such a cauldron as no Efnisien could shatter and here' — he handed Pencarn the sword and turned to his cloaked companion —' is the living proof of the regeneration that, by Christ's mercy, can be worked.'

He started to pull the cloak from the man's head.

For a moment I thought that he meant he'd literally raised somebody from the dead and I expected to see some waxen, unspeaking corpse. Cadi with an absurd, unkempt moustache, a caked rill of blood from an appalling headwound. And suddenly I saw the sword for what it was, understood Gwrgant's words afresh.

But the damp cloak was unwound from the head of an ordinary looking youngish man. Pallid, admittedly, but no corpse yet. His hair was dark and showed signs of having been tonsured, though it was grown back. He wore a leather belt but I was surprised that he carried no knife.

'There' Cadell said. 'Meilyr. Restored to his own country, and to himself.'

Another murmur.

I'd listened to talk of Meilyr before this in fragments overheard. I may even have seen him, without knowing it, soon after coming to the southern part of Gwynllwg. I'd heard of Meilyr the idiot and the madman, so I'd imagined one of those popeyed, thicktongued unfortunates who clutter the gateways to monasteries like this one for a few years and then die young in ditches.

I looked at the man again as Morgan, Iorwerth and others went to him tentatively and embraced him. He looked around nervously, between rather than at us, as Rhun had, and his hand went up to his crown, tugged and twirled the strands of spiky, regrown hair. He stood with his weight on one foot, looking, somehow, slightly more lopsided than I thought he should have been.

There was a buzz of talk among us. Those who'd known Meilyr before he'd been sent to Penfro, to the care of the monks at Ty- ddewi, showed astonishment at his transformation. I heard some trying to explain to others how he'd been. There was a ripple of thank you fathers and congratulations for the priest. Meilyr, a porridge finger and thumb still twirling at his head, continued to look at the gaps among us.

In the hubbub I heard him say, quietly, 'They're still here.'

Cadell quietened us and spoke. So far he'd given a performance worthy of a bishop but he now, as it were, lowered the mask little, gave the impression that he was letting us in.

'I must explain that my young friend still sees demons which by god's grace are forbidden to our eyes. It surely would have been wrong for us to have deprived him of this finer vision, though the vision itself brought torments that are perfectly understandable. Rather his long pilgrimages, both of body and of spirit, have brought him some tranquillity, an acceptance that, arbitrary and mischievous as the interventions of these spirits may be, the great hand of god is somewhere at work. As I've often observed, the ways of —'

Meilyr, meanwhile, started to wander around us and look in a kind of innocence at the smith's instruments. Suddenly he stopped and put a hand on a man's shoulder.

'I know she's dead' he said. 'Don't you pretend she isn't.'

'Who's this, Meilyr?' Cadell interrupted himself, spoke with a practised gentleness.

'You know she is. I told you. Ellyll Llwyd came to me at the cathedral door last year and said. I call him Ellyll Llwyd. He whispered she was dead.' He spoke with a grotesque lisp which, in other circumstances, we might have laughed at. It was because many of his teeth were missing. 'They've all got names. Ellyll Llwyd and Pwca Buga and Pen Tewdrig and Pidyn Pab and Indeg Wenwyn. But that time it was Ellyll. His voice first and then I saw him on the roof. She's dead, he said. He knows.' He squeezed the man's shoulder.

The man, a good soldier called Athrwys, looked into Meilyr's face and spoke. 'He means his mother. She was my third cousin. She died last winter.'

'There. I knew she had. Old bitch. She's up or down I don't care which. Ellyll tried to gloat but I praised god like the monks taught and he went.'

There was more murmurring among us. I began to wonder what he must have been like before his cure.

'Do you still grow wheat, Athrwys?' he said.

'Yes.'

'River rolling on the plain. A harvest full and certain.' He dropped his hand from his uncle's shoulder. 'And who keeps cattle?'

Everybody owned up to this except the priest.

'Farmer tending to his herd. Ten thousand years remembered. And I've seen sunlight fingering a hill, the way its fingers move around a cloud and gild the cattle scattered at the hafod and then there's no Ellyll, Pwca, Pen Tewdrig, Toilu, hil Elidyr under banks, only sunlight fingering a hill. Mountain sprawling pass and ban can give a glimpse of heaven.' He went to Rhun and held up the smith's hand, which still held the tongs. 'Up. Right up. Stuff it right up.' And then Owain Pencarn's hand holding the sword. He spoke to Rhun. 'Doctor doctor will you pull my teeth?' He displayed his mostly empty gums. 'Too late too late. At least I'll have fresh breath.'

Cadell looked apologetically at Morgan.

'We had to do it' he said. 'You remember how he was.'

Meilyr said, 'Then whose will you pull?' He dropped Rhun's hand and turned to Pencarn, glanced from him to the prince. 'And is this of the true line of Caradog ap Gruffudd, king of men?' He extended his free hand on top of Pencarn's head. 'Yes. You'll have a crown that shines but it won't be gold or silver. As a prince you'll never fall in battle. No ravens will come as your crown to peck your eyes. Beware of modern doctors. Goose grease for colds. Try not to lose your appetite and look after your teeth.'

I could see Owain Pencarn, terrified and enthralled, trying to remember every word, his lips moving slightly as if he were being taught a catechism. Iorwerth held his hand on his moustache. Hywel his son didn't look scared as I thought he might, but intent. His eyebrows were drawn down on his blank eyes, but this may have been because of the dimness of his sight. Meilyr took his hand from Pencarn's head and placed it with his other on the young man's hand where he grasped the hilt. There was a pause, then Meilyr released the hand, moved quickly to Morgan and embraced him.

'Iorwerth' he said, 'why has your hair gone red? I dreamt I saw you murdered.'

Gwrgant, next to me, made a small breathy noise.

'Meilyr' he said, 'this is Morgan the prince. Years ago Iorwerth was mistaken for Morgan and some men tried to kill him. That was what you dreamt about.'

Meilyr wasn't bothered by this. He pulled away and looked into Morgan's face.

'The sea's like a big polished shield there' he said, 'by Dewi's bones, and when there's sun and broken cloud god's fingers play on the shield and the air is full of light lovelier than music with his fingers on the ocean strings. The light catches under people's chins and on the shadows under their noses. It glows on the underneath of leaves. Trees glow, stretch out like woken men. They were kind to me there, the monks, even the French ones were kind to me and talked, kept women away from me, and the others too. Well, they tried. Demons have no need to hide. The Churches were like honeycombs and they were bees clustered on doors and windows crawling on the thatch looking for customers. Inside if the singing ever stopped I could hear them whispering on top. Important people go there. I've seen them riding weightless on their backs, crawling from the purses that they bring to make oblations and some pilgrims leave followed by a troop that dance and imitate their walk. Over rich women they buzz like shitflies where the cows are grazing. People came and gave me money for me to talk but I saw them coiling in the purse. Cadell was kind and took the coins away. Sometimes he spoke in French to visitors, told them what I said. The shittalk squelching in their wormy teeth. Pwca Crwca follows him everywhere. He's outside now.'

Involuntarily I looked at the door, where Angharad was still standing. The rain had stopped and water was dripping from the frame. But nothing could stop Meilyr.

'Cadell is strong, though, and do you know, he can't see him? But

91

as I've often observed' — he crossed his hands as if tucking them into the sleeves of an imaginary habit — 'the ways of god are never unjust, though they are sometimes difficult to understand.'

We laughed at his imitation of the priest and he smiled round at us gummily, not understanding the laughter. His hand went up and twirled at the spikes.

'Nine years ago' he said 'you kinned me, Morgan, with a kiss. It's Cadell who has told me this. You'll rule Gwynllwg until you die. Iorwerth smeared the arrow on my face.' He turned to Iorwerth, who stood with his head turned aside, presented at three quarters, as if he couldn't face the returned man direct. 'Penteulu, penteulu. Semiautonomous Iorwerth. I've had seven years of holiday. Let me serve. River rolling on the plain. A border for a captain. Mountain sprawling pass and scree. An outpost for a sentry. You'll fight yet be a maker of amends.'

Iorwerth's face relaxed. His hand dropped from his mouth as if he'd speak but Meilyr went on.

'Broken tower broken men. The butchered lie forgotten.'

He looked down to Hywel, crouched and stared into his eyes for a long time. I was surprised that the boy didn't waver or turn to one side but merely looked interested.

'Cloudy as sperm' Meilyr said judiciously. 'A mole.' He looked up to Iorwerth. 'Moles cheat death too. They live in their graves and it's they who eat the worms.'

We laughed again. The startled gummy smile. He ruffled Hywel's hair.

'He'll claw through the mud. You've seen the spirits in the trees. Live long. Fear nothing. Ghosts walk where the living sing. The end of life is nothing.'

He turned again towards Gwrgant and me, Hywel looked disappointed, Iorwerth relieved.

As he approached I noticed Gwrgant glancing from him to me and back and I realized he was observing a bizarre resemblance. Meilyr was about my slight build then, and of the same height; we both had dark hair, grey eyes and the same pale skin. But my hair was neatly trimmed, my white teeth carefully cleaned and polished every day. I stood straight shouldered. His crown was hacked, his shoulders skewed, his mouth broken.

'When they get into me' he said. 'Then it's the worst. And I think of the polished shield being worked and slid and all that space over the sea and sometimes they go and I can sleep.' He came close. 'I know you, though we haven't met. Gwrgant.' He turned to my master. 'Your son?'

Gwrgant glanced at me, gave a small nod.

Meilyr turned to me again. 'Trees link fingers overhead. For some a roof is wanted. You've buried grieving for the true. Now comes the grieving for the false.' Again he turned to Gwrgant. 'Old friend. Old head not old enough. You'll follow the prince to the best song, be like wheat with a wheat man. Poets shall judge who is of heart. It gives me little comfort. Eat more fish. Never play throwboard with a Benedictine.'

With this undeniably sound advice Meilyr stopped. He looked around and, smiling shyly, restarted his twirling.

'Well, friends' Cadell said, moving smoothly into the silence, 'far be it —'

But Meilyr cut across him, moved quickly across the smithy and pulled Owain ab Iorwerth out of the crowd and close to the hearth, which was burning low by this time.

'See' he said. 'Cadell soothes the time, leaves no dark gaps where they can creep back in. So *he* thinks.' He laid a finger to the side of his nose as if to say we all understood but could keep the secret. 'Who are you?'

The redhaired boy smiled. 'A mole's brother. My name's Owain.'

'Tell your uncle to watch out for dwarfs. A man of blinding strength will be glad when you feel the warmth of a shining fortress. Tell your cousin the hawks should be kept in the barn when there's a fire in the hall.' He raised a finger. 'You see that don't you, Cadell?'

'Er, indeed, yes' Cadell said.

'I forgive you the perjury. It was well meant.'

We laughed.

'Soothing the memory marred' Meilyr said, 'is a difficult art. You can't always be expected to get it right. My countrymen will guess you've had a tiring journey.' He looked towards Morgan.

'Yes' the prince said, taking the cue a little slowly. 'Yes. We must wash your feet, father, Meilyr, and give you food. We'll all have food to celebrate my son's growing up and Meilyr's growing back towards himself.'

## 22

Cadell, to give him his due, must have had a more than exhausting journey, especially if he'd had to listen to this sort of stuff all the way, not to mention the seven years off and on before that. Later he preached to us at Cadog's church and I supposed that Meilyr had been sent to Tyddewi to punish the priest for the quality of his sermons.

Meilyr became a favourite of the teulu and people came from all over the place to visit him, to consult him on all sorts of matters, then spent whole evenings trying to work out the meaning of what he'd said. They usually gave him food or clothes so he never went short, and this was how he started to get a bit fat. Morgan had a small house built for him outside the beili where he could be with his spirits and meet his clients. Once or twice a well armed group of French people turned up, usually priests or monks, regarding us, as well as Meilyr as mainly of curiosity value. They'd offer him money, which he always refused. Once even an Englishwoman, who'd lived most of her life at Bryn Buga after her family was moved there in the time of the first Henri, came to talk with him. But as you know, he's scared of women and often shouts for them to go away without even coming to the door.

But I've run ahead of myself.

The day Cadell started back towards Penfro, Owain Pencarn took Meilyr, me, and others out to hunt. Cadell had stayed only a few days, taking advantage of the first good weather to set off.

He'd turned out to be thoughtful, not wishing to impose on Morgan's generosity, and brave, as he travelled alone. Except, that is, for Pwca Crwca, who, Meilyr said, was hanging on the tail of the priest's horse as it ambled through the gate. I looked carefully at the tail and it did seem to me, from the way it arched, that it might be depressed by some invisible weight.

Towards the middle of our day of hunting, after we'd travelled north a while, we turned east till we came to the river and stopped to rest.

94

It was sunny, cloudless. The air was still. We were at a slow bend, and across the water's rippled light, a little further down, a heron was fishing. Owain ab Iorwerth and his brother Hywel, at the water's edge, watched the bird carefully and each had an arrow to his unbent bow. Pencarn, Meilyr and I squatted on our haunches a little above them. The leaf fall had started. The rust mottled blaze of branches over us was softened with shifting bars of light reflected off the water.

None of us felt the need to talk for a long time, and I began to think that Meilyr was quite ordinary after all, was cured and had given us a show in the smoky forge.

'I enjoyed your performance in the smithy, Meilyr' I said.

He looked from the heron to me. Light was cast upward on his face, under his brows, his jaw. The look contained nothing but its own openness. I felt I might have hit a mark, but he was giving no clues. His eyes shifted slightly, as if he was looking at something over my shoulder. I began to turn to look where he looked, stopped myself. I started to smile as an admission that he'd caught me, but his lips didn't move.

'Meilyr' Pencarn said, 'how do you see the future? And how do you see things I can't?'

'Don't worry' Meilyr said, still looking at me. 'He's gone. It's going to be a quiet day.'

He lay back, stretching on the bed of leaves, which were dry at the surface.

'How can I answer?' he said to Pencarn. 'I know what I'm told but sometimes they might be lying. They're like that. A lot of them have gone to follow the king of England. They get a lot of work from him these days. Blindness and darkness are sorts of brothers. The one is akin to the other. You can't see the darkest things because of the dark.' He placed a palm on each eye socket and rubbed. 'But I can. I can see the flames leaping now.'

Pencarn and I laughed. Meilyr laughed too a moment later and he placed his hands under his head.

'People pretend' he said. 'They pretend they can't see, but sometimes they can. I've seen people look round for the spirits when they think nobody's watching. People pretend all sorts of things. Nothing could please the spirits more. They pretend to be generous when they really want to stuff their own gut. They pretend to pray for their kin when they're really praying for themselves. They pretend to love god and princes when really they want rich land and a good hard shag.'

He sat up and passed a hand over his face. There was birdsong and leafnoise and me and Pencarn laughing. Down at the river's edge, Hywel and his brother threw stones that sent shimmering bands of light over us and the arching trees.

'I've seen you both' Meilyr said. 'Staring at that redhaired servant's arse, imagining it slipping in. I'll bet you've given her a knee-trembler already, Owain, nice and quiet round the back. God gives princes more freedom and that's what they do with it. That and make heaps of corpses.'

'I'll be a better prince than that' Pencarn said.

'You think so?'

'Come on now. You must have been imagining it too.'

'Oh yes. I won't pretend otherwise. That's just it. I won't pretend. I'll leave performing to the priests. And the poets.'

'And princes?'

'Them too.'

'There's many aren't princes from choice. If they pretend it's because they're compelled to.'

'So they're the least free men of all and I pity them.' Meilyr shrugged.

'What's left then?' Pencarn said. 'If you take all the pretending away what's left of you, Meilyr?'

'I don't know what you're on about' I said. 'Pretending.'

'Well you started it' Meilyr said, looking at me hard then back to Pencarn. He paused. Unlike me, he seemed to understand the question, but showed no sign of having an answer.

I looked from him to the two boys playing, the smooth river, the bentnecked heron perched on a root, looking into the water.

I would have liked his clarity, seeing through to what was needed. I wanted to get away from the others, be away from people.

'In the old days' Pencarn said, 'you could have gone off on your own and been a hermit like Saint Iswy.'

'I did that' Meilyr said. 'Nine years ago. I wasn't much older than you are now.' He looked at me. 'You'll understand this. You both will. I ran into the woodland and stayed there for months, they tell me. You won't remember, you were too young.'

'I remember them tying you up' Pencarn said. 'I was visiting my father. They tied a rag round your mouth and four men were holding you down and they fetched the old priest, only I had no idea who you were.'

'Neither did I.'

'What happened? '

He looked at Pencarn a long time, as if deciding whether to tell his story or not. Of course he decided that he would, or I wouldn't be telling you this now.

'I used to love a girl' he said. 'Over that side of the river where our land was.' He pointed to the eastern bark. 'One day a great grandson of Caradog will repossess it.' He looked at Pencarn then at me, dropping his arm. 'I ached for her. I'd seen her washing a green dress in a stream and talked with her one day. Her head was uncovered. She had a gold tongue of hair and she tipped her head like this and like this to move it from her cheeks. I said I'd see her there the next Sunday. Always nice on a Sunday because you're not so tired. Anyway,' his hand went to his crown and started to twirl slowly at the regrown locks 'she didn't turn up.'

I stifled a laugh. He sounded startled that she should dare not to go, but he was there before us, toothless, lopsided. I tried to imagine him nine years before, a young man, perhaps fifteen, sixteen, perhaps well dressed in a neatly hemmed cloak, his hair carefully trimmed and groomed for the tryst, his teeth even, perfectly cleaned.

'I went back the next Sunday and still she wasn't there. I waited ages, till it got dark. Then the third Sunday, there she was, sitting on some treeroots in the bank of the stream.'

There was a long pause. He stared down into the water.

I said, 'And?'

'We talked.'

'What about?'

He looked at me and smiled. 'How should I know? Does it matter? It was Palm Sunday. I remember the processions, and I'd had some mead. I remember that. There were dog violets growing there, and primroses on a bank nearby.'

I thought of the girls I'd had in Cyfeiliog and Gwent Uwchcoed, and could remember nothing of what I'd said to them or they to me.

Meilyr looked back into the water. 'She seemed very shy and looked down modestly like this when I looked into her face, but I'm sure it was she rested her arm on my leg first, but forgetfully, as you

97

might with a relative or an old friend. All the time we were talking and smiling but I didn't hear what we said. It was coming towards dusk but it wasn't cold and it must have been very slowly we slipped down and slipped together, to one another.

'She was — I've never seen such white skin. She had a straight nose and a broad forehead. And I lifted the rope of her hair and here on the nape the hair was so fine, the skin was so fair. I thought I'd burst as soon as I got into her but, I thought it was a miracle, we kept going and she showed me ways I'd never have — well, I was young.

'The light reddened as the sun started to go and we were still fixed on one another, fitted as tight as the halves of a cut apple pressed back together. She had a gentle voice and made lots of sighing noises but suddenly she raised her chin and made a long sort of screech. You've seen the way ravens tip forward and raise their heads and open their throats to scare the cats away. Like that. And her eyes opened wide and I could feel her nails in my back and sides and god released me then. And as that was happening I started to see and feel as if I'd just woken. The nails were sharper. I looked in her wide eyes and there was the glaucous, ravelled iris, my own ghost staring at me in it, and the pupil was a black slot. I passed my hands down her arms and tried to push myself away. The gold hair lay all along her arms, but under my hands it writhed back, coarsened like a horse's mane and blackened and curled. I pulled one of her hands from my side and the nails cut me. It was like a huge cuckoo's claw, two talons forward and one back. I must have been trying to break from her but I remember looking back to her face and it was changing. It went red and then the red was hair, fur, short hair packed like thatch across a roof. Her chin and her mouth grew forward.

'This was all very quick. I got up and started to run before the screech was finished. I stumbled in the stream and I ran into the trees and I was still running when I heard my voice screaming and her cawing was gone.

'After that they came and tortured me. They whispered a lot so that I only heard some of the words and sometimes there was shouting a long way off. Sometimes I heard my mother's voice calling my name but she was never there. I heard the Cyhyraeth groaning and Ellyll Llwyd would whisper the name of the soul they were taking. I hid but they were still there. That must have been when I lived in the woodland. I found bowls of food. Cadell told me my family left them. Instead of hiding I tried frightening the spirits. I ran at them and shouted and I think I remember knocking one down, hurting him, but it's all jumbled up. I don't know if you can do that.'

Meilyr looked at us both as if asking our opinions, but saw that we could hold none.

I got up and walked a few paces among the trees. Meilyr spoke quietly and without feeling, the way you know he does on a good day, as I'm trying to now. I heard his voice behind me, getting the impression that he was pointing his face after me.

'There was nowhere' he said. 'Brambles, trees. I tried. The green hill near where I used to live. It must have been June, gone, by then. I remember the foxgloves out among the gorse. They were seething with them and when I looked up they were moulded in the clouds. There was nowhere.'

I turned back and saw that Meilyr was watching me, Pencarn was watching Meilyr.

After a pause Pencarn said, 'So, did you see her again?'

'What?'

'The — the girl — the spirit. Whatever she was.'

'No. I don't think so. I imagined her often, but that's different. She may have come when I slept. I think she may have come then. Sometimes I woke up and things were crawling on me and sometimes I ran and there were claw gashes on me. But I'm not sure. When it went quiet I got more scared and prayed for god to take me then. It's a bad sign when they come. They come for men and women. Usually it's war. After she came to me she killed a man among the trees where she lived. They found his body. They told me. After she came some of our neighbours were attacked by the French and the chief man was killed and the sons were taken as soldiers and the daughters as slaves.'

'You know this?'

'Ellyll Llwyd told me. Some of them hide in monasteries. Some monks attract them. The holier the man often the more of these will live in his room. But they don't often see them, or let on they do. They pretend. Cadell knows about them. They've got a name, the ones like the one that drove me into the trees. Sickbo, Suckbo. Something like that.'

◆I went back to them.

The two boys at the river had given up stonethrowing and taken up their bows again. Owain ab Iorwerth and Hywel stood brandishing them, arrowless. I looked across the river and saw the killed heron, grey and white, twistnecked on the stones beyond the root-tangle he'd fished from. There was only one arrow in the bird but I don't know which of the brothers had hit him.

Pencarn looked down to them and said, 'Why're you wasting your arrows?'

Hywel looked up, frowning to see us better.

'Words' he said. 'That's all you know.'


## 23


That was the year that King Henri came into Wales for the first time, on the side of Cadwaladr against Prince Owain in the north. Though he never came anywhere near us we were all scared. Morgan paid tribute to Iarll Caerloyw and hoped for the best. Nothing, happened to us except for a brief shortage of food and a few old people starving. But it was then Owain Gwynedd bent the knee and Arglwydd Rhys too and the king promptly gave most of Rhys's castles to the French. This was all far away to me, though I heard Pencarn and Morgan discussing affairs with messengers. I remembered being startled when Iorwerth offered to send me and Gwrgant and some footsoldiers to serve Rhys and I realized I might fight against the king's army. But Rhys was already deciding then, having heard what that army was like, to volunteer submission. I remember, too, the anger in our country when we heard of how the king paid Rhys with such a kick in the teeth. Pencarn, I think, would've taken up arms there and then but the prince and his brother would have none of that.

Iorwerth told him, 'A rebellion's like any other war. It doesn't just happen. You have to calculate. Then wait.'

When Gwrgant and I talked about poetry, something similar arose. I remember him saying, 'Most doing is waiting. Most waiting is thinking.'

I was of an age to be irritated by his declamations and disagreed. I cited children dancing, ourselves talking, as examples of doing without much evidence of thinking.

'I'm talking about what should be' Gwrgant said. 'Not what is.'

'What? For everything?'

'No no. For poetry. For some things.'

'For war?'

'What? Yes. Yes, that too.'

It was early winter and we were in the house, our house. He'd been out arranging a marriage for Mair. Rainsoaked and tired, he felt he'd been done out of his waiting and thinking that day. The rest of us had sat inside shivering round the hearth while he'd been out, doing. He and I and Non shared a bowl of dinner on the floor. Mair, Hywel, Lleucu and her husband and their surviving children, I think there were three then, shared another nearby.

'So war and poetry aren't like the ordinary things of life' I said.

'That's right.'

I thought, then said, 'So your poetry has no life in it.'

Gwrgant paused in his eating, his hand holding a chunk of dry meat near his mouth, and looked at me. Non looked down into the bowl and went on eating.

He'd been on tour again recently before that and had visited Arglwydd Afan to sing at his November Calends. In our journeys we were often quiet, though never for very long. When we talked we talked shyly, about inconsequential things, like strangers without common ground. I still served him when we travelled, getting his food and looking after his horse, but what little talk passed between us was the talk of people equal but remote. I generally managed to mask the pity I sometimes felt for him, for the strain that there was between him and Non, for his use of women at courts in other lands. Our half drunken confessional in Cyfeiliog was never mentioned. His legs were getting thinner and he was developing a little paunch. His voice, though, was as good as ever and had grown deeper and richer. Anyway, my respect for his craftsmanship had continued to grow, though I never told him that. To watch him work, to listen to him, was like watching Rhun shaping metal. The skill itself said everything. The unspeaking attention it commanded was the highest kind of praise.

But here around the bowl, there was the nasty familiarity of the winter hearth and there was Non and the others. An audience. Something brushed my sleeve. Non had laid one hand on my wrist and the other on Gwrgant's. She was still looking down. I think I and my master had stared at one another a long time. Gwrgant put the meat back in the bowl, rubbed his mouth.

'You prefer it all instinct?' he said.

Suddenly there was no issue. Only us and an audience, a need for proving, and it didn't matter what I said, only how I said it.

'Dead' I said.

He looked down to where his knife rested on the edge of the bowl and then up again. Again he looked away and said, 'Well.'

'Well? Well what?' They weren't words. A challenge noise.

Non tried an admonitory mother's voice. 'Griffri, if you —'

'Shut up, woman.' He shouted. Then quieter, 'Mind your own business.' Then, quieter still, 'You're old enough. You can leave if you like.'

'Oh yes, there it is' I said, though I didn't know what it was or where it was. 'It's just an escape to you, war and poetry.' Oddly, we carried on eating. The food in the bowl, the fingers moving round it, were different. I'd changed things; moved things to a new place.

Suddenly Gwrgant started to cough. Instead of stopping, it went on until he turned a murky red and got up, wiping his mouth. He left the house, still coughing.

'You —' Non said.

I saw her hand too late. It clapped me so hard I rolled sideways into the straw and hastily tried to get up, rubbing the side of my head, trying to straighten my shirt and my dignity at the same time. My audience at the other bowl, the snotlipped children, each of them with a hand frozen in the act of delivering food to an open mouth, stared at me, and they knew me, and I was bewildered.


## 24


What am I talking about? One moment kings disputing and the next me rolling in the straw. No good for your book. You need lists of dead bishops. But who's to say what counts? In one life the fractional shifting of an eye might be the most important event and eclipse all the kings and cathedrals that ever were. Not that I knew that then. So remember Gwrgant who was — though I'm not impartial I say this unblushingly — the greatest poet who ever sang, and who never wrote a poem down.

The following spring, at the age of eighteen, I completed my apprenticeship and I was kidnapped.

The first of these — the second too, I suppose — was one of those king-eclipsing moments. I was tested at Seisyll ap Dyfnwal's little court in Gwent Uwchcoed by three poets who did their best not to yawn. Seisyll's young son, Morgan, whose mother was Dyddgu and who was fostered with Iorwerth and Angharad, came with me and Gwrgant to visit his father. He was only five or six at that time and so kept us busy and gave us a centre for our talk as we travelled, and that made it easier between me and my master. Gwrgant had to explain to the boy that his father was remarried to Gwladus and that Dyddgu was dead. The child discussed this with a detached innocence. Later in the journey he'd reexplain it to us, fuddling the details in various ways. But he grasped quickly that his stepmother was the sister of Arglwydd Rhys, and though Rhys's fortunes in the west were low then, this cheered little Morgan ap Seisyll considerably.

Seisyll's court is in a lovely place, high up on a densely treed shoulder of land looking north over the Wysg. To his left at the bottom of a steep hill is a church to Cadog. To the south behind him is meadowland and then trees and then a mountain with sheer cliffs, but far back so that the court isn't in gloom. From the huge trees around his court Seisyll's men can watch all the traffic that tries to pass into and out of Brycheiniog along the valley. As a matter of course the French and English going from Abergafenni to Brycheiniog make a detour north and then west across the mountains to avoid the prince. Still they're strong and Seisyll has to see his people taken away sometimes to work on the interminable buildings and pullings down that the French are always at. A few of them have been taken to work as servants, some of them even uchelwyr and their wives. Although their condition is close to slavery, it's not all bad as they're a good source of intelligence. Seisyll's people talk with them on the odd time they can sneak past the town gate at Abergafenni.

That's a terrible place. They kill people there just for stealing, maim people for hunting, won't allow divorce, treat their women like dirt, put no faith in oaths on relics. To be fair to them, the English who live there have grown ingenious under this tyranny and are skilful at growing a lot of strange but tasty plants on quite pathetic little strips of land and seem to survive for quite long periods without eating any meat at all.

At that time Gwladus was pregnant with Seisyll's son. She's probably visited you here when she's come to Rhys's court. She's a devout and modest woman and I remember her playing with Morgan ap Seisyll more like a sensible older sister than a stepmother while Gwrgant talked business with her husband and I flirted with the concubines.

I'd prepared two songs; one in praise of god, and the other to Seisyll. I still sing the first, though it's not the same one I sang for the abbot here earlier tonight. Seisyll and his wife often ask for it when I visit them. Seisyll himself has praised it for its economy. 'It's the pithiness of the thing, Griffri' he says. 'That's what I like about it.'

That day I was completely convinced of the greatness of my work for minutes at a time. But though my confidence was a wide vessel with a gaping mouth, it had a narrow base. I've tried to remember that on the few occasions when I've attempted to teach some of the rudiments, but it's very hard. Too many fools have been encouraged while the talents of others have been spilt with their confidence.

The three poets listened. While others cheered at the end, they were silent. I'd been nervous at first and then more controlled as I was absorbed in the song. It was a fine afternoon and I sang in the open air, which any poet will tell you is a lot tougher. Children wander away and play. People watch the sky, swat midges. There was a breeze, so sometimes the harpstrings spoke out of turn. None of this seemed to matter though. I was facing south and slightly west towards the cliffs and broken cloud slid over them slowly and I was aware of the blur of watching faces. A slight movement of the eye and I could shift from sky, to rock, to woodland, to the crowded people, to my fingers at the strings. At first I felt that the hands were someone else's, remembered my terror at the tree, the sitting man with an arrow in his chest. My fingers were a little cold. I had difficulty drawing a deep breath. But I warmed up, spiritually anyway, with the song to Seisyll. It was in the conventional modern style, competent enough, though I sang it badly at the beginning. You know the sort of thing —

I praise a giftmaker, true line of Tewdrig
I raise up ap Dyfnwal harrier of Wysg
Right lord of Uwchcoed, bowbearing Seisyll,
Rock of his people, slayer of stags,
River his rampart, his tower the crags.


Somewhere around that line I felt something of what I'd felt when Gwrgant sang Marwnad Eneas and the action at Bryn Buga, except that it was I who sang now.

I finished and the sky, the cliffs, the trees, the people, my hands on the stilled strings reassembled themselves and the breeze sang faint harmonics in the harp again. There was a moment's quiet and then a murmur among the people and I felt myself smiling in a kind of innocence, like Meilyr smiling in the smithy. The base broadened. I became myself again and started the second song with better technique. The mountain, trees and people, and I too, disappeared into the song, or we all became stronger in it. There was a sense of a healed totality and as I — we — reemerged at the end I knew that it was all right.

As I say, they cheered.

Seisyll's curled head came to me and he was raising his arms to me, smiling and applauding.

Gwrgant came to me and took the harp, said, through his unnatural smile, 'You're a bit flat in the treble. Always retune between pieces. Listen to yourself. You missed a line in the first but they won't notice that.'

The praise from the three poets wasn't unequivocal. They picked holes here and there the way we always do. One of them, an older man from Ewias, was very sniffy. I don't remember what he said about my singing, but he looked at me as if I'd crawled out of a cheese.

None of that mattered. They said that I was qualified to ply my trade at any court that would have me and after they'd crossexamined me on a few technicalities thought I might be fit to teach to, though the sniffy one told me not to take that up for another seven years. He said, 'The law is that no man shall be a lawyer before he's reached the age of twenty-five and lived through the heat of his manhood. So it should be, too, for a teacher of poets.' But I'd felt the purity of the song. Their words — though they were probably all justified — were just background noise compared to that.

## 25

That evening, though there was no great feast, Gwrgant behaved like a second uncle at a wedding. Which is to say he got meaded so that he could scarcely stand, made a shoulder slobbering display of ineffectual lechery with the most modest and therefore least likely women in the court, and, to everyone's approval, rendered with perfect technique a selection of the kind of late night verses that never will be written down.

My singing of Seisyll's generosity paid off, as you might expect. That day he gave me this cloak, I'm wearing it now, and as he threw it round my shoulders he said, 'Griffri Brydydd.'

There was greater praise than any poem. I felt the uncontrollable burst again. My nose pulled my face upward of its own accord and when I tried to walk a few steps I couldn't stop it from becoming a triumphal strutting. For which reasons, for the sake of some new seemliness, I tried not to get quite so drunk as Gwrgant. Not quite. The trick is to empty the horn with a flourish when you're called but to drink quietly otherwise. Besides, I thought there might be a chance of —

Once in Cyfeiliog I went, staggered, with a girl into the barn after a feast, while the rest were still singing. I woke the next morning in the hall next to Gwrgant and the prince of Cyfeiliog's penteulu, with dried puke in my hair, and a little wooden splint had been tied to my penis with a length of ribbon. I saw the girl later. She was wearing a different gown and a big smile and her hair was loose. A lot of people made jokes about not being able to stand. Experience teaches us about these things rather than advice. You get the advice, then you have the bad experience, and then you realize what the advice meant.

So I sipped my mead and watched Gwrgant with resigned condescension as he slithered away in drink. People I didn't know topped up my drink and talked to me about poetry.

106

'Your father's enjoying himself' one girl said.

At this point Gwrgant had keeled over onto his side and was speaking fragments of his boastsong. They eat seated on the floor at Seisyll's court, so this wasn't quite so noticeable as it might have been were we following French fashion.

'What's the matter?' the girl said.

'What?'

'You started. It's all right. Don't be embarrassed. Nobody minds. He's important enough to have that freedom.'

*Father*, she'd said. I thought of a pale sun through trees, a hand on my shoulder.

I looked at the girl, obscurely grateful to her for not talking about my status, about song. She had waxy, dark straight hair that had a reddish tinge when it caught the firelight. As I turned to her she turned her face away, though I sensed her reading me as she did so. She was shy of me and yet curious. I was to become familiar with this when I visited other houses to sing on my own. The totality of the song didn't extend here. My qualification, I realized, made a kind of ditch around me for which I had no bridges yet.

Later, when the meal was finished and the music had stopped, I saw her leaving the hall. I got up and followed, though she hadn't looked at me. Gwrgant had already lurched out, helped by a servant.

I stumbled towards the door, surprised that in spite of my new greatness I was a little unsteady. The doorpost leant towards me and hit me on the ear. Outside I ran-fell down the few wooden steps and then stood exaggeratedly still, straightening my new cloak and palming my hair into place. It was cold. There was a half moon and Jupiter stark overhead and I was in the empty yard.

She'd disappeared.

I called, 'Rhiannon.'

I had no idea what her real name was. I was being extremely clever, referring to Pwyll and Rhiannon in the story. How ever fast Pwyll's messengers followed her they never caught her up. I thought she'd smile when she heard this gem of allusive skill. The half moon and Jupiter weren't impressed. Two sniffy critics waiting for more.

I walked. The earth twitched itself away, a little lower than the place where it should have been, every time I went to put my foot down, which made walking problematic. I stopped walking. There was a crackling sound. At first I thought it was fire.

'The hall's on fire' I said. Then I identified it as the sound of someone pissing in the straw litter of the yard. Then I noticed it was me. I felt hungry and thirsty.

There was a sound. *Yyyrch*. Like that, and then a sploshing. I thought, Jesus, I'm being sick. But I put my hand to my mouth and It wasn't me. I smiled at my two critics. There. Not me.

There was the sound of troubled breathing.

'Rhiannon?' I said.

Someone breathing more firmly, becoming resolute, standing up, saying, 'That's better.'

My eyes were recovering from the sting of woodsmoke and dim in the moonlight I could see my sickspattered master in poetry.

'Gwrgant?' I said'

'Griffri?'

He walked towards me with perfect control and then fell over. I leant and studied him carefully, though I could see little except that he was flat on his back with his arms flung out.

Again his genius struck me, that he should find such a wonderfully decorated sleeping chamber while the rest huddled around ashes in the aftermash of food.

I allowed one of my legs to do as it wished — that was to collapse and I thumped down on my back next to the pencerdd.

I stretched. The earth was luxuriously cool and wet. I dug my fingers into the mud and the stars and the moon more or less stopped swaying.

'If we don't see a shooting star' Gwrgant said, 'I'll give you my, I'll give, I'll give you something, my, I'll give you my —' he made a turbulent, gurgling belch '— white Jesus.'

'You all right?'

'House. I'll give. If. Yes, fine. Pissed. Drunk as a monk and covered in puke. Missed as a cunk and povered in cuke. Kissed as a wank and cut into chunks. Chunkatupunk a plunkatuthunk. Wunkatuwunkawunkatuwunk.' The syllables turned into laughter and then coughing before he stopped. He sniffed, like a critic. 'Well. Poet. Qualified songmaker. Wordheaper. Keeper of memory. Lister of princes. How is it?'

'What?'

'H-how is it to be peotified. Poetificated.'

'Good —'

'How g-good is your memory? Can you be the cauldron to contain a people? To remake them? Do you feel m-made? Are you c-completed?'

He sat up and rubbed his face, looked at me. The moonlight had strengthened a little. I thought I saw a kind of smile on his bluegrey face. He paused though — or because — he knew there were no answers, then looked up.

'The moon is a genuine critic' he said. 'She knows it's all s-so much shitsmashing. Look.' He paused again. 'She's turned her back on that, that star.'

'Jupiter.'

'Jupiter. Ah. Oh yes Jupiter. She's turned her back on Jupiter. She knows all about him.'

I looked. The curved edge of the half moon was towards the planet and suddenly she was a hunched figure. Gwrgant's work was often very visual.

'She's constant. K-keeps a rhythm. Moves with the sea and women's blood. A wise man with a book will tell you exactly where she'll be and how big ten months next Thursday at an hour past midnight. But h-him. He just wanders all over the place. Nobody knows what the hell way he'll go next. He's wayward. He can swell. There might be some disaster. She doesn't care. She sails on, swelling and shrinking like — like an eye opening and closing, but never put off by anything she sees.' He sniffed again and turned to face me. The head was unsteady, rocked a little. 'You've seen it. The way birds sing through a battle. Skip in their colours after, among what's spilt. Threadworm. You wake up in the night ready to tear yourself in two and there's the trees the byre, and —' He nodded skywards and nearly fell onto his side '— her. There she is, not batting an eyelid. Doesn't care. So it's good, is it?'

'What?'

'And they can come to you now when they want to know if they're descended by marriage from Saint Dingat through the child of a concubine of King Ithel. Or somebody. It's good then? That's very good. I'm glad. I'm glad it's good. I'm.'

'What?' I said.

'What?'

'What are you? You said, "I'm." So what are you? Tell me what you are.'

109

There was a pause. Drunk as he was he saw that I was hurt by his attack and he knew the contempt in my voice.

'Oh, I think you've d-decided that' he said. Then, 'Do you think we'll ever be free?'

'Come on' I said. I knew he was trying to slip away.

'No no. Rhys had a look at Henri's army and he had to back off and look what happened.'

I was up on one elbow and I clenched the hilt of my knife where it stuck from my belt. He talked on, only occasionally coherently, about alliances and payments of tribute.

'— and Seisyll' he said. 'Your new p-patron. Do you think he'll ever get the rest of his land back? It's pitiable. They ship in monks and masons. They even get our people to do the labour. Old Bledri had the right idea. Learn French and fuck you lot.'

I sat up. 'Yes' I said. 'Yes of course he can. The whole country's against them. Do think they can ever win?'

'And can they e-ever lose?'

'Yes' I said. 'Gwrgant, how can you —'

Suddenly I realized what he'd done, how he'd slipped away. I brought my fist down on the mud between us. The knife I held went in to the hilt. I looked at the place where it was in the dark, surprised, then back to Gwrgant.

'Tell me what you are.'

Another pause. I sensed that he was smiling.

'Released' he said.

'Free, then.'

'Oh no. No no. Not that. That's not the same. A man who's been freed can never be the same as a man who's merely free. Unless he loses his memory.'

When my fuddled mind caught up with this I snorted. It was the kind of aphorism he liked to have in store.

'So how good is it, chick poet? Your memory that is. It's a high calling. You will be it and I am released. How many horses? And what was his age? Not that. Those things d-don't matter. Twenty. Two hundred. Three hundred. Call it three hundred under Morgan's thigh to remember the Gododdin.'

In half a dozen words his voice began to choke with emotion as he rambled like an old man. My anger turned back to something between contempt and pity.

'I thought it was all shitsmashing' I said. But he wasn't hearing me.

'Or twelve. Or thirteen' he said. 'Meaningless. It says nothing. Releases nothing.'

There was a different kind of silence. I was impatient with the maudlin quick changes of emotion, sensed that he was about to start whining, wanted to hit him, to stick his head in the little stream that runs through that yard.

But he sniffed again and his breathing became more controlled. Away in the trees an owl called. I saw Gwrgant's head make a small sharp movement and he gave a forced laugh.

Something of the darkness that was in him moved across my mind. Then, looking at his shape in the dark, I thought that this was a performance. He was trying different tactics at random, seeing how long he could keep me from my newest saint, or trying to provoke me, to get me to hit him, as you idly look for the place where a stone, balanced on a ledge, will just topple.

'What about this whatsername then? Rhian?' he said.

'Rhiannon.'

'Rhiannon.'

'That's not her real name. I don't know what she's —'

'What about her then?'

'What? '

'Think she will?'

'Jesus, Gwrgant.'

'Looked a regular knobgobbler to me.'

'Look —'

'You've had your pride crowned and some dinner and a nice new cloak. Why don't you —'

'You bastard.'

'You know the s-saying. Chief poet chief ram. In fact I think I had that one the last ti—'

I was on my feet and dragging him up. He was revealing not his own nature, but mine. For a moment he was genuinely startled, and too drunk to find his feet. At last he managed to stand and I shook him. I thought I could actually hear liquid swilling around.

'Is this what you want, wise man?'

'You don't get wiser you just get older.'

'Evidently, you bastard. '

I don't know what other names I called him. But I don't think I actually hit him. I pushed him away. His feet slid and, arms milling, he fell onto his back with a hollow dunt. He turned quickly on one side and propped himself on a hand. I heard him vomitting and groaning, 'Mair, Mair.'

I felt idiotic, in the wrong, but that somehow I had nothing left but defiance. I felt I'd misread him, that this hadn't been calculated after all, that he had no more idea of what he was doing than I did. The next day we'd have to travel back to Gwynllwg together with Seisyll's son in our care. The dark had reasserted itself, we were teetering on the old brink and the healing totality, the king-eclipsing day was in ruins.


## 26

The following day I felt that I ought to hide, that everyone was staring. I was of course being over dramatic.

Gwrgant was quiet, his face bloodless, the colour of grass that's been under a stone. He couldn't open his eyes wider than the narrowest slits, but he managed to read the shame in my face and tried a sheepish smile. Even smiling seemed to hurt and he gave up, but managed to say, quietly, 'Mud on your new cloak already. No bad thing.'

I wish my memory was less good for such moments. You relive them trying to play them different ways but nothing is ever changed.

On the way back, little Morgan ap Seisyll, who shared my horse, wanted to know why the pencerdd was all quiet and mushroom coloured. The persistent, innocent questions irritated me but Gwrgant laughed, despite its hurting his head. The boy turned then to talk about the new sister, as he called her, whom his father had married, and the new brother or sister she carried for him in her belly. While this was going on I wondered how much Gwrgant remembered. Mead can tear whole pages from the memory. Indeed, I felt uncertain about some moments myself. What had I shouted? And was there a ring of faces watching? And was it me who helped him up, or was I helped or dragged away too?

The daylight in the trees, though the sky was shingled with cloud, made everything unbearably sharp. I should have gloried in it. The fact that I couldn't made me feel sicker.

The world is either miraculous or hellish, especially at that age. I looked at my hand where it held the reins under Morgan's arm and the mud of the courtyard was under my nails, on my palm. I tried to rub it away, but it was the hand itself I wanted to get rid of. Can you understand me, monk, I wanted to say, *this is not me*.

This desperate condition may have lasted as long as all day. But if I recovered from the mood quickly enough, its shadow fell across me many times in the months afterwards, especially after —

## 27

— well, we'll come to that.

First let me say that I spent much of that time away from Non, Gwrgant, Lleucu and the others. I toured with Iorwerth, helping to drive the tribute of cows and other goods back to his court from his tenants and then I often went with Iorwerth's tribute to his brother's court. After Henri had given most of Rhys's land to his French friends, Iarll Caerloyw started to get greedy for our land, so while Morgan feigned negotiations with the Iarll's men we went out at night to destroy earthworks and sometimes to ambush small numbers of his troops. They wore too much armour and tended to lumber along in valley bottoms so with a skilled man like Toothless or Iorwerth leading we picked a number off easily. By keeping a careful balance of hostages and making agreements when he had to Morgan kept the land intact.

These summaries are so easy to make when the events are so hard to live through. Iorwerth often talked with me, asked me many questions about the business of learning poetry. I told him what I could without giving any secrets away and like a good servant I told him the things that I thought would please him. He wanted his surviving sons, Hywel and Owain, to know something about it. Hywel's lack of aptitude was becoming obvious but still Iorwerth wanted him to learn a little, which made Gwrgant's life more miserable, as well as Hywel's. Owain ab Iorwerth, still fostered with his uncle Morgan, had learnt to read a little with the thinfaced lawyer, and even had a few words of French.

Iorwerth talked of these things in a dead sort of way. He has the habit of looking somewhere else as he talks to you, taking you in with sliding glances. In matters of the teulu he becomes more open. That moment of satire when Iorwerth came across me in the woodland with Cristin was rare for him. I don't mean to denigrate my master. He's a great leader, full of strength. But the only other time I'd seen him as — alive — as that was when he smeared the blood on me at the court.

Don't let me give you the impression that I was an astute observer of the scene, or that I was his confidant. I marvelled at Pencarn's grasp of events, and his young cousin, the other Owain, seemed ready for the world, young as he was. They and Iorwerth and his brother the prince moved around the the land with a kind of urgent purposefulness which, to me, was full of mystery.

She, Cristin, was more my concern than all of that. For weeks she kept away from me. I wasn't consciously making wary circles of her, but I suppose that that was what was going on. I've got a picture of her turning away from me as I walk round, her head endlessly averted. My sense of the ditch around me grew. First Cristin pushed away and then Gwrgant. The meticulousness with which I cleaned my teeth, the care I took with the trimming of my hair and wispy moustache, the artful disposition on my shoulders of my new and laundered cloak, became more the symptoms of fretting on my imperfections than of my pride.

There. Princes and wars and then me rolling in the straw again. I don't want to make too much of the way my vanity flickered in this little breeze, but the feelings were real. You've watched fervent prayer become fervid. Think of all the stone and armour clutter in the world. Sometimes the most powerful of assertions is the most pathetic admission of frailty, of doubt. Only someone with a feeling for the strength of what's ungodly would bother to build a cathedral. I was like that then, I think, masking my uncertainties with arrogance.

But in the end she came to me.

I was in the woodland one morning, on the hill near Iorwerth's court. Morgan had been there administering the law. I stumbled away from the busyness with a melancholy that wasn't entirely affected.

I came to a place where a tree had partly fallen and was leaning crazily into the branches of another. This seemed an appropriate spot to be thoughtful in, so bunching one shoulder against the bark and resting a hand on the crown of my head, I stared down into the wounded roots.

'Meilyr?'

I started, looked round. A green dress and a moon face — looking anxious at first and then relieved to recognize me.

'I thought —' she said. 'Thank god.'

'You thought I looked like —'

She nodded.

'Do I look like him?'

'From the back, with your hand up like that. Well, he is here with Morgan.' She sort of laughed.

There was much looking to interesting things that we noticed over one another's shoulder, and an awkward pause. We stood close together for a long time, neither of us quite knowing what move to make next. So we fumbled uncertainly towards the embrace and when it came it was filled with huge relief, that sense of wanting to press through one another into the same space.

For me then stillness was a rare thing to achieve. Things had happened in those actions with the teulu to make more turmoil and unbidden remembering. When it happened — stillness I mean — I knew it with great clarity, felt the stinking ditch miraculously smoothing and greening itself into a level meadow.

She said, a long time later, 'I —' and hesitated.

'You.'

And we laughed.

Look, I don't mean to bore you with all this adolescent stuff, but bear with me. Few things can be more trivial, or more important.

We walked. She wanted to walk to the north and west, across Gwrgant's land and into the woodland, towards the disputed territory, where we knew it would be quiet. It wasn't a warm day. Cool lifts of wind sent talking waves through the late spring branches. I would have preferred us to lie by the fire in Gwrgant's house while Non worked at her distaff, but Cristin pulled me across the meadow.

Little Hywel was there, happily kicking one of Lleucu's children, and Gwrgant was at the door of the byre with Lleucu's husband and a priest, praying for a sick cow. The priest had written a benediction on a piece of parchment and tied it to the cow's ear in the usual way. Gwrgant rubbed her flank and made shushing noises, as if that might soothe her. Her dugs were withered and she trembled. My master looked up at us as we neared the northern fringe of trees. He was a bowshot away, but I thought I saw a tiny, Rhunlike moving of the corners of his mouth, or a fractional inclining of the head, before we disappeared from his sight.

Cristin and I walked a long way in a silence that had no sense of being strained. The earth was wet, but we came to a strange tree that curved out of a bank and on its thick, looped back we couched ourselves and made our limbs into a loose plait. Though our wariness was gone, the old frantic physicality hadn't flowed back into place. There was something slower burning, more intense.

I took off her headdress and observed her hair, the exact singleness of each strand where it entered the scalp, then ran my finger in the flute of her upper lip, looked at the small, extraordinary teeth.

She half laughed, murmured, 'What're you doing?'

'Worshipping creation.'

'Buying a horse. They always check the teeth.' A pause. 'I've missed you.'

A long time later she spoke again. 'Listen. Angharad says we should marry.'

'All right.'

'All right?'

'Yes. Please. Does that mean —'

'Not now.'

I growled, then said, 'Where'll we live then?'

She shrugged.

'We could go to Pencarn' I said, 'and you could serve him if Angharad would let you, ready for when—'

'We'll see. I was thinking —. Well, perhaps.'

'Gwrgant'll be pleased. I'll be out of his way.'

She looked at me and pursed her lips.

Suddenly the wheel slipped its rut.

'Wait a minute' I said. 'Angharad said? Is this what *you* want? Did she just decide to fix it? I mean —'

Cristin knew what I meant.

'No no' she said. 'If it was that, just an arrangement, Iorwerth would have gone to you or Gwrgant.'

'He has been talking to me a lot recently, Iorwerth.'

'Hm. He was just seeing if you were all right, I expect. Angharad saw me moping. She asked me about it and I told her. She said we should, you know, marry, to help me. If she hadn't said it would've been harder for me to come to you.' She paused. 'Impossible.'

'I could love Angharad for that.'

'You always did fancy her.'

I looked at Cristin, wondered if she saw straight through me.

'She fancies you' she said.

'Don't be —. You don't talk about things like that do you?' She nodded.

I reconsidered. A rapid fantasy wove itself in the branches. Iorwerth catching me and Angharad on their mattress. Iorwerth killed in single combat. Myself a great and greying penteulu sharing a chamber with Angharad and Cristin. I tell you this in confidence. And before you ask, I confessed it and did penance. The dream ended with me and Pencarn on horseback, people cheering.

But I looked down at Cristin who was suppressing laughter.

'I mean it' she said, too insistently, pulling herself back to her game. 'I bet you could if you wanted to.' She paused again, saw that I wavered into believing her once more, and laughed out loud.

I shook her so that we almost fell out of our loop of tree.

'She's past it' I said. 'Her tits are all shrivelled.' I laughed too.

'Want a bet?' she said.

'Aren't they?'

'No. They're not and she isn't. And she's a fellow poet.'

We stopped laughing and looked at one another.

I said, 'It's you I want.'

'Is it?'

I didn't answer in words. We just looked.

'She's a poet' I said at last. 'So what? You're a storyteller. I prefer your stories.'

'I wish *I* could make my way by talking and singing like you do. Then there'd be —'

'Yes?'

'No. Never mind.'

'No, go on. Then there'd be what?'

'No no. Never mind.' Her gaze flickered over my shoulder to the trees and the extraordinary teeth bit at the lower lip. She spoke slowly. 'Did I ever tell you the story of the Afanc King and the sons of Teyrnon?'

'Never heard of it.'

She often came up with odd stories from her own country — still does. Even Gwrgant didn't know some of them. Amateurs often pester us with their poems and stories. The poems are generally excruciating but sometimes the stories can be interesting. Anyway, Cristin, as I think I've said, is a good storyteller, and in those circumstances she could've recited the lineage of Gwilym Bastart and I would have been enthralled. So I set my head on her shoulder and in an overelocuted parody of a mother at bedtime she began.

'Well, in the days when Teyrnon Twrf Liant was —'

But I never heard about the Afanc King and the sons of Teyrnon because it was then that the arrow hit me in the neck.

## 28

I felt something hot but not immediately painful across the back of my neck and everything disappeared in a glare of white light. I know we fell and slithered on the bank and I heard someone distantly calling 'Idiot' and I felt annoyed, but I couldn't stand up. Crumpled on the earth, I found I could move a little and I saw Cristin standing with blood or her dress and hands.

She held her hands up like this and she was gasping as if she'd been scalded, but the blood was all mine.

I tried to look round for the archer but couldn't move my head much. Let me confess to a moment of valour.

Turning back to Cristin I managed to shout, 'Run.'

Well I thought I shouted. She tells me it was a voiceless rattle.

She looked at me with her mouth open and her eyes wide, then turned and started to stumble away. She lifted her skirt and I saw the dirty soles of her feet as she started to run.

The sound of feet approaching. I lay still, waiting for the finishing off. A pair of feet was near my face.

'Oh shit. Don't tell me you've killed him.' It was a light, rather high voice.

'Well this is a bit of all right.' The second voice was lower, subdued and apologetic, but its owner was starting to pull off my tunic.

I felt that none of this mattered at all and deduced from my odd nonchalance that I was already dead. But the blood that had flowed around my neck and onto my face touched the corner of my lip. It was hot and tickled and when I licked it it tasted salt and wonderful and I knew I was alive.

Somehow my realization showed itself to the two men. The looting stopped and a hand rubbed at the blood on my neck. It hurt.

'Shit. It just gouged him a bit. Come on. Up.'

The hand was slapping me on the head and I was being dragged to my feet. I stood unsteadily, trying to pull my tunic back into place.

'Shit. You're lucky.'

The light voice belonged to a heavy, short man with dark hair and a stubbly chin. He was perhaps thirty. The other man was thinner, my age or younger, and scrawny. They wore blue and black cloaks.

I didn't feel lucky.

'I fancied his belt too' the scrawny one said.

'Shit, Dafi. As well as being an idiot you're what my dear old mother would've called a thieving git. Go and find your arrow.' To signal his displeasure, the shitman hit his assistant on the temple with the flat of his hand.

The arrow retrieved and my knife taken from me, these two crucked me along, one at either armpit, as if I was an old friend with no head for the mead. Lightvoice even spoke soothing words from time to time and helpfully held my collar away from my back so that the blood wouldn't stain so badly.

'There' he said. 'That's it. You'll be all right. You'll see.'

Then, as if because he'd forgotten to say this at the beginning, 'Shit, aye. You'll be all right.'

'Yes. Keep it clean' the other one said, referring to my collar. 'I might have it yet.'

I'd like to be able to say that thoughts for Cristin filled my head and that my attack of selfless valour persisted, but I was merely physically terrified, and when they tied me and slung me across a horse and I saw the water spurting around its hooves as we forded the river into Senghenydd, I was too scared to remember the cocksure archer with an arrow in his chest for whom I might be galanas, or to be reminded of Eneas dead and drained of blood.

## 29

Pain, a little later, claimed its kingdom and for a time I was too preoccupied even to be scared, or to listen to the conversation of my captors.

When we reached the place of Ifor Fychan ap Meurig's main court — though I didn't know then that that was where it was — I started to see, trussed and tipped up as I was, chickens and the lower halves of people and small children entire. Some of the children simply watched. One little girl walked alongside me, and stooping slightly, looked up into my face.

'No he's not' she shouted. 'His eyes moved.'

We stopped. Shitman dragged me from the horse by my elbows and as I was whirled more or less onto my feet I saw I was in a small, stockaded yard. A few people had gathered to watch, silent and staring, edging forward curious as cows.

'Shit. Go on. Clear off you lot. There's nothing to see. Dafi, go and tell the prince we got him. Try to hold him off for a bit, will you.'

He threw me into a small building that had a damp, earthen floor and smelt of urine. The hurdle door was raised into place and the room darkened. Through the chinks in the woven hurdle I saw the shape of someone standing a casual guard outside.

There were two voices in the dark. I'd heard English once before, among some foreigners in Llandâf, but I was surprised to recognize it here. One voice was hoarse and halting, as if the speaker had difficulty finding the words. The other, when it came, was more fluent but less talkative.

They discussed me, I supposed. I managed to pass my feet through my tied wrists so that my hands were before me. I'd just leant myself against the slimy timber wall and started to finger my caked backhair to examine the wound on my neck when a shape and a noise came towards me. It spoke. The halting, hoarse voice began to speak more quickly and certainly. An articulated barking. I know French no more than I know English and anyway as the man searched me for a weapon I was too scared to speak. Finding no knife he stood before me, evidently able to see me, though all I saw of him was a dark shape. He spoke urgently and was suddenly silent.

A question. I started to stutter that I was wounded in the neck. Before I'd finished, the shape spoke some squashy, ugly sounding word. There was a gasp of surprise from the darkness behind him.

I guessed that the nearer man was telling his companion that I was a Welshman and I cringed against the wall as the shape leant nearer, placed a hand on my shoulder.

As they talked quietly, the Englishman fetched some vessel of clean water and the Frenchman attempted to wash my wound using his fingers. As the light grew stronger I saw that they wore smirched, greywhite shifts. Their outer clothes had been taken and their feet and wrists had been fettered. The Frenchman had dark hair and a full beard and the Englishman, who was younger, was fair, wispy chinned.

I drank some of the water and for a moment the world was miraculous. I loved the urinous, faecal stench, the oozy floor lightflecked from the gaps in the hurdle.

The Frenchman spoke quietly in French and English, asking me questions, I think, but gave up when he realized I understood nothing. I never found out exactly who they were, or how long they'd been held hostage, but I supposed the older man wanted news of the outside.

I don't know how long we sat in silence after that. I felt lightheaded. What thoughts I had whirled uncontrollably. I huddled against the wall and felt I'd never be able to move.

Later that day the hurdle was removed and Dafi and Shitman dragged me out into the yard. Briefly in the blast of grey light I saw the other two prisoners, ashfaced and dazed by the sudden movement. Outside I was shoved on a stool and an old woman — she could easily have been fifty — came to me with red ointment. She was in such a hoop that she scarcely had to bend to treat my neck. Dafi dragged my hair up and she rebuked him for his clumsiness. Out of the corner of my eye I saw her face close to me, examining the wound.

She was proficient, expressionless. One of Toothless's lessons to us was to show no signs of surprise when we looked into another man's wound. She practised that art. She didn't look at my eyes but cleaned the cut with a damp cloth and then smeared it with the ointment.

'Nothing' she said to Shitman as she turned away, waving the rag. 'Hardly worth bothering about.'

This satisfied the two men, who walked me quickly towards the door of Ifor's little hall.

The blow had something to do with this, I suppose, but I remember that time as if it was something out of a drunken night. I could swear that I floated, and the door, I swear, opened on its own as I moved to it. There was a distance to everything, as if I watched someone else experiencing these things rather than living through them myself. The doormouth was small but the three of us passed without any sense of cramming. I thought the men at either side were ghosts who moved through the jambs as if impalpable.

Inside there was dry air. The smokesting and crackle of a small fire, movement into the radius of warmth. Men older than myself stood there, four, perhaps more of them. They watched me come, as if interrupted in some subdued conversation. One man was seated on a short bench near the fire. He had an unusually large cloak which he'd furled round each of his legs and its brass clasp was worked with living coils like the churchyard crosses. He had a large head and dark, crinkly hair that was greying. His moustache too, which was cropped unusually short, was greyed. His face was pale, his cheeks deeply lined, and his eyes set very deep in their sockets. He sneezed and wiped his nose on the shoulder of his cloak.

I looked again at the standing men and recognized among them Rhys Ddu, no longer living up to his name as his hair, too, was greying. He'd continued to use Morgan's permission to visit the court over the years, but only occasionally and only when the tensions were at their slackest. He and Gwrgant had maintained the professional courtesies as well as they could in the circumstances, though I'd always felt that Gwrgant's higher rank chafed at the storyteller's pride.

The man on the bench glanced at me, levered his shoulders as if they were stiff, sniffed, and stared into the fire. He mumbled something, then there was silence.

I felt a fist between my shoulderblades and Dafi said, 'Answer.'

'What?'

The man on the bench shouted. 'Name. I said name. What's your name.'

I tried to answer but only unvoiced air came out.

He stood up. Standing, he was hardly any taller than he'd been sitting down.

'What?' he said quietly, coming towards me. 'What? What did you say? Did you say something? What was it?'

I tried again, produced the same hissed whisper. He stood close. The crown of his head was level with my chin. As Ifor Fychan ap Meurig looked up at me I imagined that he slept badly. I saw him drag himself off the mattress, rub and rub the sunk eyes, the lined cheeks, wait for the sun to rise.

'What?' he said.

Before I could try a third time he said again, 'What? Griffri? Did I hear you say Griffri? I thought he said something. Did he say something?' He looked round.

'Yes' Rhys Ddu said. 'Griffri ap Berddig. I heard him.'

'He heard you. That's who you are then is it?' He sniffed again.

'So.' He looked down, as if thinking, rallying his ideas, then up at me once more, became conversational, essayed a smile that transformed his face. 'So, Griffri. My boy. Tell us who you serve. Who do you serve? Who's your lord, then?'

The smile encouraged me. When you're so scared and weakened any signal is seized upon. My voice came, though it sounded distant.

'Morg —'

Before I'd finished the word — I thought even before I'd started it — his face was twisted by a look of pain and enormous astonishment.

'Morgan?' he shouted, stepping back. 'Morgan? Did you say Morgan?' He looked round. 'Did he say Morgan?'

'He said Morgan' Rhys Ddu said.

'I thought that was what he said. Not him. Not Morgan of Gwynllwg. Not Morgan of Caerllion. Not Morgan ab Owain Wan ap Caradog. Oh, Griffri, you disappoint me. Not him, please. Not the Morgan who comes here bristling spears and tells me not to pick on him. Not the Morgan who confuses good pasture with his own. Not the one who shoots Welshmen in the chest and licks the arse of Iarll Caerloyw.'

I felt my mouth opening and closing and heard incoherent noises.

For a wild moment I tried to think of some other Morgan to pin my loyalty on. Thank god I couldn't call one to mind.

Just before that time, perhaps a few days before, I'd been out with some of the teulu, working on the ambushing and wrecking of the French I've already mentioned. Why didn't I think of that then, as I stood there gagging? I felt irresistibly that this man was right, that I was caught, guilty. It was me, whatever it was. I looked at his face again, saw that his pain, amazement, was unnaturally sustained, and that made it worse, so to be fooled with.

'Yes' I said.

One of the standing men started to cough loudly and covered his mouth with his hand. I looked at him over my questioner's head.

'Don't look at him. Look at me' the short man said. 'Look at me. Look. Here. There. That's right.'

The coughing stopped.

Another considering pause, the rallying and the smile.

'Well, never mind' the short man said. 'Never mind. God gives us so little freedom. Not many men can choose their master, ey? Not many. You can't, I suppose. I can. You can't. Your master thinks I can't choose my master. He's wrong there, though. You know he's wrong don't you? Tell me your master's wrong. Go on. Say it. Say it. Say it. Tell me it. Go on.'

Sheepishly I started to say, 'My master's —'

'Yes?'

I stood silent, looking not at his eyes but at his chin.

He pulled a face and looked round at his audience.

'A little bit of pride' he said, like that, singing the words. 'Come on. Try it again. Try it for me. You're safe here. Come on. Just say it. That's all. For me. Come on. My —

And I spoke the words. I can hardly say them now. Then I'd lost all sense of their meaning, of any meaning they might have had. They meant nothing in themselves, were kinds of counters in a game. I yielded them up as I felt I had no choice.

'What?' The astonished shout again. 'Is there no loyalty in you? Is this the way you are as soon as your master's back is turned? Is that the sort of man you are? He's not much of a master I know, but still. Oh, Griffri. I don't know if I want to be associated with you. How could you say that?' Looking round. 'How could he say that?'

'He said it' Rhys Ddu said. 'I heard him.'

'You heard him.' Turning back. 'He heard you. You said it. I don't know if I want you here. I don't know if I care to have you here. I might send you back. This isn't the place for the likes of you if that's what you're like. I might just send you back and say, no thanks. But then I could just cut your balls off and ram them down your throat.'

I don't remember my legs giving way, but I know that Dafi and Shitman were holding me up by the elbows when the little man grew quiet and conciliatory again.

'Aw. There. Look' he said, 'nobody's going to hurt you. Nobody. We're all friends here. Aren't we?'

I staggered as he waved the guards away and tried to put a hand round my shoulder. I say tried as he was far too short to reach. His hand did touch my wound in the attempt, though, and I gasped.

'What's this?' He stood on tiptoe and examined the hurt. 'How did this happen?' His voice had become flat.

Shitman pointed to Dafi. The little man looked at the young soldier, who seemed to shrink, but no words were spoken between them. Ifor turned back to me and I sensed that he was resuming his mask, his performance, felt almost lucky this time that he should veil himself in satires for me.

'Yes' he said. 'Nasty that. Nasty. But it'll mend. It'll mend. You can still move your head, ey?' He started to walk me about the hall as he spoke, putting his arm through mine as if we were to be married. 'Look at all these nice people.'

The man who'd coughed stifled another spasm with his hand.

'Look at them. They don't mean you any harm. You don't mean him any harm do you?'

There was a chorus of noes.

'See. A big strong man like you, after you've had a bump like that, I'm surprised, surprised, Griffri, you'd get worried about a few words. They're only words. Air.'

The look downward and the rallying smile. The afternoon light was beginning to fade and the timbered belly of the hall started to become visible as the unshuttered windows grew dimmer and the firelight stronger. Ifor's face was lit grey on one side by daylight and redyellow on the other by the flames.

'So tell me' he said. 'In what —' he milled a porridge finger in the air as he seemed to search publicly for the word '— capacity, yes, do you serve your lord? Tell me that.'

125

His smile widened and he looked into my face. I fancied his eyebrows started to lift, registering surprise, before I began to answer.

'I'm — a poet.'

The eyebrows were fully raised but the sunk eyes still seemed dead.

'Oh. A poet.' Turning. 'He said he's a poet.'

'I heard him say it' Rhys Ddu said.

Turning back. 'Well, so he did. That explains it then, doesn't it, Griffri? I understand now. You just want to please a lord or two, don't you? Doesn't much matter which. So it's this to one lord and that to another. Give them what they want, ey? That's right isn't it, Rhys?'

'Yes' Rhys Ddu said. 'He's a yesman.'

'I admire your consistency in that. And I do believe it's so important to support the arts. Rhys there, you see, he's a poet and a storyteller. Where would he be without me? I do my little bit, don't I Rhys?'

'You do, Ifor. I don't know where I'd be.'

'There. But tell me, Griffri, I thought Morgan's pencerdd was an older man. What was it? Geraint. Gwgon.'

'Gwrgant' I said.

'Ah yes. Of course. Gwrgant. Yes. That was it. I knew it was something like that. But tell me.' He frowned, seemed to search his mind. 'He's been here hasn't he? Hasn't he been here?'

'He's been here' Rhys Ddu said.

'Yes. I knew he had. He sang for us. The people love it when you turn up with your little harps slung in your little bags. Where would *we* be without *you*, ey? Yes he sang. What did he sing about now?'

'He sang about how great you are, Ifor' Rhys Ddu said.

'Yes. That's it. He sang about how great I am. What a privilege. Mind, I've got to be honest with you, Griffri. I didn't understand a word. Modern poetry. Modern poetry leaves me cold, you see. So many long words. Still, we have to support these things don't we? After all where would you be without people like me? Sitting around hungry somewhere, probably. Telling the truth. No no no. I'm sure you're all much happier to be paid arselickers. Which is probably why you get on so well with your lord, isn't it, Griffri? Tell me it's why you get on so well with your lord.'

There was a sound of horses and voices in the yard outside.

126

He smiled up at me.

'Go on' he said. 'Tell me. Tell me that. Say it. Tell me the reason you get on with your lord is because you're just two paid arselickers together. You see that's true don't you? Go on. Say it. Tell me it. Say.'

He kept on smiling. I stared at his chin.

# 30

I sometimes wonder what I would have said. Nothing, perhaps. And what then? I've tried to work out what alternatives I had — to say my catechism and be shouted at again, to be silent, to be defiant, to fall down in a faint. To cry. I was near to that. But when you're there there aren't alternatives, only the chaos of the moment and things happen by some mysterious impulsion, by god's will or the will of his enemy and you're left with nothing but a sense of the inching on of obscure destinies.

When the door burst open I was too frightened to realize that I should have felt relieved.

The young man who came in was redfaced from riding and a little out of breath. He seemed on the point of blurting out some message when he looked round and saw the static clusters of men, and me, a stranger with his master. So he checked himself and fetched some deep breaths.

Ifor turned away from me.

The man came forward, presented himself, so to speak, then looked from Ifor to me and back.

'It's all right' Ifor said to him.

The young man looked down and with a release of feeling said, 'They make you kneel.'

'Yes' Ifor said.

'They held me on my knees while I spoke with him.'

Ifor looked away from the man but said nothing. Like the old hoopwoman looking into the wound, he showed nothing.

At length he looked into the man's face. 'And?'

127

The man returned the look briefly then his eyes dropped and he made a tiny shake of the head.

Ifor breathed out and his head sank at the same time.

'All right' he said a moment later, stirring himself. He motioned Dafi and Shitman to my sides and then drew away with the messenger and the other men. They talked in a quiet group.

I watched them. The grouped heads talked quietly as if they were, say, discussing cattle. For them the tense stillness of a few moments before was gone. Ifor seemed to talk in quite an ordinary way and I wondered how it was that I could be so frightened of this.

Suddenly he looked towards us and my fear returned.

'Has he eaten?' he said.

Dafi said that I hadn't.

'Well give him something then, give him something.'

Dafi fetched me some porridge in a wooden bowl. There was no spoon. They let me kneel and, my hands still tied, I ate with my fingers. I was preoccupied with this for a few moments. I was very hungry and the bowl was quickly emptied. When I looked up, Ifor Fychan was issuing instructions. Still he seemed shrunk — if that's the right word — into ordinariness, into something like reasonableness. He'd consulted with his uchelwyr as I'd seen Morgan and Iorwerth do scores of times and, it appeared to me, they jointly reached some considered decision.

'In the yard' Ifor called to one of the men who was leaving the hall on some errand. 'Fetch somebody to translate as well.' He turned to me. 'Do you know any French?'

Cheered by the food, I almost said, 'Of course not' but I managed to hold that back and just shook my head.

'Pity' he said. Then to my guards, 'Bring him anyway.'

He walked out quickly followed by the others. I was dragged to my feet.

Outside fine rain had started. It would soon be night. Looking up, I saw the wisps of cloud were very low, was reminded of days at the hafod in my boyhood and I opened my mouth to feel the tiny pickings of the rain on my tongue and lips, like a child catching snowflakes. There was a cawing of crows. Over the wooden wall of the yard I could see, at a little distance, the crowns of trees. The court was evidently an upland stronghold.

Shortly, a young and nervous looking priest appeared. His hair was tonsured in the Welsh manner. Next was dragged forward my fellow prisoner, the Frenchman, who had tried to speak to me and washed my neck. He too was tasting the clean air, tilting his face to catch the fine wash and stretching his eyebrows upward. He was tall and a little fat, the dark hair threaded with grey.

Ifor nodded to Dafi, who left my side and went to help with the prisoner. The fetters on the man's feet meant that he had to move by making absurd, hopping little steps. Ifor spoke quietly to the priest, who spoke to the prisoner in Latin. The Frenchman shrugged and shook his head. The priest tried again more slowly and loudly, I think trying to hazard a few words of French here and there. After this there was a pause. The prisoner looked down. The slightest movement of a shoulder. I thought that this time he'd understood, but the priest spoke once more. The prisoner looked at him dazedly, then turned his head to look over the wall to the treetops where the crows were calling.

'Oh great Christ' Ifor shouted, interrupting the priest. 'Come on. Bring the bench. Bring the bench. Here. Here.'

The bench he'd sat on in the hall was brought out and the prisoner was laid face down on it, his head overhanging the end. Dafi and the other man held his chained hands to the ground underneath his face. Ifor gave some instructions to Rhys Ddu, who sat astride the man's back. People, the little girl who'd stooped to look up into my face among them, appeared from various buildings to watch. Ifor nodded to Rhys who caught hold of the prisoner's hair and jerked his head up. The man grunted and then started to speak quickly and quietly. I assume he prayed. Ifor took out his knife and knelt in front of him. He held the blade by the man's cheek, then paused, dropped his hand, squinted up at the sky. The light was poor. He looked around as if expecting to find a lamp nearby, but then settled to his job once more. He wiped the speckles of drizzle from his knife on his shirt, said, quietly, 'Hold his legs' which two young men did, and, with admirable speed and a kind of bored expertise, he dug out the prisoner's eyes.

There were screams that could have split rock and I heard an explosion of wingbeats from the trees. Dafi half crouched at the hurt man's arm, eager to get up.

'Turn him round, Ifor? ' he said. 'Top and tail?'

'No no no no no' Ifor said, smiling at him as he got to his feet.

129

'Minimum force. Minimum force. In politics, my boy, restraint is everything.'

He wiped his knife again, this time on Dafi's shirt, and waved an arm.

The signal was for the hoopwoman, who waddled forward carrying a bag and turned her attention to the mutilated hostage. He was still conscious and whimpering. She had him turned and sat on the ground so she could treat him with her ointments.

'Silly boys' she said.

The people started to move away, murmuring about the show. A few crowded round the woman to see the wounds.

Ifor turned away from all this, tucking his knife into his belt with the sigh of a man much troubled by affairs of state. He called forward his redfaced messenger and I heard him say something like, 'Sleep here tonight. You'll go back and tell them about this in the morning. Your brother's in Gwynllwg on the other business. Rest now. I'll need you back day after tomorrow whatever he says.'

His words were fragmented by the distance and the scene too was breaking in the coming dark, sapped colourless. Still I saw him turn to me as the messenger went into the hall and I was conscious of myself shrinking away as Dafi had. Instead of beckoning for me to be brought to him, he came to me, smiling.

'All right. All right' he said. 'My apologies for all that. No no, Selyf. Let his arm go. I think he's got the idea.'

Shitman uncertainly released my arm and moved a pace away from me. Ifor resumed his bridal position, started walking. Shitman was rejoined by Dafi and they both shadowed us, awkwardly, as if not sure they were doing right.

'You see' Ifor said, 'god allows even princes only a little freedom. Our glorious king set the example that I've found myself forced to follow this afternoon.'

We walked in silence. Presently he stopped. By this time the yard was empty except for us. An enlarged fire in the hall splayed its flickering glow from the open door. People would be turning towards sleep. In the half dark I could see the wet gleam of Ifor's eyes as he turned to face me. I tensed, expecting a blow, but none came. Nor did he resume, as I expected him to, the game that had been interrupted in the hall. It occurred to me that he needed an audience. Here there was only Dafi and Selyf to perform to and they, it seemed, hardly counted.

'Griffri' he said. 'Was there ever a time when things were easy? Was it ever simple?'

He wanted no answer from me, or at least I felt that he didn't expect to get one. I was grateful that he'd forgotten the game.

'All I want' he said, 'is to keep my cattle and collect my rents and give law to my people. That's all. Why should it be so hard? Why is everything such a struggle? They say it was better before the French came. There's nobody alive can remember those days now. What did they say then? They looked to the time before the English didn't they? Was there another perfect time before that, just beyond their memories? Does the delusion go right back into the loin of god? Tell me, Griffri.'

He paused. The questions were unanswerable — they were scarcely even questions — but I began to make noises as if I was looking for a word.

'Tell me' he said, 'what can we do?'

I like to think that if I'd been whole and nearer to my right senses I would have concocted some clever words. But I said nothing. It was cold. I was wet as well as dazed, and had started to shiver. There wasn't the teasing pressure to his questions this time. His eye caught the little light as they moved, watching me, and I felt that he really wanted to know. The words were more, other, than just the machinery of a kind of torture.

The eyes seemed to disappear as, I suppose, he looked down.

'Your master' he said. 'What about him?' The gleam again. 'What might he do? What? What do you think? About this. About you. What do you think he'll do?'

I realized that he hadn't forgotten the game, had just switched back to it with a movement of the eye. The teasing pressure came back into his voice, though he spoke much more softly, having no audience, or, it occurred to me, because I was the audience. He seemed to me always at the point of exhaustion but always managing to carry on, as if living itself was an unnatural burden to him.

'M-morgan?' I said at last. Ths shiver got into my voice so that I stuttered, as Gwrgant sometimes did when he was drunk.

'Yes. Yes. Him. What about him? Do you think we could talk?' He paused. 'You see, Griffri, I don't want to hurt you. You understand that, don't you? It would be so distasteful, wouldn't it, and me a pa-

*131*

tron of poets? I'd hate to be remembered as a harmer of poets. That wouldn't be a nice memory would it? I'm sure good Welshmen everywhere would prefer not to remember such a thing. But we mustn't appear weak either, must we? That would be unfortunate. It won't happen. There will be nothing unfortunate. You see, Griffri, perhaps one day I could invite you back here to sing for us. Oh, I know it's all froth, but it's such good form, isn't it, to be seen as cultured and generous.'

He talked on like this. I had no idea what he wanted and somehow that made things worse. I felt that he didn't know what he wanted either.

At last I managed to say, 'What do you w-want me to do?'

The gleam stilled for a long moment.

'Nothing' he said. 'You're already doing it. Believe me. You're being very helpful. All you have to do is to be calm and patient. That's the best way for you to help us, as they say, arrive at a satisfactory outcome, ey? And you'll go back home in the end, duly rewarded. You watch. One way or another.'

And suddenly he went. Dafi and Selyf were at my sides, dragging me towards the prison.

'Shit. Thank god for that' Selyf said.

'I'm wet as a cow's arse' Dafi said.

'Sometimes —'

'Sometimes what?'

'Sometimes I think he's.' Selyf grunted instead of finishing the sentence.

'What?' Dafi said.

'Never you mind what. You've already landed us in enough shit with your archery display.'

Dafi was disinclined to answer this point in words, but commented by punching me in the back as he pushed me into the prison.

## 31

I lay in unbearable silence and the damp litter of the prison floor. My shivering became uncontrollably violent and at last I cried, plentifully, but as quietly as possible. I was, even in this condition, oddly aware of the guard outside the hurdle door, the chained Englishman and the eyeless Frenchman lying still, embarrassed by the thought they might be listening. Pride, you see, extends even to those places. I think we must be afraid of what would or wouldn't be left if we peeled that away.

Anyway, so reduced, I watched daylight and dark come and go three times. That first night I heard subdued music and gusts of voices from the hall, which stimulated my selfpity wonderfully. But I had things to be thankful for. Though my wrists were tied, I was never chained as the others were and when we were fed — once each day — I was given more than the others. Selyf would stand and watch us eat, I think to ensure my safety. Certainly when there was enough light for us to see one another the Englishman looked his hatred into my face, though he was too prudent to make any attempt on me. The Frenchman, in spite or because of his injury, talked a great deal at first. The other man sometimes listened and made conversation, but much of the time seemed bored and ignored him.

Should I say I turned my face towards god? I didn't. I thought often of Ifor. Sometimes I saw him thoughtful in grey, early light, looking from the stockade out over the treetops, his face lined and tired after brief and useless sleep. Sometimes he was shouting, but I heard no words. I dreamt him smiling, welcoming me into his hall, his arms extended, gesturing me towards the splay of flickering red light where a woman was sitting on the bench by a cauldron of glutinous stew. Sometimes I shouted in my dreams, cut out Dafi's eyes and wore a large cloak. I don't know what I was. When my mind stilled a moment I imagined walking from Gwrgant's house to the court, every hollow, tree and stone, getting them into order, remembering the patterns of moss on rocks, and there were strange intrusions sometimes — a still place where no water ran, a massive fallen tree, lush angelica to soothe a fever.

Sunlight too is a great soother. I remember the lightflecks through the hurdle door one morning, and the stillness and the small sounds of people working in the yard outside, the caw of birds, with the kind of clarity that comes when you recover from sickness. I began to decipher the sounds, to notice how many horses, for instance, to guess at the arrival and departure of messengers, strangers, to recognize individuals, children. And naturally, as I became more myself, I began to work.

The cawing, I think, was the start of it, at least of the technical putting together. Looking at the intense points of light on the earth floor I remembered the fraying low cloud, the wet blade in the gloom. I won't pretend that what I produced was great work, it wasn't, but I did it, and there. The Englishman and the blind Frenchman must have listened to me chanting and stopping over and over as I tried to assemble the piece and thought I was possessed — but I was merely self possessed. So my pride was overtaken, or perhaps I was showing off. I sang

> Clouds low overhead
> Dusklight smothering.
> Far my lord and the land I love.
>
> Wave breaks on the rock
> Moonlight shattering.
> Far from her and the home I love.
>
> Crows break from the tree
> Black wave scattering.
> Far my home and the girl I love.

Overweening stuff. Anyway, I wasn't very far from home at all — though it felt that way. Yet take it out of the context of my life and it gains a little strength. Bareness suits it. The wave again, notice. Her moon face when she called to me in the woodland.

I worked at the poem all that day and made many other stanzas, but kept only those three, felt a great satisfaction with my technical rigour. I was scarcely aware, I think, of how images of darkness, the blinding, suffused the thing, how there's a movement towards dark in every part. Gwrgant would've called it old fashioned. Llywarch Henish, lacking the intricacy and opacity that seem obligatory nowadays. But to articulate chaos, desolation, can be, in a man's heart anyway, to subdue it. That third night I slept without dreaming.

## 32

The next day I woke to the sound of much movement in the yard. The Englishman moved around a lot and tried to watch events through the chinks in the door, sometimes describing what he saw to his companion. The Frenchman had become silent and lay with his face to the wall.

After a short while it became unusually quiet and there was nothing but the noise of birds and occasionally a dog barking. We weren't fed. In my mind I tried to walk again, all the paths I knew. Up to Cadog's spring with the buckets and the clear water slopping and the dark billow of September trees. Three men coming from the woodland and Gwrgant smiling, waiting to see if I'd recognize. Walking in the trees an arm's length from Cristin. Her chin going up. My hand a fist snarled in her back hair.

I don't think I thought of the negotiations, which must have started, thought of the disputed meadow, or what payment there might be. The hunger gnawed quietly. I thought they'd forgotten us, except that now and then the shadow of our guard would flit across the hurdle.

At length — I've no idea at what length — I heard some horses and shouting and cheering. Laughter too, and talking, some phrases coming through clear. A voice spoke quietly for a while and there was a sudden explosion of many voices laughing. This all seemed oddly other, as if these weren't real people. I didn't think these silly noises could be made by true men and women with lives, histories.

The sounds subsided, became the normal traffic noise of the yard. Something was over.

There was another long wait. Eventually the guard came in and gave us cheese and milk. He and another man stood at the door and watched us — not Selyf this time. A grinning head appeared, startlingly low, round the jamb. It was the hoopwoman. The rest of her came into view and she actually clapped her hands and laughed, looking at me as if she expected me to reply in kind.

I didn't. She scuttled in.

'Let's see, boy' she said, turning my head in her hands so that she could examine my neck. 'Away from the door, please. Hm. There. Lovely, lovely. Good boy.'

She laughed again and I felt in danger of being kissed, but she merely gave my downy cheek a horny squeeze between her thumb and porridge finger.

'He'll do, he'll do' she said as she passed the second man at the door and scuttled out.

In spite of my hunger I ate with difficulty, gagging on the cheese. The two men at the door were watching me, I felt, waiting for me to finish. The other hostages evidently didn't count. The eyeless man ate nothing, didn't even move, though his companion tried to persuade him, but the guards ignored all that. They watched me and I watched them as I ate, feeling, absurdly, that I was obliged to force down all the cheese and drink all the milk, which was nicely warm but dungtainted. Giving up his efforts at persuasion, the Englishman took his friend's portion for himself and watched our dumb- show while he ate.

When I'd finished, the two men, who'd been lounging against the doorway, got properly to their feet and with an odd slowness moved towards me. I was aware of the Englishman's chained hands like callipers holding a lump of cheese, frozen half way to his open mouth. As they dragged me out I wasn't comforted to see the cheese disappear behind a faint, ruminating smile.

Although the sky was overcast, the glare of daylight hurt my eyes. The new guard having established the tenor of our relationship by producing a large knife, he prodded me away from the prison, leaving the other man on duty.

'This way, shitface' he said.

'Are you Selyf's brother?' I said.

Well, all right. I might not have said it, but I certainly thought it.

Falling again, or floating towards the door. He'd be smiling, his arm extended towards his hearth, or greyfaced after sleeplessness.

Inside, the messenger who'd been redfaced was standing with the young priest who held a rolled parchment, a seal pendant. There was a small fire, the smell of green wood burning. Smokesting, dryness in the throat.

He was sitting on his bench, drinking milk from a bowl. The two standing watched him. He looked up at them, guiltily I thought, with the bowl at his lips, and then to me. He held the bowl away.

'Nothing better for griping guts' he said, as if he had to explain.

His lined face wrinkled into a sad smile. I thought then that he possessed some huge wisdom that he couldn't explain and that did him no good. I felt that if he'd been able to speak it I wouldn't have understood. He knew me better than I knew myself, saw all this in an instant, without having to lumber through thought as I did.

'Well, poet' he said.

Even those two words, as I stood there then, seemed full of meaning. He saw through to what was left of me, or that pride that pretended it was what was left of me when humilition had scorched off the rest. Either I'd arrived at the essential, or at the essential sham. It's like what I said about remembering, hours ago. Do you remember? About whether we remember things because they're important or they're important because we remember them. The first is constant emotional truth, the second is endless expedient contriving.

It shows you how I was, to squeeze so much from two words. But worst of all, his voice was unbearably gentle.

He read something in my face, or I thought he did, and he stood up, small and skewshouldered. he gestured towards the bench.

'Here' he said.

I looked at the bench which stood waiting like some mutilated animal, thought of the unspeaking prisoner with his face to the wall.

I don't remember starting to run, but I remember colliding with the man with the long knife in the doorway. Perhaps I was shouting something. The man dragged me back in towards the seat and I resisted like a pig at slaughter. Ifor was shouting. He was pulling my front hair, his other hand clamped around my chin, and he was shouting.

When I was still they sat me on the bench and his voice softened again.

'There now' he said. 'Mustn't panic. Sh. You're among your own kind here. There. That's it. Calm. I was as you are once. As I am now you might be one day, if you're lucky. We're all one person, you see.

Forget those things I said. Forget them. This is a different day.'

He sat next to me.

'All one. We must strive to be civilized about these things. Learn to unlearn what can only be hurtful. You see that, don't you, Griffri? That's the way of it. It's as well to avoid unpleasantness, so let's just remember the nice things about one another, ey? We're kin, in a sense. All descended from Brutus, after all. And Seisyll ap Dyfnwal's a patron of yours isn't he? His wife and mine are sisters. There. Did you know that? Arglwydd Rhys makes wise matches. There have been bad times. Why hang on to them? We've shrunk into —' he glanced away from me and then back '— into the core. But we'll resume our full selves, won't we, ey?' He smiled and his eyes flickered away from me again. 'And perhaps even be fuller than before. Morgan did a shrewd balancing act. I suppose we all must these days, so how can I blame him? There. I forgive him. It's all forgotten.'

The priest shuffled his feet in the straw litter.

'It's such a strain on us, on all of us' Ifor said. 'This balancing. So often I feel that things are about to —' he actually wiggled the bench so that I almost fell and cried out suddenly '— topple.'

The man at the door started to laugh and stopped when Ifor glanced at him.

'Modern life, modern life' he said. 'It's like modern poetry. Uncomfortable. Difficult. And let me tell you this. Have I told you this? Perhaps so. I'm getting forgetful, you see. Sometimes I wonder whether it wasn't always this way. Perhaps it — no. No. I'm determined to be optimistic. That's why we must put behind us the dreadful events that can serve no purpose but their own perpetuation. You see that don't you, Griffri? Don't you?'

His voice remained gentle and slow. I didn't want it to change, and, full of undigested cheese and dry, smoky air, I said a voiceless yes.

'So do you know what I'm going to do with you, Griffri? What would you imagine? I think we can begin that resuming. Some of my men will take you for a walk. The people are happy at the moment — you've noticed, I expect. Have you noticed that? Just now things feel good for them. People are like children, you see, they forget the larger problems that you and I are aware of. And while they're in such a good mood it wouldn't do to have more mess in the yard. Not today. You'll be taken for a walk. Some of my men will take you. They'll enjoy that. I must apologize, by the way, for the damage on your neck. I've been busy, these last few days, but I'll have a word with Dafi later. All right? Forgive us for that. Ordinarily there'd be a fine or something, but' — he shrugged — 'things aren't within the normal course of law just now. I hope you see that. Not yet. So.'

He nodded to the man at the door, who went out.

'Now, Griffri. Now, we can each begin to become himself. Each can claim his own kingdom. God's blessing on you.'

Have I used that phrase before, about claiming? You see, it was Ifor planted it. The words rang like a sword in my head as the man with the long knife returned with another soldier and they led me away.


## 33


There had been a shower of rain and the yard was slippery. It was that strange piebald weather with short bursts of sunlight breaking around dark swags of cloud, turning the sheets of water in the small puddles brilliant for moments.

I slithered between the two men — it's surprisingly difficult to keep your balance when your hands are tied and your arms held — towards the gate. The little girl appeared with some of her friends and they shouted and cheered after us.

As we went out through the gate two small boys were coming in. They carried hazel switches and were herding half a dozen pigs before them.

'Looks like a good one tomorrow' the knifeman said.

'About bloody time too' the other one said.

They talked across me as we walked, as though I was a lugged sack. We were on the open back of a mountain ridge. There was heather, a slippy track beaten through it to the fort, no houses near. The land fell away on either side and I could see the crowns of trees, hear the cawing and all the spring birdsong. The land was strange with the shifting light, going dull and smudged and then clear greens and browns, exact with the detail of leaves and the hill rippled as the broken cloud was dragged across the sun.

The children stopped following and calling, as dogs stop barking when you leave their territory. I tried to see the opening of the clouds as a good omen, but I couldn't. The sense of the world waking crushed me with a feeling of the indifference of things to people.

Still, when they put the bag on my head and started to draw the cord I felt a moment's panic. This passed. I let my head loll, smelt the odd mixture of rancid bag and green things growing. I could still see — a picture made of flecks of green light, dulling to grey sometimes, through the weave of the coarse material.

The men continued discussing the feast they were to have the next day. I thought of the driven pigs, the switches, felt blown with the un-digested food. More than anything in the world I wanted to take a twig of hazel and clean my fouled teeth.

They fell silent and we walked for a long time. Different shadows, flecks. We had come into trees and the birdsong turned into a cage of sound over us. The sound of a river at last, and then voices approach-ing. Familiar voices. One of them light, rather high.

'Well shit. What's this? Why the decoration? You haven't —'

'No' Knifeman said.

'Thank god for that. Come on. Let's see him to say hello.'

There was a fiddling at my neck and the bag was pulled away. The green and yellow and brown mottling of the woods in sunlight. I gasped the clean air and sneezed.

Selyf the Shitman smiled at me.

'So why the bag?'

Knifeman shrugged. 'You keep a hawk hooded to keep him calm.'

'Hawk?'

Selyf laughed and a bass laughed to his treble. Dafi's laugh was a kind of guttural, blown mooing. He showed his large yellow teeth. My two guards laughed at his laughing.

Selyf had a bow and quiver. Dafi was armed similarly and in his belt I noticed a number of knives, among them my own. He carried a bul-ging sack. There was something different about him. I couldn't tell what.

'Well' Selyf said to Knifeman. 'It's all set.'

'Clear?'

'No bother. You know where?'

'More or less.'

'We left an arrow in the tree. Oh shit. There's a thought. Bring it back with you when you're coming. It's all sorted.'

And then Selyf looked to me.

'Young man' he said. Looking down he extended a hand, stretching the fingers like this as if measuring the air. For a moment I was bewildered but then I understood and lifted my tied wrists forward.

Believe that standing there in the lightdapple, to birdsong and the noise of the river, he solemnly shook my hand, and Dafi copied him.

'No —' Dafi said and then mooed briefly '— no hard feelings.'

He smiled a yellow smile and his eyes strayed a moment on my shoulder. He was either looking at the scabbed neckwound or my cloak.

'No. And Ifor said he wants a word with you.' I observed the momentary freezing in his eyes.

The two waved and went. I turned to watch them, saw the sack bunched on Dafi's back, but the bag came back over my head and my guards pulled me on by my elbows. I sneezed again. Though the clouds had cleared and the sun was quite strong, I was shivering. The river noise grew louder but above it I could still hear the breathing of my guards, which had become shallower, as if they were anxious, and a blackbird singing.

Without warning we were in the river and I was stumbling on the slimy stones, shocked breathless by the sudden cold. I fell forward and felt my arms and chest go into the water. A hand was at the back of my head, gripping my hair through the sacking, and I went under, still being dragged forward.

I had thought that this was it, but I was dragged to my feet again and punched on the head and Knifeman said, 'Come on, fool. Walk.'

But I was near paralysed and it wasn't only river water that ran from me. They dragged me out onto the other bank. I could tell it was the other bank from the way the shadows fell — the sun was still at our backs and I was grateful for its warmth. The second man complained that they should have found a better place to ford but Knifeman told him to keep his voice down.

The blackbird's song receded and we were in trees again. The patched shade and the soaked clothes chilled me. Faintly there was the smell of offal, which made me think we were approaching a house, but it grew fainter as we walked on.

Suddenly I was pushed to my knees. Through the weave of the bag I saw the large blade near my hands and I closed my eyes. A moment's tension then release. The cord was cut and my hands were

*141*

wrenched to my back, retied. I was pushed to lie on my side on a gentle slope. Through the sacking I could see the legs of one of my guards, standing near my face. He paused, stretched on tiptoe for moments, then moved away.

I lay still. All the noise of our movement, the bag rustling, was stopped. I could hear my own panting, birds, the river distantly, the wash of air in branches. Vaguely I was aware of a shadow at my head. One or both of them, I thought, were standing there but he, they, were very still and quiet.

I suppose I wasn't there very long. I don't know. It felt like a long time. When the bag was taken off my head the sun had moved a little closer to the horizon and had begun to redden. I heard breathing and foot movements and a lesser shadow detached itself from the one at my head and moved around me. Someone squatting and the gleam of a knife.

'Keep still.'

There was a firm hand on my forehead and the blade suddenly came up inside the bag next to my cheek. I don't know whether I shouted or not. The hand tightened. Tension again and the sudden slackening. The drawcord was cut and the bag was pulled away. At my back another knife was cutting the cord on my wrists.

With the bag in one hand, his knife in the other, Toothless looked down at me, the late afternoon light spilling around his head. Throwing the bag away he knelt, looked at the wound on my neck professionally, expressionless.

I cast my eyes upward and tried to say a prayer of thanks. The shadow at my head was an alder tree. Looking up its trunk I could see the stump of a snapped arrow, broken near where the head was buried in the bark. The guard had stood on tiptoe, unsuccessfully tried to wrench it out.

And I was standing, rubbing my wrists, and Toothless was smiling and a boy with reddish hair, Owain ab Iorwerth, was holding the knife that had cut the wrist cord.

'Come on' Toothless said.

We moved quickly through the trees, though I shivered and staggered.

It was — how long? — a few days since I'd seen these people, yet they were strange to me as if they were entirely remade. Toothless's large chin, the worked clasp of Owain ab Iorwerth's cloak, the hard edges of pattern in the feathering of his arrows where they stuck from the quiver. You've seen a kestrel's feather on the bare rock of a mountain, seen the dark bars on the tan, the perfected shaft. There was that strangeness.

Toothless was talking to me as we walked but I don't know what he said. He talks quietly, almost shyly, and seldom looks into your face, rather like Iorwerth. But subduedly he was telling me something. Being kind, I sensed.

I talked too. I listened to myself, heard a voice flatly — bar the shiver — giving facts, quiet and without feeling, the way Meilyr talks on a good day.

We came over a treed lip of land to a hollow. That smell again. It must have been a lift in the breeze that had brought it to me the first time. We stopped talking. A little away, two of our soldiers were squatting on their haunches, hanging on to spears, the two who'd been with Iorwerth and Toothless once when they found me and Cristin in the woodland. They didn't talk. They were so still, draped by their cloaks, that a thrush with a ravelled spray of dead grass in her beak passed quite close to them. I watched her run and she led my eye to the corpses. There were half a dozen of them, stripped, laid in a row. The bird foraged another blade from near one of the stiffened feet and flew to her building.

My shivering continued as we skirted the hollow. The sun, huge and pale red, was tangled in the trees, and I remembered another time a palm came on my head and there was pale low light in the woodland but there'd been no cage of sound then because it was winter and thawed ice moved in the streams and I'd run towards the horses and the people.

I turned my face to watch the dead as we passed them at a distance. Without looking to them, Toothless crossed himself mechanically and murmured a scrap of prayer. There were four of the best men of the teulu — Ynyr and his brother Dyfrig, Athrwys and Abram. And among them, stiffarmed and unremarkable, Morgan and Gwrgant.

My master in poetry's elbows were bent, his hands above his chest, close to his face. His fingers were doubled and the wrists bent back. Like this, not in fists. As if he'd been holding something delicate in both hands. His eyes were half closed and his mouth was hanging open, the jaw dropped. Morgan's mouth had been tied shut with a length of bowstring and his eyes were closed. The whiteness of their bodies was spoilt by mud and the hackmarks. Gwrgant had a blackened vertical wound in his belly. Morgan's moustache was crusted with blood from his nose.

Perhaps we can see something of what Meilyr sees. Dead, people are so shrunk — I'm sure your spirit literally enlarges you. Singing, Gwrgant stretched out to fill a hall, held darkness outside. The corpses were like bits of driftwood dragged up on a riverbank.

I'm not sure what happened then. If I'd known rightly who and where I was I might have thought of something clever, expected a sign, like a shooting star or an owl hoot away in the trees, but I didn't. There was some absurd conversation I think, silent tears in Owain ab Iorwerth's eyes. Morgan had fostered him of course. And some sudden movement, an embrace or a restraining, I don't know, somebody holding me up or back.

And then things stilled and we were standing by the bodies, or I was. I waited, shivering, for something. For a Rhunlike movement at the corners of his mouth.

It was coming dusk. Shadows in the hollow were turning opaque blue. The waxy paleness of his skin began to glow, the way certain flowers do when the light is going.

Looking at them all stripped, I remembered the crammed sack, the beltful of knives. As they'd put the bag back on my head — something different. His cloak. Dafi wore a cloak of one of our teulu. He carried their clothes in the sack.

I stood and waited as more shadow solidified and the glow faded. For something. For some sign. Fragments hung on smoking dark. Fingers tightening on my shoulder. I don't turn or run. For a palm on my head and the question. Icethaw and branchtangle. Ask now.

### 34

The fever lasted a fortnight and more. I remember, vaguely, being tended by Non and Lleucu and mostly Cristin, her moonface. Waking and seeing her dimly by the low fire, the same look on her face as when she'd backed away in the woodland. Iorwerth's face swimming up and Owain and Hywel his sons, keeneye and blankeye. Iorwerth facing me and then his eyes sliding away when he sees me surfacing.

I missed the funerals and the intensest excitement of those days and when I began to walk out of the house and look at the byre and the apple trees in blossom and the meadow and the May woodland I saw them all with the same strangeness that had covered Toothless and Owain ab Iorwerth at my rescue. It was something like floating, being unconnected. The blaze of things and the tumult inside were uncoupled.

Still life was good. I avoided looking into the furnace of sunsets at first, but liked to be out and working with Lleucu's husband on the days when clouds soothed the air. For a long time I was racked by uncontrollable imaginings of Ifor Fychan. I saw myself killing him — or no, never actually killing him but up to the moment of doing it — by every method thinkable. These pictures never went beyond that point. There. This is a kind of confession. I was crazed so that I had no notion of consequences, either for the world or my soul.

After I was over the fever, Cristin said that Iorwerth wanted to see me in Caerllion.

She'd neglected her duties with Angharad for days at a time and had slept with me and Non. I'd told her all I could remember of what had happened after I was taken, and that was a sorting out, an organizing, part of my cure. We were careful, though, only to talk of these things when Non was out of earshot. This was out of respect for my master's wife's feelings, though I must say she lived through her grief with a huge dignity which I, then anyway, had no touch of. Each time the wave broke on me I was destroyed. At night when they all slept there was the bare table, and the leaning harps wrapped in a cloth.

When Non was away, too, Cristin and I returned to our devotions. Our arrival together at the shrine of the true church was the most emphatic evidence of my recovery, or of my need for solace. There was a great luxury in stretching out, extending arms and laying hold on the air between spread fingers, letting your feet burrow mud like roots.

As we travelled to Caerllion, Cristin explained to me how things were. Iorwerth had taken his family there and Toothless was made castellan of the penteulu's old court.

'Shouldn't Iorwerth and most of the teulu stay on the border?' I said.

She was quiet, then said, 'He thinks there won't be a war. Angharad says we can avoid it.'

'Avoid?'

How can I explain to you? I can hear the word now. It echoed as hollow as an empty hall.

She said, 'She says he thinks we should. Thinks we should avoid it.'

'What?'

'Wait. You'll see' she said. 'He'll explain it.'

I'd been imagining the teulu and all the men of the country rushing from the trees, across the heather, heard lines in my head. Skull of air cleft. Three hundred horses. Spearclash.

I went before Iorwerth in the room off the hall in Caerllion where a long time before I'd lain with Cristin and we'd seen the two Owains at mock swordplay. Seisyll ap Dyfnwal was there, visiting his son Morgan, I assumed. Just weeks before I'd sung for Seisyll and he'd given me the cloak and there was an owl hoot — and confusion. He had with him a couple of his best men and there were the remaining teulu, apart from Toothless. As I went in there was a cheer and Meilyr was smiling crookedly. Iorwerth raised his arms and said god's welcome and embraced me. A corridor of smiles and raised arms.

Iorwerth sat on a chair at the base of the post on which a French shield was hung. He was wearing the iron torc. I looked around the room uncertainly and there was a strained pause. Cristin had come in with me and was standing behind me, to one side. I was too numbed with selfconsciousness to be surprised to see Angharad at the council too, standing near her husband's chair.

The thinfaced lawyer stepped forward and spoke. A lumbering lawyer's speech welcoming me, talking about Dark Days, something about Coming Through It. And though there was no fire I felt smokesting and Morgan's ghost spoke to me as clearly as if he'd been there in the flesh. 'I don't know why we have to go through all this rigmarole.'

I must have looked round startled then. I remember the lawyer's face reacting. He glanced round too and said that he was sure I'd excuse the absence of Owain Pencarn. A messenger had been sent to him and his mother at Pencarn but they hadn't arrived. Understandably, they were still distressed.

The lawyer looked to Iorwerth, who spoke warmly, invited me to tell everything that had happened.

Most of the people sat on the ground to listen. Seeing Seisyll there, on a stool near Iorwerth, I thought of my singing at his hall. With a movement of the eyes I could look from the French shield to my new prince, his head sunk forward in listening, hiding the rim of torc at his neck, to his two sons, each of whom had lost a foster father, sitting at his feet.

I stuttered. Cristin helped me sometimes. Her being there helped me to tell the truth. A man's likely to soften his humiliations when he speaks them, but I'd already talked to her and it would have been a double humiliation to know that she heard me lie.

When I'd finished I looked at Iorwerth. I could see him and others making their own messages of what I'd said, sorting and shaping. No doubt I'd said a deal that was irrelevant or incoherent.

'The best time for striking back' I said — I added it quickly before their thoughts could settle — 'the best time for striking back's already gone, when they were complacent with celebrating. But, Iorwerth, I'll lead the teulu to the fort if you'll equip us for it.'

A couple of men murmured approval, but there was no more than that, and then a silence. Iorwerth glanced at Seisyll and then looked at me.

'Griffri' he said, 'you must sing marwnadau to us for my brother and your master and, and those others. Seisyll's man sang at the funerals but you were ill then. You sing your own poems for them at the three feasts.'

He looked down. We all waited. It was difficult for him. It's not easy to learn performing, to become someone else when you're so old. Even then he must have been getting on for forty. The lawyer was about to speak when the new prince looked up.

'But understand this' he said. 'When the French fight one another we attack and gain ground. Twenty-two years ago I killed with my own hand Ricert ap Gilbert. A few of you are old enough to remember the time and some of you were with me and my brother at Coed Grwyne. I wasn't long come to manhood, younger than you are now, Griffri. I know what it is to kill a great lord and see the fire that follows it. All the Welsh rose and we started to regain our country. Dyfnwal, Seisyll's father was with us. You've sung us songs about it, Griffri. It was near the time when the king, Henri ap Gwilym Bastart died and Estefyn the new king was weak because his own people attacked him.

That made our circumstance.

'The king now is old Henri's grandson. You know he humiliated Rhys, Seisyll's father in law. He only gives land to the French. Only god saved Prince Owain in the north.

'Now if we make war in Senghenydd, we'll make the circumstance for them. You stand at the heart of things but you don't see the boundaries. In wars people go hungry. People round the edges, the ones with relatives held hostage, the ones with an English parent, the monks with French abbots, the ones who're starving, they falter. People must ache to fight in their bones before we can move. If we make war on Ifor Fychan we'll suck Iarll Caerloyw into these mountains as a long cloak sucks up the damp.'

That last part stayed in my mind. I thought of Ifor, sneezing, with his huge cloak wrapped round his legs, the wet gleam of his eyes in the dark.

Unusually, Iorwerth looked straight at me when he'd finished speaking. There was no sign of it in his face, but I think he was pleased with his speech. A few men called out approval of his words but many said nothing.

There was the boiling of feelings in me that had nowhere to go. My mouth was too narrow a place to issue them and I was choked quiet for moments, then said something disjointed, something about the families of the dead. I'm ashamed of how I behaved now, with hindsight. There were a few people there willing to side with me but the prince was calm and kept his hold on things.

'We're all in those families' he said.

More murmurring, more general murmurring, and I knew that whatever I was, I was thwarted.

I turned and saw Meilyr.

'Meilyr' I said. 'Athrwys. Your uncle. Did you see him? I saw his cloak on another man's back. All their knives in Dafi's belt.'

There was a touch of poetic licence about this. I couldn't know that it was Athrwys's cloak, but I think as I spoke I believed it was.

I remember the moment as grotesquely comic. Meilyr skewed and slantheaded, I holding my own head stiffly to one side because of the scar on my neck. He leant towards me, touched my cheek.

'I killed them all' he said. 'When Ifor's messenger called the meeting to bargain for you, the slippery demon called Cala Dewi Heliwr came and told me all things would be good in Gwynllwg because of it and I told Morgan this and he believed it as I did.'

His eyes dropped and for a moment I wondered if this was a performance, if the lawyer had told him to say this to me.

But he looked back and said, 'A crushed man won't notice new weight. Give me some of it.'

'What?'

'Your guilt.'

I had no words to answer this.

Seisyll said, 'These two men, Dafi and the other one. Who is there to swear Ifor knew all they did?'

Iorwerth spoke across him, 'Meilyr was tricked by the devil. How can we trust you, Meilyr, when your advisers lie about the future?'

Meilyr smiled. 'Oh I don't think he lied. We have a great prince now. In that much it's been good for Gwynllwg. Nobody can lie about what hasn't happened. And looking forward and getting it wrong sometimes isn't mad or dishonest. When you're untrue to what's happening now or what happened then, there's the sin, when you know what was and won't own to it.'

Iorwerth opened his mouth to speak but the lawyer raised his hand.

Meilyr looked back to me and leant closer, whispered. 'There was a red sun wasn't there? And you were shivering and wet. Did the sun make his hair redder?'

And the lawyer was speaking loud across the whispering. 'I think we can — Meilyr. Thank you. I think we all know the keenness of this loss and share this young man's sense of hurt. I know many of you will feel the need of redress as strongly as if it were for insult to your own persons' — you know the way they go on — 'Blah blah. Even Lord Seisyll here must feel torn and know the need to act —'

Seisyll nodded and broke in. 'Yes. But in Gwent Uwchcoed the people are on their knees. Griffri knows this. I'm kinned with Rhys and through him with Ifor. The foreigners live in their towns, under endless half siege and we live half the time like hunted things. If we could be one all that could finish. Understand that.'

He looked at me and I had to look down. Iorwerth and the lawyer were talking quietly. Angharad leant towards them. I saw her straighten, place a hand on her husband's shoulder and look at me.

'Are we just to forget what happened?' I said.

Keeper of memory. Lister of the dead.

'No' Iorwerth said. 'You sing it. In twenty generations it will still be sung. If we withstand the French.'

'Yes' the lawyer said. 'Look, we all of us feel for you, for the insult you've had.'

'*My* insult?' I said.

'Ah.' Meilyr again. He was still close to me, whispering, a hand twirling at his head. 'I've seen them dancing on some tongues today. Is it because his master died? Or is it because he's hurt his pride?'

The lawyer's face dropped in exasperation at Meilyr's obstructing him, but the words buried themselves into me.

The lawyer said, 'We all feel it. Iorwerth himself, many times over the years, warned Morgan about Ifor, urged him to act, but we're not free to make a real choice at the moment, for all sorts of reasons. I'm sure that everyone here has seen the rightness of Iorwerth's intentions, as he's suggested them today, of peace and consolidation. After all, there is no threat to our land from that quarter.'

He paused. There were calls of assent.

'There. And let me add we do not intend to let this matter drop.' He glanced to the prince and smiled. 'I think we can promise all parties that there will be payment for these deaths. I think you'll find that matters will work out in a more satisfactory fashion if you leave this one with us.'

Iorwerth pointedly did not smile. Without turning his face from the lawyer, he looked to me and said, 'I promise you, Griffri, and all of you here who have felt this grievance, that payment will be made for every death and every hurt.'

This better measured making of the lawyer's words was enough to draw shouting of approval. Seisyll said nothing. He made an involuntary movement of his face which could have been a wince or a smile.

## 35

It's hard to imagine myself speaking to the prince as I did. It was a measure of my indignation that I did, and of how deeply I trust him.

After that, many words were wasted on the affair among the teulu and everyone else for days. Iorwerth's strength and the presence of Seisyll were persuasive among us all and messengers told us about Ifor's troubles to his south. We knew he was preoccupied but it would be dangerous to be drawn into an alliance, or look as if we were being drawn into an alliance, with Iarll Caerloyw while Rhys and all the Welsh in the south were looking for ways to gather strength.

This was a dozen years ago, and a few months before the action that made Ifor famous. After he snatched the Iarll and his wife from Caerdyf and held them till all his lands and borders were restored we all had to see him in a different light, and my times at the court were touched with an unclear sense of shame, as it is when you've been drunk and can't remember the next day exactly what you said or did. Can you imagine that Rhys Ddu came to Caerllion in the autumn and I had to sit and listen to him sing a poem about it? A bad one too — Rhys was never much good with verse, though I don't mean to speak ill of the dead, not even him.

Before that, in the summer, Iorwerth gave me all of Gwrgant's wealth, an arrangement which Non agreed to though she had plenty of cause for a lawsuit over it if she'd wanted to get her inheritance. There was some hunger among the poor that year as many cattle had been taken for some tribute or other during my illness, but my marriage to Cristin in the calends of August, and our entry into my inheritance, with Non installed as honoured matriarch, is as close to a happy ending as I'm able to give you.

A bell did you say?

I sang a dadolwch to Iorwerth and another to Seisyll — not that the situation really demanded them — and with those songs I grew up.

I did sing a marwnad for Morgan — I adapted Gwrgant's to Eneas which he'd adapted from one to an old uchelwr in Erging, but nobody noticed the borrowing.

And I've sung to the teulu drawn in battle order, fought in a dozen small wars. I've been Iorwerth's messenger to your Arglwydd Rhys and that's how I first came to this house, with Owain Pencarn, how I came to see the sea close to for the first time, in Penfro. Meilyr's shields sliding and the illumination of the undersides of things. I sat in a high place too and watched the water boiling like treetops in a storm. That Owain, Pencarn, who'd lost his father, lived out his grief apart from us and I don't think he's ever heard my marwnad. After a long time suffering what you people call a conceived affliction, he bent the knee to Iorwerth and — well, you know him — he's one of our best men. It doesn't pay to be in the teulu of a prince who loses.

I never did sing a marwnad for Gwrgant, or not directly, anyway. That time Rhys Ddu came and sang his piece of mediocrity he brought with him Dafi and Selyf in chains and Iorwerth hanged them in the beili for killing his brother. Ifor was in a generous mood, I think, after his successes against the French. The lawyer said that all payment had been, as promised, made, all galanas blah et cetera and no one should henceforth and some such legalese. I felt nothing.

Meilyr said a curious thing to me that day. He looked at me and said, 'Well, poet. Wifed and landed. No coincidence wars come thickest in spring and summer. Scratch the itch in the bag, empty the cauldron the right way, and making amends turns meaningless.'

So I never sang. Non, my mother and my children's nurse, asked me about it once. Made no demands though. She was just curious I think. Wanted to know how much I was like him. There was another little song. I made it pretty much exactly a year after the deaths. I sang it here once and one of your colleagues insisted on writing it down, though he spoilt it by adding some lines of his own. It's strange how many people who've never carved a poem think they can improve the work of those who have. He ruined it. The original was like this

> Intricate May the loveliest month.
>   Birds' clangour. Branches writhe and wind.
> Ox in yoke. Ploughs rutting earth.
>   Green ocean and the mottled land.
>
> When cuckoos call on greening trees
>   Grief hurts the worst.
> Smoke in the eye, long sleeplessness
>   For kin I've lost.

152

It was all there was. Perhaps a little oversweet. Your colleague thought it was too pessimistic. He didn't see that words that tell a grief can do more than tell.

Talking of telling, I've told too much. Almost talked myself sober. No penance for this confession, please. I've told you how to grow, I had to be cut down, and to become myself I had to see the death of one mother and at least two fathers.

Yes, the bell. I know.

Go to your Office, then. Pray for me, Idnerth. I'll sleep.

# The Second Hearth

# 1

No need to offer me more drink. I've had enough. Old men look even uglier drunk.

Don't worry, though. I'll tell you about it anyway.

See, I've acquired some of poor old Meilyr's prescience. I've prayed that god has eased his torments, but I wouldn't bank on it. His demons didn't warn him about his own death. I suppose you might construe that as a sort of kindness.

I knew you wanted to ask about it as soon as I saw you tonight. You've gone very respectable in your magpie outfit now that you've got the mud face like a dry river bed and your natural baldness has overtaken your tonsure. But I could see the fire in your eyes. Like I saw it in Owain Pencarn's eye once, in Rhun's forge. Did I tell you about that all those years ago in Hendy Gwyn? I rambled all night, I seem to remember, but you stayed the course very well. It was a kind of lust. The light, I mean. Or an energy. A desire to consume, to use the world up. Sorry, no. In your case to consume words. A juicy story.

I'll tell it. But don't let me ramble this time. I'll try not to keep you up quite so late. Besides, I'll have to take more care to get it right. Now that you live here in my country you'll have the chance to check a thing or two. How do like it here, by the way? Is it three years now, four, since Prince — sorry — Lord Hywel endowed it to you lot as a daughter house? It caused some trouble, I can tell you. A lot of people had to move because of your bloody sheep. But there. It was the best way of keeping the land out of French hands.

Please don't pretend shock. He's Frenchified to the extent that he can combine a good territorial move with a bargain for his soul.

I'll tell it. It might be a kind of sorting out. Another bargain for another man's soul.

It's the best part of a year since I stuck a knife into the head of Siryf Henffordd, which is the nearest I'm going to come to clearing the whole matter up. A lot of the others we wanted to get have died too —

some of them by the hand of god alone, which makes me wonder whether I need have bothered. Except that I needed to prove —. Well. We'll come to that.

I did it without any compunction. Without any feeling, actually. Killing the Siryf. He might even have been already dead. He'd certainly taken some knocks by the time I got to him. You may have heard something about his calling for a priest and getting his rites before he died. All shit. That's the sort of story that goes down well in their castles. He died like a pig in a ditch. Come to that, he was in a ditch. We embroider important deaths that way to make them bearable. A bit, I suppose, as a poet affirms who we are, or who we think we are, as if that might hold everything in place, or shift it to a better place. I think I used to believe that.

Not that he was the main culprit. Word is even the king may have had a hand in it. Well, he turned out to be a bigger bastard than any of us ever expected. Had he already murdered his archbishop by that time I talked all night? I think he did that a bit later. At least, barring tantrums, he's a clever enough bastard to be able to make the sort of compromises that have given us a little — a very little — space.

Us. That was force of habit. I'm not sure if I'm *us* any more.

You see. I'm ill. Feeling unconnected in this way makes singing hard. It takes an energy to sing, an appetite. Teeth. A point of firelight in the pupil. I've been in places so stony that every fibre is abraded, everything is unwoven. It's hard to fulfil commissions when the earth is slipping away under your feet. Hard even to talk. But it's a story I've rehearsed, or parts of it. There are parts I've never. Parts rehearsed uncontrollably in the memory. You see, I'm reduced from song to a sort of storytelling. It starts with the loss of a patrimony and ends with a meeting between ghosts.

Listen.


## 2

When the king took Caerllion from us, a dozen years and more ago now, Iorwerth was already an old man. Us. There I go again. The one side of his face had already started to droop. The outer corner of the left eye hanging down on the cheek and that cheek a little hollower than the other, that corner of the mouth pulled down.

When you live among the same people a long time, you stop seeing them as they are now. As they change you see them through a fog of what they were. But I was away often enough and long enough — at song in other courts or at campaigns fighting with Pencarn for Rhys sometimes — for the strangeness of familiar things to be restored to me. So I could see the unmatched halves of his face, the hair grizzled and gone crinkled as strands of vetch.

By that time we had no illusions about the king. It was after the time he'd taken Rhys away in chains and blinded some of his sons and all that. After the wars I think he thought he couldn't risk that sort of thing again. The siege at Rhuddlan showed what we could do. He needed us to prevent his own countrymen who stole our land from getting too strong.

Us.

Still, we knew what sort of man he was. Is. Everybody said the king was running away in going to Ireland, the edge of the earth, as far as possible from Rome after killing his own archbishop. Besides, some of the French from hereabouts had gone to Ireland hoping for rich pickings there. With that on his mind and the fact that Rhys had gone to meet him in Llwyn Danet and promised him all sorts of tribute and any number of hostages to buy his friendship, we thought we were safe. Rhys had started to rebuild his power by then and I remember Seisyll telling me that his great brotherinlaw was planning to build his own stone castle in the west.

And when he came — the king, I mean — I've never seen so much shiny metal or so many pairs of shoes. They were all got up brighter than bishops. Or so much mail, and those lumbering, useless horses they seem to like.

Morgan, Seisyll's son, who stayed with us — us — at Iorwerth's court after coming of age, was amazed and terrified at the show. Iorwerth, wisely I think, had instructed some of us to leave our weapons in the forge, where a few of his men guarded them.

I saw all kinds of irony. A priestkiller with a retinue got up like a holiday procession. Books in every other hand. A fat, bearded murderer waving a mockery of benediction from his horse. What must it cost to the spirits of our chief men to bend the knee to these people? What god lives in the churches they build? And all the priests with

*159*

him. Throats and eyeballs seem to outweigh souls in these matters.

There was one particular French priest, a tall young man with a snooty expression, who got friendly with the thinfaced lawyer and they jabbered away, mainly in Latin and occasionally French. It was a case of like attracting like. The lawyer introduced him to Meilyr, who was forced to perform a few of his tricks. The Frenchman tried the few mangled words of Welsh that he'd learnt from the slaves at the castle where he was born in the west. The lawyer told me this man was known among the French as 'the Welshman' and treated as a great authority on all matters concerning us. They say he's a cousin to Rhys. You've probably met him. He talks loudly over the music at meals and has a reputation for blundering nosiness. You'd think he was a divine idiot, though they say he's a ruthless bastard when it comes to tithes, and it's generally reckoned that he sold his soul for an uncomfortable cartride with a king's son and the gleam of a bishopric. It's comforting to think that the king's intelligence about us is likely to be so defective, though I've heard Rhys himself say that this strange man may be useful and must be kept sweet.

I saw the lawyer hovering as near as a Welshman dared to the priest while he — the French Welshman — showed the king the ruins from the age of giants and spoke at length in French. The king paced around like a dog anxious to get outside and a shoal of bright acolytes darted back and fore in unison with him. They switched direction quick and glittering as minnows. It was as if the moon had uprooted herself from her right way and was dragging the sea about arbitrarily.

The king looked up and north westward, towards where we are now, to the trees. He half listened to Snooty and murmured something. I thought — but I was a long way off — that I heard the word 'forest'.

Then he did a curious thing. Suddenly he started running on the spot. I expected the minnows to join in immediately, but they merely stood respectfully silent. A nervous laugh passed among the Welsh. Then the king started bowing to the priest, violently and repeatedly, stretching his fingers to touch the earth by his toes. He stood straight again and milled his elbows, flexing his shoulders. Some of the smaller children started to copy this and were cuffed by their mothers. I was glad my children were at home with Cristin.

The freckles on the king's face made a livid marbling as he purpled with his efforts. Suddenly he stopped and his articulated barking was

*160*

sharp. Some minnows broke from the shoal and glittered off severally.

God allows us so little freedom. Perhaps that would be the damned priest's excuse. For me a dozen years of abrading, of unconnecting, of unweaving, were ravelled on the whim that ran in the king's head at that moment.

## 3

The mechanics of it are boring as well as humiliating.

The king left. A few hours later a large number of French soldiers arrived, walked and rode in through the open gate. And threw us out. The weapons in the forge were seized. A few swords were held at important throats. Some young men were beaten up and one — well I won't go into detail. Except that I saw one young soldier take down Rhun's — Rhun was still alive then — take down Rhun's neglected leather cap from its peg, drape it over his helmet, and execute a grotesque, hipwiggling dance for the amusement of his colleagues.

The people most likely to struggle — Iorwerth's sons Owain and Hywel, Owain Pencarn and Morgan ap Seisyll, had all laid down their arms in the forge on the prince's orders, which was probably just as well. Pencarn, anyway, hadn't brought his sword, but had come to the court armed only with a bow.

A roll of parchment with a seal on it, for what that was worth, was read out in the yard. I stood with Pencarn and Morgan ap Seisyll as this was done. The barking. Tense limbs.

This time, when the translation was finished, Iorwerth nodded, could find no words. His two sons and Angharad approached him. He and his wife and the lawyer talked quietly and then the prince spoke.

'The only wisdom today' he said, 'is to leave. The teulu will meet me again at the old court.'

The lawyer spoke. 'Lord Iorwerth' — it was the first time I'd heard him called lord instead of prince — 'Lord Iorwerth will leave last to see us all safe.'

There was little talking. Nothing like panic. A hurried attempt to gather possessions. A soldier barred my way into the hall where I'd left a harp. I didn't argue.

There was a strange quiet over the town. People moving away seemed merely businesslike, as if this was something they'd always expected. Nor was there great jubilation among the enemy soldiers. I don't think they knew what the hell they were doing either.

You could see it as more than a whim. The storytellers in Erging as well as Rhys Ddu and old Bledri had made Caerllion Arthur's main court for years by then, which is plausible enough, if wrong. I felt I could read the king's mind when he looked up. A man afraid of his own gut seeing himself as the great king, the mechteyrn, and seeing a pleasant reserve for the hunt, if only the inconvenience of the people could be shifted. Snatching at a scrap of destiny and a little sport at the same time.

## 4

He didn't stay to enjoy any of that. He went on westward and in the part of Penfro where the foreigners live he waited for good weather for his aimless voyage.

But all this idiocy is prologue.

I was with the two Owains — Pencarn and ab Iorwerth — when Iorwerth moved an army against Caerllion a little later that year. See what I'm doing. Trawling a threshing confusion from the dark. Better a few songs than all that stuff coiling in the bag. Some old veterans who did the most appalling things find tears easily, just as some people who go silly over a big hunting dog have no trouble in beating their children.

We destroyed everybody and everything that could help the French, to the wall of the fortress. Hywel ab Iorwerth distinguished himself in this work particularly.

Iorwerth called Meilyr and Meilyr consulted his advisers one night. The following day he told Iorwerth that the fortress would be rewon, but not yet. I remember the old prince's face, half dropped,

162

intent on Meilyr that early evening in the old hall, and Toothless there and the two sons, and Morgan ap Seisyll and Pencarn. I'd always thought that Iorwerth distrusted Meilyr's advice, but he paid attention to this and laid no siege that summer. We were short of arms and horses anyway, so much having been left. Hywel held Bryn Buga to the north and the land round about was empty of food. Most people with any sense moved away to safer territory north and west. Meilyr told Owain ab Iorwerth that there was danger for him in going to the castles, at which Owain and the rest of us laughed. It was a warning of stupefying banality.

Things settled into the routine of attrition, the French installed in the fortress having no people around them to rule over and no supplies except what they could sneak up the river from Casnewydd, ourselves not ready to attack.

Old soldiers are apt to get technical at a point like this. I'll spare you that.

Instead, let me snatch a memory, a whim.

That autumn I sang at Owain Pencarn's hall and many of the people, three or four families, gathered in the area, so there was plenty of work for poets and storytellers. People who're not quite starving can be good listeners.

Late one afternoon he and I hunted together on foot with nothing but bows and arrows to remember our boyhood. We shot some hares on the hill and when we stopped to rest on our way home, we talked.

'Griffri' he said, 'I think I need to marry.'

I believe he'd littered several bastards among the slaves and taeogion. Crises tend to force thoughts of marriage on young people. Youngish. He was in his late twenties then, I thirty odd.

'Anybody in particular?' I said.

'That's what I wanted to talk to you about. Iorwerth will never make a match for me. Any tips about somebody appropriate? You travel enough to see what's available. I'd want to make the right move.'

That's the way of an uchelwr. I've never really got used to it. I'd been incapable of such calculation — but then, he was that much older than I'd been when I married.

'Iorwerth's suffered a terrible insult' I said. 'You'll have to wait I think.'

He looked down.

163

He was already balding even then and the weakish late sunlight shone on the place where his forelock had been.

'To lose a patrimony is hard' he said.

It was my turn to look down. There was a silence.

He went on, struggling for words. 'And to —'

'Yes?'

'Never mind.' He paused again. 'Iorwerth is my father now.' He gave a sort of smile and looked up. 'All the years of fosterage should have been a good training.'

'They were very alike' I said.

'That doesn't make it easier.' The struggle again. 'When one man stands in another's place there are all kinds of — complications.'

The clumsiness of the words somehow made them stronger.

I looked at the glazed eyes of the dead hares at my belt, remembered Cristin in her girlhood, the pelts in her hand, her eyes widening. Blood on the chin. Stolen bread. A man smiling, stretching his arms like a tree and another openmouthed, his hands crabbed stiff on the air before his face.

Pencarn was looking at me for advice.

'You'd be as well asking Meilyr' I said. 'What do I know?'

He looked away.

'Hywel and his brother will find wives soon' he said. 'Has the prince asked you to help with that?'

'Not yet.'

'What do you mean "Not yet"?'

'I mean he hasn't.'

'I wonder. I wonder what division will be made.'

It was an inept attempt to disguise his question as thinking out loud.

'I don't know' I said.

'The French order these things better. Just one to inherit.'

'You admire that?'

'It's clear cut.'

'And look where it leads. Their sons looking outward. Wars and fortresses erupt across the world.'

'You prefer to keep murder cosy and in the family.'

'Their king godforsaken, scurrying to the earth's rim after wayward cousins.'

'We've spent this summer destroying our own country, killing collaborators, for the sake of a few dozen of them in a paling.'

'There was no other choice.'

'Exactly. They risk nothing. It's a venture for a bit of land. For us it's everything.'

'We'd better win then' I said. 'Or there'll be no patrimony to talk about.'

'Yes.' He paused. 'I've been loyal in the teulu a dozen years.'

I don't know why he said that.

There was an obscure sense of contention between us, though we disagreed about nothing important. There's something in the nature of conversation that draws up submerged resentments.

I said, 'You'd do well to marry after all this. When I was your age I already had plenty of children.'

'I've got *them*.'

'I mean ones I could own to. If god spares us I'll make enquiries for you the next time I sing abroad. Rhys might have some cousin or other he hasn't managed to marry off yet.'

'Would he bother? There isn't enough advantage in an alliance with me.'

'Unless we win.'

'Even then.'

'The prince is generous to you. You've done him good service, gone when he's sent you to serve others.'

'Do you think he ever wanted me to come back?'

'Yes' I said, too quickly.

Pencarn was looking down, his fingertips kneading at the hard hilt of his knife.

I went on, more slowly. 'He sent me with you sometimes. Told me to keep an eye on you.'

I thought I saw the corners of his mouth twitch, but his eyes didn't smile. He looked down for a long time and I didn't know what to say.

'Remember Meilyr's story' he said at last. 'That day on the river-bank. I've known those places. Been pushed into places where there's no pretence.'

That was all. He looked at me, his eyes moving slightly as he looked from my one eye to the other, trying to judge, I suppose, how far I understood. Which wasn't very far. Autumn, I thought. The itch in the bag.

'Find a girl tonight' I said. 'Save the rest of your energy for the

French. There'll be a war come spring.'

'Yes, yes' he said. 'Stuff it up them. I know. Do you think only kings can be godforsaken?'

And the gleam of his eyes and his balding crown seemed written on the air of the space he'd left. I remained, stupidly watching his impatient walk away.

The true church.

Remember that? Lovers among trees and the roots plaited like the old carvings.

I'd forgotten. I owe Pencarn a great debt for reminding me like that. Yet I was angry, followed, feeling myself to have been caught out, tested and found shallow.

'What is it you want?' I said.

He looked at me and then forward — we were walking quickly, the ground was uneven. He shook his head.


## 5

I spent much of that winter at home. Lleucu, who was still alive then, and her husband had got used to Cristin's commanding them after Non died. Our children and the presence of some of the refugees from around Caerllion — some of them lived in the byre — made food a little scarce, but I believe we lived with little squabbling.

When spring came there was no assault. Iorwerth sent messengers to Rhys, whose tribute to the king had paid off. While Henri had deprived Iorwerth of his home, Rhys was building his new castle in Aberteifi, just as Seisyll had told me. So Iorwerth still hoped, I think, that Rhys might be able to intercede on our behalf and we held back and quietly gathered arms and men, and built many ladders.

Toothless, though he must have been forty or thereabouts, led skirmishing forays sometimes. It kept the young men happy to snatch some spoils occasionally. We went often into Gwent Iscoed where Iarll Ystrad Gul was less strong than before. His being out of favour with the king made winning the support of many men there even easier. The Welsh he'd pressed to his army had gone into Ireland with him and sometimes I went there expecting battle and ended up singing.

One time that spring I went with Owain ab Iorwerth and some others at night to wreck the boats the French used to bring supplies from the new castle at the mouth of the great river.

We went on a night when there was a slice of moon and slowmoving broken cloud, so that we could choose moments of darkness to move in. She — the moon — had sucked the sea, the river, whichever it was, off the fields of tidal mud.

Owain ab Iorwerth was a good leader. Apart from anything else, he was physically easy to distinguish because he was tall and strong and because of his curling redgold hair — though on this night that was silvered by the moon almost to the colour of the wet mud. With us were eight or ten young men with little experience of battle. Iorwerth, I think, wanted to prepare them for what was likely, though he still hoped to negotiate his way back. Owain was skilled at this kind of training.

We hid among trees within sight of the river and the clutter of buildings round the new castle, waiting for the right conditions, and Owain ab Iorwerth knew that keeping the men quiet and patient before the work would be hard. Doing the same after it would be even harder. So he told them, whispered to them — and can you believe I sat by? — of how old Ifor had gone into the great castle at Caerdyf and taken Iarll Caerloyw and his wife, and how that had been no matter of casual cheek but the product of a sense of great wrong, a firm purpose, and exact skill in execution. I almost cheered. Then the head of curling silver turned to me.

'Isn't this so, Griffri?'

I was used to my senior position by those days — did I tell you I was officially pencerdd by that time as well as bardd teulu? Only rich courts can divide these labours.

'Yes' I said. 'Even the king had to wait for the right wind to take him to Ireland. Owain's great grandfather was a king. God's given us this night for our work.' I nodded towards the moon. 'All we've got to do is to wait for the rhythm in things to allow us space for it. And what firmer purpose can we have than the freeing of a people? Or the restoring of a patrimony?'

These are the sortings out I presented them with, the kind of sieving that has to be done, the words that have to be said to make action

167

possible.

Owain handed round the skin of mead, warning them to take no more than two mouthfuls each. As they sucked on the neck I thought, in the dark, that he looked at me uncomfortably long.

The kind of sieving off of what's not needed so that they don't see the moon except as a lamp, they don't see people but the enemy.

The work itself couldn't have passed off smoother. The men stayed quiet, and even some slithering round in the mud induced no panic or false hilarity. We prised the planking away and smashed it, floated the pieces off on the water for the moon to scatter. Burning would have been more dramatic but we wanted to raise no alarms and get away without hurt.

Which we did. I imagined every cracking plank waking the king in Ireland and his thugs despatched as he'd sent them from France to Caergaint. But no one woke and no one came. A great cloud lay like a lover across the moon and we ran with short steps, each an arm's length from the man in front, Owain ab Iorwerth leading and myself at the rear. Once we were some distance from the scene of our heroism one of the men in the file squawked a very creditable imitation of a duck which, given our disposition, was appropriate and provoked, from some of us, laughter. I didn't laugh myself, not out of restraint but from lack of breath.

We got to the old court after dawn and some men went straight to work, but others had excitedly to tell their story, complete with actions, to anybody who'd listen. One young man, the squawker himself, discoursed feverishly to an old woman who was carting dung, for no particular reason that I could see, from one heap to another. She didn't listen. When she left the yard altogether the squawker, not breaking his sentence, went on talking to a solitary hen who listened politely except when she occasionally turned aside to pick a piece of nothing up from the yard.

The rest of us threw ourselves down in the hall and slept until the middle of the day.

This could be invention. I could be making this up for the sake of a pleasing irony. Still, when I woke, my mouth feeling sticky and my limbs stiff and aching, I saw Owain ab Iorwerth stirring in his sleep. A bar of sharp spring sunlight fell on him through the unshuttered window, metalled the redgold coiling of his hair. Though he lay on his side, a crooked arm under his head, his features were balanced, neither of the lightly closed eyes slipped, neither cheek hollower than the other. When his time came I would call him the expected names. Hawk. Dragon. Wolf. Oak door of Gwynllwg.

No other part of his face moved, there was no movement of his moustache, as his eyes opened, stared at me as if the pupils had been in place waiting for the covers to slide back.

The bar of light — which I suppose had woken him — began to fade as slow cloud dragged itself across the face of the sun and the redgold metal dulled like an ember.

I tried, a little slowly, to look away, as people do when they've been caught staring.

'A good night's work' I said, to shut the silence out.

He murmured something, stirred again. I think he was still asleep, blind, as some people are when they're near death.

'Griff' he said, sitting up and seeing at last. 'Yes. Work. You think so?'

I shrugged. 'It might slow them down a bit.'

He looked round the little hall and nodded to two of the men who still slept, their heads close together and their bodies diverging, their chins up, giving an inelegant display of mouth and nostril.

'It's for the sake of the children really' he said. 'Look at them.'

There was the unsynchronized drag and blow of the two sleepers' breathing.

'Every one a Culhwch. They'll be full of strength next time. Ready to cut throats.'

I thought of a man sitting down in a meadow, my bowhand rattling against a tree, Toothless peeling fingers from the blade.

Owain looked at me. 'And how are the senior members of the expedition after the action?'

'Bloody stiff' I said, stretching my arms. 'All the senior members.' And as an afterthought, 'Except one.'

He laughed.

'Perhaps I'm getting too old for this.' I dropped my arms in exaggerated exhaustion.

'If *you're* too old, my —' He hesitated and I looked at him.

I could swear he was about to say the word 'father'.

I spoke to stop the darkness of his hesitation.

'Soon my sons can do all this' I said. 'And I can fart by the fire and talk about old tragedies.'

*169*

And, behold.

Owain, like a good chick prince, asked after my family, relieved, I think, to be helped from his stumbling, listened politely to anecdotes about my children.

'Yet' he said, 'you spent the winter with Pencarn.'

'No' I said. 'No.'

He\waited.

'I was with him in the autumn' I said. 'After all the. After being in the field I wanted to be with my family.'

This was half true. It was talking with Pencarn that time that had made me want to be with Cristin. How could I have explained that? The true church. She was near the end of her time for children then. To watch the lifting of a dug from her shift and the stoppering of an untoothed face. The rituals were a little different from our youth but the religion was the same. Think of all the stony jaws of churches crunching on the bones of saints compared to that, the milk communion.

'But not straight away' Owain said.

'What?'

'You didn't want to be with them, the family, straight away, if you were with Pencarn in the autumn.'

I didn't answer for a moment.

'People there needed song' I said at last. 'War always brings good business for poets.'

He laughed again.

'Pencarn's been loyal in the teulu a dozen years' I said.

Owain said, 'Hm' and paused. 'So. Just the autumn, then, you stayed there.'

'You'll need him if it comes to a siege.'

'You mean he's going somewhere?'

'No. No, I mean he'll be needed. He's useful.'

'Oh. Oh yes, he's that. He's made himself useful all right.' Owain sniffed as punctuation to this comment and rubbed a hand across his face. 'Yes. He is a useful man.'

'Made?' I said.

'Well, yes. It's his own efforts.'

'Your father's always liked him.'

'Yes.' Owain looked at me, but without seeming to see, as if his thoughts clouded my face. 'Yes' he said again, something like that, a

170

little more quietly.

Another sniff and again the salving palm across his face.

'I might be going away for a bit' he said. He glanced suddenly at the snorers and then back to me.

'Really?' I said.

'My father the prince wants me to go to see Rhys.'

'A match?' I said.

He shrugged. 'But now. With things as they are.'

'Things are always as they are' I said. 'He might be able to help us. Rhys. Now that he's so well in with our great king.'

I so overdid the irony that even in his disgruntlement Owain smiled.

'You might even meet the king' I said. 'If he's back. Will you go?'

The smile went and he looked down.

'It's so bloody galling' he said.

'Imagine what it's like for Rhys.'

'Caradog was a king. They don't even call my father a prince officially any more. You know what that lawyer told me. You know the Frenchman, the priest, the one the French and English say is Welsh. The one who showed the king around. He told the lawyer, he said it's only matter of their deciding. The king deciding he wanted it. A blockade, an army. Some more castles. Expendable men. They can use men up as we put logs on a fire. They buy them when they run out. It's just a matter of how much they want it. And we've got to smile and yes sir no sir and do business and retreat and retreat.'

I said nothing.

'Of course I'll go' he said.

I watched the sunlight come and fade, its bar through the window glowing and dulling on him.

'So you were just there in the autumn then' he said.

'For a while. Not long.'

He had the anger and sense of his parents. I think he might have made a good prince if he had lived.

## 6

A heavy dug lifted out. Think of that. A warm purse. Its roundness.
And the pull of the mouth and the small hand kneading. A little
pulse. Tonguing and half sleep. Take the nipple away and nothing
could be more awake. Then the eye shows itself, the perfect white,
and the cleanness of the inside of the mouth, a voice that enters living
bone. There's loss more real than any other. Grief is the only emo-
tion. We come awake, know ourselves best, when we lose what it is
that defines us. The rest depends on that.

I was with Angharad and Iorwerth when they brought the news of
Owain's murder.

Her legs buckled as suddenly as the legs of a cow under the axe at
slaughter. Iorwerth was standing with his weight on one foot. His
face tilted down a fraction and — perhaps this wasn't so — but I think
the eye in the dropped half of his face glazed. Otherwise he didn't
move for moments while I and the two men who'd brought the mess-
age watched him and others attended to Angharad.

At last he stirred and motioned to his wife. 'Take the lady to an-
other room' he said. 'And fetch her the priest.'

After that he sat for a long time and would respond to no ques-
tions.

'Lord' the taller of the messengers said, 'I'll tell you what we know
about the matter —'

But his companion touched his arm, indicated Iorwerth with his
eyes and made an all but invisible shake of the head.

They backed away and left the room in the foreign way.

He and I were alone. Suddenly I remembered him a youngish man
on horseback, his face wet with rain, his cloak wrapped on his head.
Gwrgant looking up at him, his hand resting on the quiver.

'He was a good man' I said. 'An intelligent soldier. I'll — I'll make
a poem for him.'

Iorwerth looked up at me without seeing, unreachable in his self-
knowing.

'Send for Hywel and Pencarn' he said.

Sorry, I'm not explaining this very well. I should have said that this was after the king had come out of Ireland. From the new castle at the mouth of the great river he'd sent Iorwerth one of those letters he's so fond of. You know the way they are. Henri King of the English and Duke of the Normans and of the Aquitainians and Count of the Angevins to Iorwerth of Gwynllwg, greeting. It ordered Iorwerth to come to the castle to parley, in the meantime promising a firm truce.

Owain was already on his way to Rhys's court at that time and Iorwerth sent men after him to call him back so that he could go with his father to the king. Did I tell you that Owain spoke a little French? I think I did.

He was killed, they say, by Iarll Bryste's men, to the north of Llandâf. We got his body back, and by god's grace and French negligence, the head was still on it, though the face was badly marked.

Angharad went for a while to my house and stayed with Cristin and my children, but Iorwerth called her back after a few days saying that the place was unsafe. We were on constant alert at the old court and he commanded that the palisade should be strengthened and kept men on watch on the little wooded hilltop that overlooks us to the north, even though it was impossible for anybody to get up there without our knowing about it.

He sent me and Owain Pencarn to see the king, rather late.

'Tell them I'm ill with grief' he said. 'They like that sort of thing.'

He pretended there was no truth to the reason.

We, Pencarn and I, went to the new castle with a few men and the king's letter to protect us, a priest to do the translating.

It was an overcast day. I remember the grey air and the silly banners on the palisade shifting in the gusts of wind. The castle was much then as it is now, a dismal, high, splintery enclosure of split timbers, one of the prisons important men make for themselves. Nothing like as awful, say, as the fortress at Abergafenni — yes, I will come to that — but horrible enough. Their true churches, but with the pretence that Christ lives there removed.

We waved the letter and got in, leaving a few men outside. I was surprised at how few soldiers there were. There were men carrying wood about for running repairs and there was some noise from a small pen ludicrously crammed with pigs. Nearby a youngish man sharpened a large knife on a stone. He looked at us occasionally but didn't speak.

At length two soldiers came to us and with them a richly dressed man. He was very short and had a deep chest. He didn't look old but his face, which was cleanshaven and pale, was lined as if newly carved from some waxy white wood. His eyes were smallish and set very deep, his hair dark and crinkly, though even then, perhaps, greying. There was a weariness in his manner that made me imagine he slept little. And this was the first time I ever looked at the king's great reeve, Randwlff de Poyr.

He rubbed his eyes, glanced at the letter, half listened to our priest, and waved us towards a door.

At the door he stood to one side and let us in. I noticed him looking at our feet as we passed, and our clothes, exchanging then a look with his soldiers. He registered mild surprise, too, when we stacked our bows and spears against the jamb as we went in. I noted his clothes. Dark shoes, a small knife in a tiny band below one knee, the scalloped edge of his dark tunic. A light sword worn on a loose belt, which he didn't remove as he came in.

The priest announced who each of us was — I heard our names — and the reeve glanced up, asked where Iorwerth was, got his answer and looked down. He spoke to our priest in French and broken Latin. He seldom raised his eyes above the level of our chests and when he did I felt that he was looking at our moustaches and hair.

'Majesty's gone' he said. The priest told me after that he talked in this way. 'Got a real war to fight elsewhere.'

There were squeals outside. Pencarn put the appropriate questions about the restoration of our country, but as soon as the priest started to translate Randwlff talked him down. There was some confusion then, as the priest had to catch up with the crosstalk above the squeals, especially as his French seemed to be no better than the reeve's Latin. But what came out was something like the king had left to attend to his great affairs having with great skill resolved the problems that had arisen in Ireland and there was no question of entering into discussion concerning the future of the king's hunting lodge at Caerllion until such time blah blah. Squeal. In any case, his majesty had with his usual magnanimity et cetera granted to the native chieftain Rhys of Deheubarth justiciarship over all the natives of the south in recognition of that lord's greatness and fealty in his majesty's service and as a token of the and so on and therefore it was to that great lord that we natives should address our conceived grievances and before him pursue our what have yous.

Randwlff smiled startingly in the gaps in his speech — stopping once when the squealing outside threatened to drown his words. Smiled that is with his mouth only. Though I didn't understand him as he spoke, I know he rattled the words off, his voice lurching up and down arbitrarily, like a child's who's learnt a poem by rote and who puts all the emphases in the wrong places.

Pencarn's eyes flickered from the priest to the Frenchman as the words were translated. He glanced then to the light sword and from that to me.

We both knew the war was coming.

Rubbing at the corner of his eye once more, Randwlff extended the letter to the priest.

We turned to go, at which the reeve started a little. Perhaps he expected us to go out backwards. He followed us to the door and as we collected our weapons exchanged a few words with the priest.

'He asked me why we left them by the door' the priest said to me afterwards a bit puzzled.

We crossed the beili to the gate, passing the place where two men were stacking the dead pigs on a small cart.

## 7

But the heavy dug. Yes. Forgive me. When these things flow in my mind the tides are sometimes too strong for navigation. I don't even own my own thoughts. I can call up memories sometimes, yes, but sometimes they come without the calling like someone new stepping into your house, into the space around your hearth, stark and alien, as if brand new, filling the space, clear as now in a tunic with a scalloped edge, rain dripping from a metalled scabbard point, entering new every time, never absorbed.

She fell as if poleaxed, but you should have seen Hywel. I forgot to tell you about him. Before I went to the castle with Pencarn, when he came, Hywel that is, when Iorwerth sent for him and he came on horseback with some men, leaving a castellan at Bryn Buga.

I hadn't seen him for a while. His entrance was a grand one and the children called us to gate of the old court when they saw the half dozen horsemen coming up the slow curve. They broke into a canter, which made the banners on the spears flutter picturesquely but the escort of foot had to run like cats to the devil to keep up, which spoilt the effect.

In the yard, Hywel leant out of the French saddle he'd acquired and bent to wrap an arm round his mother's shoulder. He spoke some quiet words of comfort to her, not heard by the crowd, and held his spear, cupped in some special place on the harness, firm and at a steep angle. The right picture. Strength one arm, tenderness the other. He let his horse, a red stallion then, dip his head and turn a few times, presenting a profile to each of the four corners of the earth in turn. Then he dismounted. Children and young women pressed forward, my children among them, because Cristin was at the court. Older wives nudged one another and observed the behaviour of their daughters.

Hywel pulled off his helmet, which had a flange that came down over his nose. His face still had its fullness then, his cheeks not graven like his father's, as they've become since. His moustache and hair were meticulously trimmed but his eyes had the same blankness of his boyhood. He raised a hand to his lip as if checking the exactness of the scissorwork.

He turned to where his father stood. There was no need for speeches. The air was strange and heavy with shared grief as Hywel, his face distorting, embraced Iorwerth with a gasp that I heard at a distance of five spears. He hid his face on his father's shoulder. The old man was slow responding. He raised one hand to his son's back. The other hung at his side.

## 8

That marwnad for Owain was a tricky thing to put together. Its publicness came too much into contact with a real hurt for it to be uncomplicated.

I went the next day to where his body had been laid in a wooden chapel Iorwerth had had built outside the beili. There was heavy summer rain. A thunderstorm would have been appropriate but god didn't oblige. I remember stepping into the dark space — there were no windows, though four candles — unwrapping the cloak from my head as I tried to juggle some likely phrases for my song.

A few women were there, employed by Angharad to pray. There was a book open on the table, near the corpse's head. Dim in the yellow candle-light and the raingreyed daylight I could see that the page was done in the old style, fretted with plaitwork that turned into living plants and creatures and people.

The droning of the prayers got on my nerves after a while and I told the women to go out and pray at the church, said I'd stay in their place. They were only taeogion and I think they were relieved to get off their knees.

I leant against the wall furthest from the door and the bier. Tallowstink, the sound of rain and incongruous birdsong, the still corpse with its face covered.

There was movement at the door. A man came in, seemed to limp in, only he couldn't have limped because it was Iorwerth. Memory and invention must be close neighbours — their stocks are forever mingling.

He went to his knees and leaning his head on the board, prayed.

I went down too and bent my head in case he should see me, irritated that I'd been interrupted. I was wondering how I was going to get out without awkwardness when the doorway darkened a second time and Hywel ab Iorwerth stepped in. I looked up in time to see him stare at the back of his praying father, who, although he must have seen the shadow fall, didn't look round. Hywel hesitated a mo-

177

ment as if he might go out again, but in he came and sliding a glance at the covered face he moved to the other side of the bier and went to his prayers too.

Only he didn't pray long. Soon his head was up and he was looking over his dead brother's chest at the crown of his father's head.

A corpse so presented is stiller than something sculpted on a church, invites contemplation as well as horror, but Hywel's nervousness, his sense of being preoccupied, broke all that.

Iorwerth made a kind of groan. I think it was 'Hywel' he said, and the grizzled vetch stirred and he lifted his head and looked at his living son.

Hywel shifted his weight as if his knees hurt already, but he didn't look away.

'This'll cost more than cattle' he said.

Iorwerth said nothing.

'What'll we do?'

Iorwerth looked from the living face to the draped dead one and back, said, 'I heard Ifor Fychan of Senghenydd has died.'

I started, lifted a hand to my neck, but they didn't notice the movement.

'Meilyr told me he would. But that's always a safe bet.' He looked at the corpse. 'He told him not to go to the castles. Some wasting disease, Ifor had. And in his last days half his body froze and he lost the power to speak, as though death came by fractions.' He raised a hand, touched one side of his own face as if finding the texture of something strange.

Hywel looked at his father and said nothing for a long time.

For moments I saw doors opening and a splay of light, a small bench waiting like some animal, with all the silence of a catafalque, and a break of crows from the treetops.

'— the king' Hywel was saying.

I was in the chapel again, my hand on my neck.

'— you know it was the king.' Something like that. 'Iarll Bryste did this for him. They even had Seisyll seized in Gwent Uwchcoed to deprive us of allies. Gwilym Brewys did that for the king although he risked the hostages Seisyll held.' He paused. 'Brewys. That bastard. And then this letter.'

There was long silence again and I don't know what passed between their faces in the half light, except that Iorwerth looked again from the living son to the dead one and back.

'The king' Hywel said, like that, insisting. 'He wants to draw you out.'

Iorwerth reached towards the head of the corpse. I thought he was going to touch the book but instead he took a corner of the cloth covering the face and gathered it up slowly like this, his fingers walking over the cloth.

I could see little of it from where I was. The jut of nose. A fore shortened whiteness little yellowed by the candleflames. Gashes. But I saw its stillness spreading — how can I say it? That's not it — I saw those two things, horror and contemplation, fix themselves in the living men.

Iorwerth didn't look long though, but turned and watched Hywel. At last Hywel turned to him but again I couldn't read their faces.

'Everybody pays' Iorwerth said.

'Exactly' Hywel said. He sounded impatient and puzzled. 'Look. Let's take Toothless, me you, Pencarn, Morgan —'

But he hadn't finished that word when Iorwerth hit him, slapped him, only slapped, and they were standing. Iorwerth had reached across the body and dragged Hywel to his feet, had hold of his hair and neck. Hywel was hunched unheroically and didn't hit back.

'Morgan ap Seisyll' he said. 'What's the matter? What're you doing?'

Iorwerth twisted his son's hair so the face turned upward and I saw the blank eyes, the open mouth. The prince held him still like this a moment.

He said, 'What I'm afraid of is that you're too much like me.'

'I wish I was more. Like you were in Estefyn's days. Like all those times you've talked about. Talk.'

Iorwerth relaxed his grip. Hywel straightened himself, checked the lie of his moustache with an automatic touch of the fingertips.

Iorwerth's face was turned away from me, towards the corpse, sideways to Hywel.

The prince started to say, 'You don't —' but he stopped and slowly turned full face to his living son again. And then his arms were raised and he was trying to embrace Hywel even across the bier. It was awkward to say the least. The board shook and two of the candles went over. The father and son watched them absurdly for a moment then Hywel relit them at one of the other candles and replaced them.

179

They stood in the threads of white smoke and Hywel said, 'Tooth-less, and me, and Pencarn, each with men, and Morgan ap Seisyll too.'

'The king' Iorwerth said, and he spread the cloth back over the broken face. 'We'll have to wait till he's out of the way.'

Hywel smiled.

## 9

And that was why, when Pencarn and I looked at one another a few days later as we stood before Randwlff in the new castle, I was certain that the war would come in its usual season with the absence of a king and the presence of fair weather.

Hywel, who had developed his techniques in the previous year, as I think I've already said, and Toothless too, and the prince and Pencarn, led us out across Gwent Iscoed. Hywel went into England, even to Llwyn Danet, and killed foresters and their families and burned their houses. But we kept away from the castles. Caerllion was too strong, though everything around it was waste. Once we attacked two supply boats that were coming up the river and killing all the crew we captured a great quantity of salted pork, but still the garrison kept itself supplied and we laid no real siege that summer.

I've never known Iorwerth so ferocious. In spite of that, and though hatred of the king among us was almost palpable, the prince sent messengers back and fore to Rhys all the rest of that summer and while spoil and supplies came into our country all the time, he still hoped for some arbitrement.

I'd sung my marwnad for Owain, after great labour in its making, before the funeral, but grief was so general that any loosestrung words approximating to the right sentiments would have opened all the sluices. When it came to the assaults, which some people had clamoured for even before Pencarn and I had kept our tryst with Randwlff, Iorwerth told me to make no battlesongs but to sing only the marwnad and so our works were seen as acts of vengeance, and that was what moved the hands of ordinary people who carried weapons.

And there were many of them. Toothless gathered people from the whole country. There was one young man called Berddig ap Heilyn who was killed in a battle beyond Gwy in a place that's called Maes Hywel now, and I believe he may have been my brother's son, though I'm not sure. He had wideset eyes, anyway, and the right name. If he knew who I was he never let on. I don't think he did. You know I've wrongly been called ap Gwrgant many years now and since Seisyll gave me a cloak — did I tell you about that? — I'll tell you how I lost it shortly — most people have called me Griffri Brydydd. But he had the eyes, and an unkempt moustache.

And it was Seisyll, talking of him, who became the means of ending the campaign. Gwilym Brewys the French lord in Brycheiniog offered to release him if we withdrew, though we hadn't moved much in his territory. It suited everybody. Pencarn saw through these things — forgive the expression — in his usual way.

One day in a smoking wreck of broken posts and thatch, while he and I watched Hywel's men practising their arts with precision and dedication on the former inhabitants as a parting gesture to the French and English who stayed put in their strongholds nearby, he, Pencarn that is, turned to me — I got the impression that he never liked watching these performances any more than I did, though perhaps to Hywel and the rest they were no mere performance but a way of being, of living through their particular art — anyway, he turned to me like this, in that wincing sort of way as we watched one of the — well I won't tell you what we watched — and he said, 'Why all this? The sooner Seisyll's out the sooner we all go home. After Rhys's preferment from the king Brewys can't hold him for long, even if it's on the king's behalf.'

And Rhys's late little love scenes with the priestkiller — only the great can conduct such grotesque courtships — were significant, Rhys being Seisyll's brotherinlaw. It hadn't occurred to me till Pencarn spoke that this was the state of things. Morgan ap Seisyll was with us too, riding with Hywel, about eighteen then, I'd say, and though he was quiet and wide eyed — Iorwerth's son fancied himself as his cousin's mentor and, as part of his education, led him to places where innards hung on thorn — though he said little, we supposed that he ached to lead men into Uwchcoed, which eventually he did, of course.

181

It was near the end of summer and most of us had had enough.

These neat concoctions. I tell you what *we* thought. What can that *we* be and what can that thinking be made of? These summaries are bound to be a kind of lie, but what else is there? Arrows clattering onto the decks of the boats, thumping into pork. Tallow. Or Pencarn one day as we were coming back holding his knife to the neck of a young man we met and then waiting and then moving it away and I watched the sharp declivity of flesh smooth itself, unwound itself and Pencarn tapped the boy on the cheek with the flat of the blade but the boy waited like a monk kneeling for his weekly tonsure and Pencarn pushed his shoulder and told him to go.

He turned to me then and stared, but I said nothing.

# 10

One day in September I stood in my house and held my youngest son above my head and looked up, making a stillness among the tumult of the others. Though there was no rain dripping from the eaves and there were no dead leaves yet plastered on the thatch, I wanted, that homecoming, a moment of perfect knowing without the need of grief. I looked at my little boy — he was two then — watched him smiling and contorting, my face not turned away.

There were the familiar smells and smokedrift, the two apple trees outside. I had the sensation that the arms holding the boy up were somebody else's.

I looked at my thumbs, the hair on my forearms, and they weren't me.

I nearly dropped him. Then it was as if I woke up and I was aware of the strength in my arms again and he was laughing as I slipped him to the rushes.

After they'd all had their hug, in all the noise of their voices, Cristin and I embraced and I was surprised a moment, as we pressed, to feel a touch of the old urgency. Gently we disconnected.

That evening after meat, when some of the children slept and only some of the youngest played around us, we talked.

'Good hay this year' Cristin said.

But I was distracted by some game of peep or other and she said again, louder, thinking I hadn't heard,

'Good hay this year.'

'Good' I said.

'Two good lots. Plenty of fine weather.'

'It has been good' I said. Very fine.'

I'd been away a season but it felt like years. Everything had to be re-made and rediscovered. I saw, felt, the solidity, the weight of the children, the strange precision of their whorls of hair. Old Lleucu, sitting with us, watched me playing peep but said nothing.

'I help hay' the youngest boy said. 'I help. And a moon big moon a big dark come. I sleep sleep.'

He pressed his precise face to me, pointing to himself as he said this, so I'd be sure who it was had slept while the family killed hay by moonlight.

'We managed' Cristin said.

'I'll bet you did with a good big boy to help you' and I pushed the good big boy away gently as I said this.

Cristin looked at me over the head of the baby girl, the youngest of all, who'd climbed onto her mother's lap and was sleeping noisily with her face squashed on a cushion of breast.

'Stock all right?' I said.

'You looked in.'

'Yes. Only a quick look.'

'That oldest cow died. In calf.' She paused. 'The calf's all right.'

'Oh' I said. 'That's a shame. Still, you coped though.'

'We managed.'

'The oldest cow.' I made the appropriate pause, made the silence speak a small grief. In my mind there were tumbled posts, the smouldering thatch, Pencarn wincing.

'Pity' I said.

I started suddenly. You know the way you do when you've been asleep. I suppose I was tired. She'd touched my shoulder, I think. My arm was raised, fending her off. She leant away, raising an arm over the child's head, then smiled with her mouth. The baby stirred a little, slurped a dribble, and I saw her mouth working as she sucked on her own tongue.

I dropped my arm and we both breathed again, relaxed.

Cristin's hand touched my shoulder a second time, moved towards my neck, her smile growing a little surer.

'There'll be weddings' I said. 'War and weddings go together. Shares from the virgin fees for us.'

'All right' she said.

'And the November Calends.'

'Will you be all right to sing?'

'What? Yes of course. There'll be a share of the spoils then.'

'We did manage.'

'What do you mean, "all right"?'

'What?'

' "Will you be all right to sing?" you said.'

'Well I just wondered if you would be. I thought you stuttered a bit earlier on. That's all.'

I looked at her face. The moon was waning. She was wrong of course. There'd been all the noise, speaking over all the clamouring of children.

She was mistaken. I went to tell her this but in our pause Lleucu got up to leave, said goodnight from the darkfilled door and, looking at how the firelight had taken over from late daylight and feeling the breath of the September chill, I forgot to answer.


# 11


The boy, though his legs were planted firm as trees, was rubbing his eyes by this time, but seeing Lleucu go and the dark that stayed in the doorframe after she went, he called to his mother,

'Story story story, Mam. Story me.'

This woke some of the others who joined in the call.

Cristin, tired in the face and sitting on the floor hooped around the baby, smiled to me and nodded me to the mattress, where I crawled as she started to tell her story to the sleepy group she'd gathered.

I was asleep long before she'd finished it, but at the November Calends, which we spent at the old court, after meat and after singing, and after I'd sung to Angharad and the women, when the call came for stories I asked Cristin to tell it then so I'd know the end.

I saw in her face that she didn't want to. Her eyes hardened at me, but no one else saw and they joined in my call, seeing only the etiquette of faked reluctance and unrefusable persuasion, like a company calling for another poem, who, even though the poet shakes his head and makes to put the harp away, knows there's no denying.

'Come on' Angharad said. 'That's one I haven't heard.'

And so she had to tell it. It has to do with this place, where we are now, or hereabouts. It's not one you hear much. I'll tell it you briefly.

I think she told a fuller version at the Calends than the one she told the children that time. Here it is.

It's called

## The Story of the Afanc King
## and the Sons of Teyrnon

In the days when Teyrnon Twrf Liant was ruler over Gwent Iscoed, it happened that after a long time without children his wife became pregnant.

Teyrnon was the best man in the world, and his wife said to him, 'Teyrnon, this is god's reward to us for the time when you restored the foundling child Gwri Wallt Eurin, to his true father and mother, Pwyll and Rhiannon.'

Teyrnon remembered the time well as, although he knew it would have been wrong to keep the child, returning him had almost broken his heart.

So he said, 'When the child comes we will name it after Gwri Wallt Eurin.'

But after the birth, when the women admitted Teyrnon to the room, he saw that his wife had given him twin sons. So they decided together that one of the sons would be called Gwri and the other they would name Eurin.

Presently Gwri and Eurin grew to manhood and they became admired and strong princes. They were close friends, equal and alike in all things except one particular, and this was that Gwri conceived that his father showed greater love and favour to his brother Eurin than to himself.

One day the brothers went out to hunt. Gwri had a spear of steel and Eurin's was of gold. Gwri's bow was of elm and Eurin's was of yew.

Chasing the boar, they moved apart from the rest of the company and became lost and they were in a valley that they had never seen before. Still following their prey, they plunged into the trees and after a long time came to the shores of a huge lake and in the centre of the lake, far off, they could see there was an island.

'I can see the boar swimming' Gwri said.

Eurin looked the way his brother had pointed.

'It has climbed onto that island' Gwri said.

But Eurin had not seen it.

'Let us look for a way to cross to the island' Gwri said.

And there and then the brothers cut down a tree and hollowed it in the old way, and, using the broad blades of their spears, paddled across the water. They paddled for a day and a night and in the morning walked onto the island.

Immediately Eurin set out looking for the boar, saying, over his shoulder to his brother, 'If we catch him people will call this island Ynys y Twrch because this was where the boar was killed.'

'They had better call it Ynys Eurin then' Gwri said.

At that Eurin turned, dropping his weapons in surprise, and saw Gwri approaching him with his heavy sword raised.

'My other self!' Eurin cried. 'What's this?'

But Gwri said nothing.

Eurin tore off a bough of flowering rowan that grew on the island to defend himself and that was how they fought, with sword and branch. Gwri swung his sword down and instantly the branch was cut in two. The blade struck Eurin on the head making a gash and so he fell.

At that moment Gwri knew what he had done and he was filled with grief and terror. He gathered the weapons and turned and ran away. But as he paddled back across the lake some of his terror left him and he said, 'I will tell nobody about this.'

Reaching the shore, he sank the boat and then went back to his father's court and Teyrnon and all the court were very pleased at his return, but because he carried the golden spear and the bow of yew and had left his own weapons in the boat, they thought that he was Eurin.

While Gwri embraced his mother, Teyrnon looked towards the gate and said, 'Eurin, where is your brother?'

'Father' Gwri said, 'I lost sight of him among the trees and then I heard a cry and I ran to him. I came to the edge of a lake and Gwri was wrestling with the boar in the water and they went under. They never came to the surface again. I searched all around the lake for three days wading in the water but never found them. See, my clothes are wet.'

And so they were, because Gwri had dipped them in the lake before returning.

Teyrnon's grief was so great that he could not speak and the whole country was so concerned at the condition of the king that they neglected Gwri's story. For three years Teyrnon did not speak and no richness of the land nor the love of his people nor the songs of his poets could bring him from his affliction. After that time, he died and Gwri called Eurin was ruler. The new king made a wise match, marrying the woman who had been purposed for his brother.

But the true Eurin had not died because although the sword had cut through the rowan its force had been reduced in doing that. Three days and nights he lay on the shore after his brother had left him and then he woke and found the broken branch in his hands and the wound on his head.

He went into the interior of the island and it had many animals and small trees, though there were no people. He made himself a house of withies and a spearhead of bone and so he lived by hunting part of that summer.

One day Eurin walked to the shore of the island furthest from the place where his brother had struck him and there he saw a city made of wood. This city was made of roughly chopped timber and its peculiarity was that part of it was built on the land and part of it was built on the water.

While he looked, Eurin saw a strange creature approaching him. This creature was less than half the height of a man and it had sleek fur and a long tail and large yellow fangs, but it had the hands and face of a man, and also a man's voice.

'My father calls you to come into his city' the animal said.

Eurin hid his nervousness and walked with the creature through the gates of the strange city.

Inside he went through many courtyards and chambers that were under the earth and many that were over the water. The animal presented him to his father, who was the Afanc King, and all the host of his family.

The king was as the other creatures were, except that he was larger and wore a great torc braided from piped gold, and his fur was silvered.

The Afanc King raised his hands in greeting and entertained his guest with food and music. After the meal, Eurin told the story of his cruel treatment to the king, who sympathised and said,

'Eurin, live here with me, and I and my family will teach you good and useful things.'

Eurin accepted this and among these creatures he was the first human to learn beekeeping and the making of mead, and from the Afanc King himself he learned magic. Their evenings were filled with song and carousal.

So for three years Eurin was happy, but at the end of that time he discovered, by the art the Afanc King had taught him, of his father's death and of what else had happened at Teyrnon's court, and he longed for his birthright and his country.

Straight away Eurin told these things to the king.

The Afanc King was thoughtful for a while and then said,

'Eurin, there is a way to bring about what you want. Every year my bees fly to your country to gather pollen. One of them can carry a message to bring your brother here. But if you leave my country you may never come back to it.'

Eurin said he would adopt this plan and though the Afanc King was sad, he allowed it.

Gwri called Eurin had begun his rule in Gwent Iscoed and his mother, his wife, and all his people were surprised that he did not rule so well as his father had.

The truth was that Gwri often thought of the blow he had struck on his brother's head, and of Teyrnon's grieving for the son he thought was Gwri, and these thoughts distracted the new king from his business.

One night after Gwri and his wife had gone to sleep, a bee flew into their room. The bee settled in the wife's hair and there it buzzed gently a large part of the night. In the early morning it flew away and the woman woke up suddenly with a cry.

'What is it?' Gwri said.

'Eurin' she said. 'I had a strange dream. I dreamt that I was standing on the shore of the lake you told us about.'

'What lake?' Gwri said, though he knew which lake she meant.

'The one where Gwri fought the boar' she said. 'I looked across the water and far off I could see an island. Why are you staring? There was a ripple in the lake and a man walked up out of the water, as if he had walked underwater from the island. It was Gwri. His face was very white.'

Gwri was angry and shook his wife by the shoulders, but then he saw she was afraid and his anger left him. He grew calmer and told her to go on.

'He had a strange branch in either hand' she said, and here on his head there was a bloody wound. And that was my dream.'

Gwri hid his disquiet after this but later in the year he decided to go back to the island in the lake and see his brother's bones on the shore so that his mind would be easier.

He went out one day saying that he would hunt alone and he made himself a boat out of skins so that it would be easy to carry and then he searched for the lake.

At first he could not find it, but at length he saw a boar which turned from him and ran into the trees. Gwri followed as quickly as he could and soon he was in the valley he had last visited with his brother three years before. He found no remains.

Eurin had been observing him from a hidden place nearby and when he saw Gwri's fear, by his art he took the form of a huge boar and rushed out. Gwri ran away into the water but the boar followed and they both went under the surface of the lake, and that was the end of Gwri. Presently the boar came to the surface and resumed the form of Eurin. So Gwri, in his invention, had foreseen the manner of his own death.

Eurin said goodbye to the Afanc King and all his people and took as a gift a sapling rowan because that was the tree that had saved his life. He took Gwri's skinboat and went back to his father's country, and he never saw the island or the city or the Afanc King again.

The true Eurin was accepted without question in Gwent Iscoed and for a long time he told no one what had happened. He ruled well and taught his people how to make mead and the country came to know of his skill in magic. He planted the rowan too, and that was how it came into this country, and it was Eurin who showed the tree's power to ward off illdoing, or, if the bad thing was very strong, how to lessen the ill effects. Because of all these things his wife, who had been the unwitting wife of his brother before that, grew suspicious and asked him about his solitary hunt. Then Eurin told her all his story. At first she would not believe him but then he parted his hair and showed her the scar where Gwri's sword had wounded him. At this she remembered her dream and saw that the strange branches were of rowan, and she remembered how her husband had stared and then grown angry when she told him about the dream, and she had no choice but to believe.

'Are you angry that I have tricked you?' Eurin said.

'No' she said, 'because you have only claimed your own name.

It was Gwri who tricked me.'

After that Eurin ruled many years and they lived happily.

That is the end of The Story of the Afanc King and the Sons of Teyrnon.


The bit about the hollowed out boat got a laugh. But when Cristin finished that time in the old court it was very quiet. One of the women had gone red around the eyes and nose and she was sniffing. I think it was one of old Rhagnell's daughters.


## 12


It was Hywel who called on me in the spring to make the battlesong for the siege. He visited his father at the old court and there he sent for me.

'Is it to be soon?' I said.

'Have the song ready.' He smiled. 'War has seasons like farming. Be ready to sing my brother's marwnad too.'

I looked at his face.

They'd never noticed me in the chapel. I waited a long time, after they went waited again, then sneaked out.

I thought to say, as I looked at him, 'That'd be popular' or some such answer, but instead I looked down and said, 'Of course.'

It's strange to think of winter as a restoration but that was what that winter had been. I watched my breath form on the air in the mornings, saw the soothed shapes of the trunks in the beech grove. The colour muting in things made them a kind of salve. Ice on the churned earth outside the byre was like the glassy skin that comes when a wound heals.

This is part illusory of course. We all come back to the hearth. Colour, light and heat in one. When I went to sing at Seisyll's court at Christmas I was glad enough to get my bones to a fireside both ends of the journey. The atmosphere was subdued there too, the country weighed down by Arglwydd Brycheiniog, that Gwilym Brewys who'd held Seisyll. A young man, they said, ambitious and godly, in the king's favour. I barely followed the talk of all that and went home glad to see cows and frozen mud and Cristin at her distaff and my table and candle.

The leaves were just coming when Hywel talked to me about seasons and ripening. Before there's green you look at a wooded mountain and the branch tips make a mauve filigree.

'I want' Hywel said, after I'd said 'Of course', 'I want to make it clear exactly what they're paying for. We can't have this. We've got to make ourselves strong. The marwnad will show us Owain's ghost.'

It was a curious way to put it, I thought, not like Hywel to use such a figure. But he even elaborated it, with a certain clumsiness.

'Ghosts' he said, looking away and then back as if steeling himself against embarrassment, 'Ghosts walk when the living sing. Last year your marwnad worked a little magic on the men.'

I remembered how Iorwerth had looked down from his horse to Gwrgant and said, when Eneas had been killed, 'Make a poem for him.'

In any commission there's some equivocation on the part of the commissioner, yet, here, unexpectedly, I felt that Hywel understood something of me and my work. I looked at his blank eyes and the unhollowed cheeks and warmed to him then, thought that one day I would call him the expected names. Hawk. Dragon. Wolf. Hammer of the French. Oak door of Gwynllwg.

Iorwerth and Toothless came to us and we talked through the tactics.

Hywel had ideas about having hurdles made, and a portable roof for a battering ram and various other contraptions.

'The crucial thing' Iorwerth said, 'is the time.'

Hywel smiled at me when he heard that.

'Let them think we've given the place up' Iorwerth said. 'They've been there two years. Rebuilt my hall as a tower and all. We need dry weather, the king must be far away, they must be unsuspecting and lightly garrisonned, the new castle down the river must be in the same condition, Randwlff must be out of the district, we must be well supplied and they must not, no lord must see an advantage in helping them, we must get other help, and we must be ready to keep up the siege for four months. More.'

Hywel's smile was gone.

191

'We'll wait for ever' he said.

'We'll wait. War is mostly waiting. You can't let the cord go till the stag's in the right place.'

'What other help?' Toothless said.

'Seisyll of course' Iorwerth said. 'Caradog ab Iestyn perhaps, and' — he looked me full in the face and back to Toothless — 'Gruffudd, the son of Ifor of Senghenydd.' He looked at me again and smiled. 'We can buy their help with cattle if we have to.'

'Could we buy them for four months?' Toothless said. 'We'd starve if it didn't work.'

Iorwerth waved his hand. 'Hywel wants to throw everything into risk now and you want no risk at all. Listen. At my death I want my sons to have at least what was there when I became prince.'

'Sons?' Hywel said.

Iorwerth talked across him, 'We'll call Pencarn and Morgan ap Seisyll and all the other chief men and hear their thoughts and when the conditions are right and Meilyr's advice is good, we'll work.'

I'm sorry to give you all this detail. What sticks in my mind is Iorwerth's vehemence, his certainty. You know how quiet he is at other times, how his eyes slide away from you. He was an old man even then. It was odd to see him so angry.

I came away from the old court towards sunset and walked home through the tame woods. The late light was strange and yellowed through the trees, submarine, like the light you see in a quiet passage of a clear river at sunset. Among the trees in overgrown places lovers after their day's work were looking for temporary nests. Some of them saw me, a respected courtier in a good cloak, appropriately greying but well groomed, the lister of the dead. They looked terrifyingly young, including the duckman, who looked younger and fresher than when, the year before, I'd seen him tell his story to a chicken for want of an audience. He and his woman leant their heads together as they went away around a tree. From above, someone on the mountain would have seen the fine mauve filigree, but here I was caged in the frenzy of birds screaming in their territories, the unbearable leaves coming, and everywhere energy bursting, even in some old men. I stopped there a moment and I was afraid and I wished it was winter.

## 13

But I was more troubled than I need have been. It was the middle of July by the time we were ready for the siege and instead of the four months Iorwerth had prepared us for, it lasted exactly three days.

I suppose you must have heard about it. Meilyr was never more straightforward in his foretelling than he was of that. When Iorwerth got news that the king was deep in a war in France all Meilyr's demons filled him and he spoke ecstatic gibberish for half a day. People pressed around him and asked his advice and went away discussing whatever snatches they'd heard. Pidyn Pâb and all the rest were never more popular. He — Meilyr — lay squirming in the beili — god knows what pinches they were giving him — saying, 'Glywysing one against the ironheads Glywysing one against the ironheads' again and again faster and faster.

There'd been good hay again that year and the conditions Iorwerth had laid down were fulfilled. I think Meilyr's friends were aware of this. Though his little house outside the beili at Caerllion had been destroyed with everything else, he talked of it in the present tense, as if it were already rebuilt and ready to walk into.

I believe his friends, too, were shrewd judges of the moment and of people's feelings. We'd watched Iorwerth meekly pay tribute of horses and cattle to the French though strictly he only owed such things to Rhys, returning a fraction of what he'd taken the year before, and that the day after we'd been getting the hurdles and ladders ready. The air among us was as full and as tense as the hour that expects thunder.

Us. Yes, us then. Then Meilyr's friends paid their call.

'Tewdrig and Owain riding a huge spear' he said, squirming still, 'smash at the bishopkiller's gate.'

It got so that we'd have to go, whether Iorwerth ordered it or not, and I made my battlesong for Hywel.

I take a certain pride in it. It was well judged, I thought, though I don't go in much for composing prophecy. I cobbled together some

of the best bits from the action of Bryn Buga and an old poem
Gwrgant taught me, but most of it was my own, more or less.

It started

> Foreseen: after battle will be our restoring
> Gwynllyw and Dyfrig will bless our going
> No greater venture since Annwn's despoiling.
> At the fort will be arrows and bladework and shouting.
> Swiftness and shaftclash will be our making
> Every killed outlander Owain's avenging.
> When walls break in battlepress men will die standing.
> Iorwerth and Seisyll will unchain Glywysing.
> In battlecrush no space will let fall the dying.
> Caradog and Gruffudd will unchain Glywysing.
> Revenge for false tribute will be widowmaking.
> Hywel and Pencarn will unchain Glywysing.
> Every cleft head will be Tewdrig's avenging.
> Mair's son and her father will unchain Glywysing.

I sang it unaccompanied, by firelight, to the teulu in the open air
the night before the assault. The four beats hit the rhythm of every
heart. It worked so well it even made me enthusiastic and I snatched
a spear out of the earth and waved the banner during the cheering at
the end. I was an impressive figure, you see, not so potbellied as Mei-
lyr, and straight and upright, not skewed and hackhaired. To see
young people's eyes shining like that is a wonderful thing.

Toothless leant across to me that night as we waited and said quiet-
ly, 'Well Griff, after all that, Hywel's got his way now whether he still
wants it or not. It's shit or bust.'

It was extraordinary to see so many princes together with Iorwerth:
Seisyll, though he'd been able to bring few men; Gruffudd of Sen-
ghenydd and Caradog of Afan; as well as Morgan ap Seisyll and
Hywel and Pencarn; all talking by candlelight while the others slept
in the hall.

Not that many of us did sleep. We moved out in the middle of the
night. The hurdles, for large shields, and Hywel's portable roof for
the battering ram were moved near the fort in the dark, it being a
moonless night. Iorwerth placed me with Pencarn's group. Appar-
ently after hearing my song Pencarn had been so impressed that he'd
particularly asked for this. I wasn't keen, having heard what was in-
tended, but I had no choice but to go.

We took ladders and laid them along the ground at the places
where we intended to go in. We knew that the garrison had given up

standing to at dawn months since and that the watches had grown careless.

Pencarn and I and one of his men, called Ithel, waited at our ladder. With no moon and no cloud and a breeze keeping the air clear, the spheres of the planets and the enormous globe of the fixed stars were at their brightest. I leant my back against the wall and looked up, realized that I was having difficulty breathing. We'd chosen the part of the wall the French generally kept away from. This, naturally enough, was the place where they dumped all the shit and it reeked worse than a calf with the scours. Caer Gwydion glowed in a great track, but it offered no help as I gasped in the choking stench of the fort.

Pencarn touched my shoulder. Of course we couldn't speak. I looked eastward across the river and a dim horizon of billowing trees was taking shape as the sky greyed. We lifted the ladder into position and there was a silence in which I knew Ithel was climbing. I could just see his shape against the paling stars as he climbed over the spikes of the parapet. Pencarn followed. Behind a hurdle nearby, half a dozen other men waited to follow us when the action started. I saw the shadow of Pencarn's arm against the stars motioning for me to follow and I went, gasping for breath but trying not to be noisy about it. The ladder shook about as if it wanted to throw me off. My round shield on my back and my bow and two quivers tangled around me as if they were alive and I actually fell over the top of the parapet and onto the walkway.

Luckily, Pencarn, who was lying in just the right place, broke my fall so that apart from his strangled grunt I caused little noise. The half dozen of us who were sent in in this way — the others came in by another ladder — all knew the beili well and though it was blacker than a cow's gut we found the way to our place, under the gable of Rhun's forge on the blind side of the mound and out of view of much of the walkway under the projecting eaves. We knew they kept no geese.

There was the smell of woodsmoke. The gatekeeper was sleeping by a small guttering fire.

Ithel disappeared and returned moments later. He risked a few barely audible words.

'Four in the forge' he said. 'Asleep.'

Dimly I saw him motion for us to follow.

Inside, by low firelight, I saw a man and a woman asleep on a bed and two men sleeping on a mattress. There were no dogs. Ithel positioned himself by the heads of the couple and Pencarn and I knelt by the two men. At a nod from Pencarn we slit their throats without incident. The one I had was very young.

I stayed there and through a shutter at the back of the building I watched the place where our ladder met the parapet. Ithel and Pencarn went outside.

When I heard the first thump of the ram against the gate and the shouting I went back to the door and looked out.

There was a grey halflight and men dressed only in shirts were running round, a few random arrows coming in over the walls, but not seeming to hit anything important. The gatekeeper was already butchered at his spent fire. Then I saw the other ladder men coming in over the top and along the walkways. I remembered myself and loosed a few arrows. I heard words shouted in French and English. Somebody was screaming, 'The gate, the gate' in French — I understood that much — and a few of them were trying to form up, half dressed in bits of harness and helmets, in one of their strange geometrical shapes in the yard. It seemed an odd thing to be doing because it gave the archers on the walkway better targets. I thought, they're queueing to be killed, like people queueing for communion. And quite a few of them went down dead or wounded before the rest saw that it was a bad idea.

Things started getting a bit confused then with the horses and the shouting, but I do remember Ithel getting to the gate and trying to lift the bar — hence the scream, I suppose, and then three or four men hurling themselves onto him. Some of the French were still trying to hold ground in the yard and at the gate but many were scurrying half armed towards the mound. Three or four of the Welsh were already on the walkway over the gate, firing downwards. Every time the ram thumped, the gate shook, and I thought the men above might actually be jolted off. Smoke was beginning to drift about the gate.

There was a lull and I saw smoke coming from the top of the escaping-tower. They'd be boiling water. A man in a mail shirt was running up the steps but the door, near the place where young Toothless had stood with one foot on the other to keep warm and I, a child, had peeped round him to see the strange men who wore woven chains, the door was shutting. I loosed an arrow to see if I could get it through the mail but I hit him in the calf and he sat back awkwardly and slid down the steps.

At the same time Pencarn came back to me in the controlled crouching run of a professional, holding his round shield over his head. Another man followed him and we held the forge. People with sense were looking for cover and for a while, I don't know how long, the yard was empty and the lull turned to silence apart from the regular thump and shout.

More men were pouring onto the walkways from the new ladders near the gate but hails of arrows were coming from the tower. The French who hadn't got into the escaping-tower had mostly gone back into their sleeping-hall in the yard and would be arming up fully. I knew, as Ithel had seen much earlier, that if the gate didn't go, all the Welsh in the beili would be killed.

'Jesus' I remember Pencarn saying. His mouth was full of blood but the words were clear. 'Break you bastard.' He looked at me. 'Next time there's thick smoke we'll go and lift the bar.'

We made our rush when the moment came. Through the smoke I saw Pencarn and the other man — they were younger and quicker than I was — heaving the bar up, and the gate opened like arms extending in welcome. The blunt ram, Meilyr's huge spear with Tewdrig and Owain invisible straddling it, came in at the centre as if it was thrown and dropped immediately to earth. At either side came a hurdle and above each a harmony of spearpoints angling down like fingers meeting harpstrings one by one. It was like a flower opening.

Sorry if I get a bit poetical about it, but it was the only time I was ever glad to be charged at with spears.

There was a shout and the men behind the spears started bursting through. I threw myself out of the way and looking round saw a man in full mail and helmet, swinging a sword. The blade passed quite close to me and cleft the shoulder of the duckman at the root of the neck, going downward. In the same moment I saw Meilyr running in, shouting, his arms forking the air. Then I had a taste of what he must have tasted and in the onrush I thought I was unkillable.

Hywel and Iorwerth on their horses were close behind the spear-bearers. It was Iorwerth and Pencarn, still on his feet screaming orders, who started the taking of hostages rather than outright killing. Holding my shield over my head I dragged my man with the leg-wound from the base of the mound to the gate and outside through the press. Staggering away from the crowds and the smoke I looked up into deep blue daylight.

## 14

Sorry.

I'm giving you the old soldier routine. I never intended that. These things happen very quickly and we're forced to remember them a long time.

That was a Wednesday. By late that afternoon, though I wasn't there, I believe we'd taken all the men and all the buildings of the beili. Iorwerth posted men in every building and archers behind slotted hurdles inside and outside the beili, watching the escaping-tower. They took an occasional shot if they saw a head. The rest withdrew.

There was a lot of singing and jeering and Pencarn with difficulty persuaded the Welsh that we shouldn't kill all the prisoners immediately. The thinfaced lawyer moved in then and Iorwerth and Toothless and I too. There was a lot of shouting between the lawyer and some helmet on the tower in Latin and French.

They had built the mound up so that it was much steeper and the wooden walls of their tower were much more solid than the palisade of the beili, as well as a great deal taller. It stood with its narrow-slotted face and shut door, blank and unspeaking like a great helmet itself.

A few men made for home after the beili was cleared of animals, but though most wanted to see the wooden helmet crack, only a few of the youngest had any thoughts of storming it. Some had energy to spare and went round the district looking for mead and women.

The lawyer waved a parchment with a pendant seal and shouted to the tower about how the fort had been built by King Caradog ap Gruffudd who had held the country from his ancestors back to Tewdrig the Great ('the Great' was the lawyer's own flourish) and how the Lord Iorwerth was the grandson of Caradog and vassal only to Rhys, the king's justiciar, and by this charter and that settlement, blah, et cetera. These words hardly any of us could understand and this parchment waved over the smoking mash of our day's work. The tower had some answer ready. The French had built it. Caradog was a vassal to Gwilym Bastart, and Henri by the grace of god, and the rest.

I left then, asking Iorwerth's pardon and saying that I'd be outside if he wanted to call me back to recite the lineage.

I sat at a fire with Meilyr and took a share of the meat he was eating. We said nothing for a long time, and I remembered Rhun and Gwrgant sitting together.

'Tired?' Meilyr's hand was on his head as he said this, his face on one side like a feeding blackbird.

I wondered how tired I must look and knew I didn't need to answer.

'They gone?' I said.

He looked up, pausing in his sideways chewing, and smiled, glanced around. Some women were stripping corpses nearby, and there were groups of men seated or wandering.

'So many souls about' he said.'You'd think the air'd be thick, but it isn't. They'll be back.'

We were quiet again.

'The reason is' he said later, though the reason for what I didn't know, 'the reason is we're getting old, Griff. God releases me now and then, you see. Old Cadell said he would, peace to his dust. You sang well. I liked the song. Got them all up fairly. I need release less often nowadays. See all these wandering men. Some'll go to church and some to sleep, and some to look for women. But you and me, Griff. People our age —' mind, he was older than I was '— people our age.' He shrugged and chewed, then waved a hand, looked round to the wall of the fort. 'This bristling vegetable oval full of mud and meat. One intrusion, one forced entry, and we've had it. Spunked dry.'

He stopped chewing, blinked as if he was waking and chewed again. A little of his food was stuck to his unkempt moustache. His belly hung over his belt.

I sucked my stomach in and said, 'What about Iorwerth?'

'Him? Ah, he's a prince' he said. 'We're autumn, he's winter. A very siege engine, the timbers weathered hard and sapless. That's a different thing. But younger men like us, they need more.'

199

'As you and I were. Iorwerth commands more out of his care for his birthright. But young men. They just itch.'

Dusk was coming and it was cooler, a little cloudy. His head sideways, he fed the strips of meat into the corner of his mouth where his few teeth were.

'Wish I had my teeth like you' he said. 'I'd choose better who to sink them into now. Look at them.' He nodded to two groups of half a dozen young men, one loyal to Hywel and the other to Gruffudd ab Ifor our ally. They were jeering and making fun of one another's clothes. 'All ballocks and no sense.'

'Worry is the son of sense' I said.

'Oh good shot, poet. A phrase for every occasion. Quoting are we? Surprise surprise. Then, I get my living quoting my friends so who am I to say? For there to be a son at all you have to have the ballocks too.'

'And a woman.'

He\snorted.

'They ought to save it' I said, nodding round the field. 'There'll be more\work\tomorrow.'

'Don't worry. They've got a good few squirts left, which is more than I have.'

'There's the escaping-tower.' I looked across at the tower on the mound. It was darkening. I tried to swallow some meat but couldn't.

'Ah yes. That' Meilyr said, looking too. 'There's a few in there. See. In the smoke. One coils up every now and then. Crammed with acolytes, mortal and otherwise. It was Gwilym Bastart invented that. Ellyll Llwyd told me. They build their dunghill specially so they can be cock on it. Raising the host, sort of. Look.'

Hywel and the thinfaced lawyer were coming out of the beili. The lawyer had blood on his gown and he wore a sword, but also his usual mask and his hands were tucked in his sleeves where he kept his book and his parchment.

'All sense and no ballocks' Meilyr said.

I'd given Hywel the mail shirt I'd taken from my prisoner and he was wearing it now, though clearly it was heavy and uncomfortable. He carried his helmet with a finger hooked round the noseguard and there was a red mark on his forehead where it had sat.

'The helmet's set a mark on him' Meilyr said. He looked back to me. 'The escaping-tower. Yes. It will fall without much pushing. Put out the lamps and they'll come round. Won't that be nice? And Iorwerth and Hywel can stride into their enlarged and Frenchified birthright wearing mail shirts and helmets. Won't that be glorious? We can cram it with our own acolytes. You and me, Griff, in the chancel, at the high altar of their shit cathedral. My friends'll love it there, crawling over Dyfrig's knucklebone. They'll enjoy the equation of sacrament and excrement.'

He laughed at his own cleverness, rubbed a hand on his crown. Then he peered at my shoulder. It was beginning to be dark and our fire was lighting us from below. He extended a hand, rubbed my shoulder, then sniffed his finger. I remembered the place where I'd leant against the wall of the fort, shaking and gasping before dawn. He laughed again.

'Now we're there' he said. 'Now we know ourselves.'

## 15

There was no second assault.

The tower was surrendered on the Saturday morning. It came about like this.

Pencarn and his few men managed to save the lives of a dozen or so hostages we'd taken in the beili by imprisoning them in Cadog's church nearby. Some of the young men, especially Hywel's and Gruffudd's were upset to be so deprived, but their masters kept them quiet enough.

The lawyer's sweet, well, sweetish reason having failed to work that Wednesday evening, he and Iorwerth and Hywel and Pencarn decided their next move that night. On the Thursday, as soon as it was light enough, Iorwerth had two of the hostages chained and presented at the gate of the beili, in sight of the tower but out of accurate bowshot. The lawyer shouted out his demands, calling for the French castellan's seal to a document relinquishing and so forth and so on.

A few helmeted heads moved about on the top of the tower but no words came.

Hywel nodded to old Rhun and his equally old assistant, who came forward with their instruments.

The lawyer spoke again, announcing to the tower, I suppose, the elegant turn the debate was about to take. One of the hostages started to cry.

Rhun approached the other hostage but Hywel told him to go to the one in tears.

'He'll probably make more noise' he said.

With some difficulty, eventually needing the assistance of four others and having to sit on the man's chest, Rhun took out the hostage's eyes. The lawyer said that we'd go away and come back that afternoon with the second hostage.

When that time came it was quickly clear that the people in the tower had been pondering the subtleties of the lawyer's last discourse and had decided that they found his arguments persuasive. They buckled as Angharad's knees had. The next day was spent in moving men away and the talking I mentioned and the castellan and Iorwerth put their seals on a parchment that Saturday morning on a board rigged up in the middle of the place where we'd butchered one another three days before.

Iorwerth kept every letter of the bargain, which was the sparing and return of all hostages in return for the restoration of his chief court and all the fortifications and land attached. The prince allowed them to take their dead away — they'd already been stripped and anyway it saved us work — and cosignatories were Gruffudd ab Ifor, Caradog ab Iestyn, Seisyll ap Dyfnwal, and the prince's son Hywel, all vassals to the king's great ally Rhys.

So notice was given to the yielding castellan. The army that had installed him on its way to Ireland was beyond the sea beyond England mired to the axles in some new work, and besides, it was just a couple of years since the king had shown how well he could be trusted by the people he installed in good jobs.

In that way Iorwerth subdued, as they say in books, the castle by force through his might and his power, and we reentered the fort, after it had been tidied up and the burnt jamb of the gate rebuilt, in time to celebrate the August Calends.

As it turned out, neither Hywel nor his father wore a mail shirt. They and Angharad, followed by Seisyll and his son Morgan and Caradog ab Iestyn, led the cortege home that day. Toothless followed as distain, and then the priest carrying the relic in its box, which he held out to the crowd to touch as he passed. The lawyer was with him. I was well down the file, standing with Rhun. I remember Iorwerth turning and looking back among us as he paused at the gate and he gave the slightest of nods to indicate that we should follow him in. One side of his mouth was crooked the way it is these days when he attempts a smile. There might have been stirring in Rhun's white eyebrows, but I could be mistaken. He had somehow retrieved his leather cap and he was wearing it. It's the only time I can remember seeing it on his head.

Perhaps it was that that made me easy prey to some force outside me that caught my nose and pulled it skyward as we moved towards the gate. Pencarn, I noticed, some way ahead, shuffled forward, roundshouldered and head down, rubbing his eyes. My shoulders grew straighter and squarer under my laundered cloak as though huge hands took my upper arms and a thumb was pressed into each of my shoulderblades. I had a notion that I must look absurd, but the strutting was irresistible. And through the gate where the flower had opened and Ithel had been snowed under by attackers and I'd seen the duckman cut almost in two, I saw myself and couldn't stop it. The staves of the beili stood blind and waiting and I heard myself make a shuddering attempt to heave air into my lungs.

# 16

No restoration ever is complete. Somebody told me once a man who's freed can never be the same as one who's merely free. The freed is both greater and less; greater because the release is tasted more strongly, as as apple's the sweeter for a bite of cheese, less because the subjugation leaves a mark so long as memory is kept. But when there's plenty some people forget quick enough, and that happened to some of us. I was perhaps failing in my job.

I run ahead of myself.

We had some new shields to hang on posts and Iorwerth presided over all the sortings out that followed concerning land and spoils. Hywel went back to Bryn Buga briefly to administer his own work and much of the payment needed for our allies he collected there. I sang, helped Meilyr to rebuild his house. The singing was the harder, believe me.

I was almost relieved one evening, after subdued eating and I was singing to the women apart, in the room where Cristin and I had lain in our childhood, almost relieved when Angharad raised her hand to stop the song. It was that time of uncertain light when the last of daylight starts to yield to a candleflame, and she was on a mattress at the base of the very pillar of my holiest trinity, she and Cristin and some of my daughters and others clustered there. It had been hot and there was that fusty closeness that seems to breed in the straw on such days. She held her hand up and turned her face away a little when I started gently on a quiet passage from her son Owain's marwnad, and I saw as I stopped in mid word that the candle had grown stronger, strong enough for her hand to cast a clawed shadow on her cheek, though the other side of her face was greyed with the going light of the unshuttered window.

The gesture was almost art, so deeply felt that it made a silence that spoke. I felt no embarrassment or rebuff, though when she turned her head back to look at me her eyes were lowered and had to raise themselves slowly. The claw turned to bars that rippled on her face as they were pulled away and left her open to the yellow light.

Strange how the mind fixes these things. None of this stuff would do if I was just telling you a story. Who needs to know it? Yet there it is, random in the memory, the ripple of shadow, one finger thickened by the silver ring her father had given her, the nose less fine, the skin puckering around the eyes and the broad forehead.

I stilled the strings, forgave the still lowered eyes by saying, 'Yes. Sometimes no song is —'

Something stopped me finishing the sentence and there were murmurs among the women. The window had darkened and those faces touched by the candlelight seemed to me the faces of angels as I looked from one to the next.

Angharad's eyes, raised now, shifted to look past me and I skewed on my stool to see Iorwerth standing in the doorway. He'd been leaning against the jamb but shifted his weight now and came in.

'God's welcome, Ior —' I said, but as he approached I saw I'd been mistaken and that it was Hywel and changed the name as I spoke so that it came out 'Iorwel.'

He smiled. The light shining upward on his face made a triangular shadow above his nose and above each eyebrow and the upcast shadow of his lower lip licked over his teeth.

'What?' he said. 'I thought words were your business.'

Before I could answer he greeted his mother, crouching at the mattress and embracing her. As he dropped to the level of the candle the shadowhorns disappeared, the cheeks, which had looked a little hollow, seemed to fill. The flame put a point of light in his eyes that I'd seldom seen there.

He'd been looking for his father, he said, wanted to talk to him about consolidation and security, or some such words. His mother, joking, scolded him for breaking the intimate song.

'What song?' he said. He looked at me and said again, 'What song?' The light there. I'd call him the names he would be called one day. Hawk. Dragon. Wolf. And the rest. I have called him them. No shadows played on his forehead as he sat among the angels and stared at me. I felt tired then, ached for sleep and an end to remembering as the light in his eye came close to glint and he said,

'Go on. Sing us to safety.'

## 17

How did I come on to this? I wanted to tell you about a tree and a cave and the pigs and Gwilym Brewys. Him. I knew your ears would prick up. Perhaps you've met him. A walking corpse. It was daylight that time I came before him. No candles to supply the appropriate imagery. Just grey December and his face bloodless and the shittalk squelching in his wormy mouth. Yet he has the same dullness in his eye, as if his mind is always elsewhere. As I think it was that day. I saw him give a nod. The slightest nod. Almost not there. Can you imagine that? And I didn't read it. They caught hold of. Wait. That was two years later, at another celebration.

He's a very religious man, Brewys. You can tell that by the way he keeps Christmas. Worships his god with his own most sacred offices on his own personal altar.

This is true, believe me. Don't think I'd stoop to irony. I owe my life to his devotion. A great French bishop of his own true church. He had an acolyte in a scalloped gown. I've been over all this with Arglwydd Rhys. He looked at me. You could tell he didn't believe. Or. Well. At best he half believed and dressed my punishment as a great avenging. You can see what a statesman he is in that. That was at another Christmas.

'Go, Griffri' he says. 'This is a mission to please god.'

And he gave me the knife. Look, this one. Told me to bathe it in the water stoop every Sunday. But after it all, after all that'd gone before, after Brewys had observed his rites and the pigs and the fallen tree and Rhiannon, I was as if dead. I walked asleep and I woke up in the ditch at Merthyr Dingat with the smirched blade in my hand and felt nothing. What could I sing, dead? Somebody else'll have to sing that.

Wait. Sing us to safety, he said, Hywel. That sneer. He's got a new daughter. You advise me later how I should sing to him now.

It was he, his might and his strength, as the books say, secured us. Secured us two years of peace, in spite of the tyrant who kills his good bishops and sets his bad ones to murder us.

After the sneer, Hywel talked with his father. I remember being surprised to see the son taller than the father and the son's voice insistent. I can see them speaking but hear no words. Iorwerth acquiescent, gesturing like this. A weak gesture, the elbow bent. Many of the teulu were keener to serve the son.

About the middle of September, Hywel did as he'd discussed with his father, rode into Gwent Iscoed again and went to the gates of the stone fortress at Ystrad Gul and left a few important corpses as his calling card and had hostages taken to ensure our border. Some men followed him from there. Half a dozen of his best archers he acquired then, men who'd gone to Ireland with the Iarll and fought the Ostmen. And that was what had been in his mind when he'd come to look for his father, cut across Angharad's best song. Security.

When he came back — I didn't go on that expedition — I stood among the people in the beili and applauded the new archers with the rest when they raised their bows in a prearranged greeting for Iorwerth. Hywel's dismounting and the public embrace of his parents was followed by a greeting of raised arms for Pencarn, who was still at the court. Pencarn returned the gesture but the fact that it was without enthusiasm seemed not to be noticed by the returned soldier. He went on smiling and spoke and kissed the reliquary and delivered gifts. And he didn't once that day show any of the tired emptiness you expect in a man who'd been at the hardest sort of work.

Many of the women approached the new archers, looked at their strange clothes and asked about Ireland and horses and archery, about everything except what they thought. Pencarn and I exchanged a smile. Meilyr, with us, smiled too, gummily.

'Wish I could bite a nipple' he said.

Hywel raised his arms above his head. There was a mark on his forehead where the helmet had sat.

'We are our selves again' he shouted, and there was a cheer.

'Want a bet?' Meilyr said to me quietly, and then turning to Pencarn, 'Want a bet? There's more to come. A man after safety will make a hole in his own soul to crawl into then gnaw the shell away with worrying. There. Teeth again.' He laughed, touched Pencarn on the cheek. 'You'll see, glowcrown, or feel anyway. It's better to have them drawn and suck porridge. In that you'll be both less and greater than he is. Pity him. He never saw a stag but a target. Never saw the sun but a lamp. Never heard words but messages.'

Pencarn's sharp eyes looked from Meilyr to Hywel and back. Hywel talked with various attendants and basked in the attention of the crowd.

'What'll happen?' Pencarn said.

Meilyr laughed. 'Oh I've said. They told me and I told you. They won't be ravens. Enjoy your freshened breath when it comes. Moles exist in foulness and alone like corpses, and that was never you. Remember that. Like all men except the moles we'll both know wounding' — he clutched my elbow as he said this though he was still looking into Pencarn's puzzled face — 'we'll all know wounding, but survive.'

## 18

A year later Meilyr was dead.

I knew you'd laugh.

He was wounded, but didn't survive, wounded when the French besieged Bryn Buga, by a blade across his ribs, and, when the castle was burning, by a falling timber that struck him on his back. Hywel escaped and most of his teulu, first to the old court and then, when he realized the French were making no further moves, to Caerllion.

They got Meilyr back to the old court still alive and he was laid on his stomach on a board in the hall. His legs were paralysed and the hair on the back of his head and his back itself were burnt.

Months before, in the spring, he'd foretold the battle, said again he'd be wounded but survive, told Hywel he would survive unscathed. It was this that had allowed Hywel to prepare and to fight with a kind of contemptuous ferocity in the siege, I'm told.

We, all the people, gathered round Meilyr in his last agony, who'd believed from his own words that he wouldn't die, watched him slip into the dark with naked horror in us.

Yes, us then.

His voice was strong, in spite of the chest wound.

'Cala Dewi Heliwr' he said. He looked around at us and seemed to see, though I think he saw more figures than any of us could. 'He always speaks a kind of truth. See, I have survived a little while. God forgive me. Forgive me, Morgan. Forgive me, Ynyr, Dyfrig, Abram, Rhagnell, Athrwys my uncle, forgive me Owain.' He looked at Owain Pencarn as he said this, though I think he meant Owain ab Iorwerth. 'Forgive me, Mair, Shigbo —'

And so he went on, naming, listing the dead, many I'd never heard of. Pencarn crouched at his head, clutching his hand. As Meilyr's voice started to become faint, Pencarn leaned closer, listening hard. I looked down at the king's great grandson's thinning hair as he listened. He was looking for some sign, some special thing that wouldn't come. So far as I know, Meilyr just listed the dead. Which is what this story's turning into, come to think of, another list.

In those last moments Hywel came in, looking preoccupied, and Meilyr, seeing him, called out. The young prince knelt and Meilyr clutched at the edge of his cloak, looking from him to his cousin and back. He said something then, voiceless and aspirated.

When he became still Hywel tugged at his cloak, tried to knock the dead man's hand away, as if afraid to touch it, half panicked, the way some people are when a moth flutters against them. At last he had to peel the fingers away one by one and he left the hall quickly.

Pencarn stood by me. I put a hand to my mouth, felt my teeth, straightened my shoulders and I dropped my hand, smoothing it over my belly. Meilyr's head was hunched to one side, his back and part of his face blackened.

Pencarn looked at me. 'What was he trying to say?'

I noticed his eyes switching slightly as he looked from my one eye to the other as if he expected to see something more there than his own reflection.

## 19

I thought of that tonight when I saw him at supper here, with that young man helping him. And another time I thought of him, and Meilyr, after the the cave, by the tree, when I looked into eyes as into some half lit significant place and saw nothing but my own ghost.

Twice he'd come to me and asked for help and I hadn't known it.

'Remember Meilyr's story that day on the riverbank?' he'd said. I've known those places where there's no. We'd stood together among the tumbled ruin of smoking thatch and known something of them together, those places, known all that unweaving, and when he turned to me I didn't recognize it, had nothing but a blank eye to turn to him. The world is either miraculous or hellish. Pencarn knew that with a bewilderment more intelligent than mine, and still god allows us so little freedom that he was caught in the tide of someone else's whim and there's no choice left to him now but to dribble at the table with his helper and play the saint.

The itch in the bag, I'd thought — and that was, perhaps, partly it, but not all, not even a major part. That's to take it in the wrong sense, to think in parts like that. Pencarn — forgive the irony — saw it a different way. To him there was the true church, or the possibility of it, I mean, like the plait of roots woven on the woodland floor, and Cristin. And in him there I saw myself when he stood and looked for some sign in me. A brighter version of my younger self. And 'Find a girl tonight' I'd said that first time, missing the point and hurting myself in the miss.

I'm an optimist perhaps, to think he'd have played the saint even if he'd had a choice. If I'd seen that then, that possibility in him, I might have found him some answer and turned the world a different way. I never knew I had any power till the time for using it was gone.

As it was, I was at the ceremony that started Pencarn's canonization. Hywel robed for the rites in the shit cathedral with his acolytes.

I knew Pencarn planned to marry. We'd talked about it. I'd agreed to be his messenger if the need arose. It's the usual arrangement. I was with him at his home when Hywel's messenger came to call him to Caerllion.

'Do we go?' he said to me.

I didn't know how to react to my inclusion in the invitation so treated it as if it was expected.

'Excuses would offend him' I said. 'He's your uncle's son.'

There was long quiet and he looked at me.

This was in daylight, a long time, perhaps a year, after Meilyr's death. Pencarn sat near the open door and the splay of sunlight made a gold foam of his thinning hair. The quietness turned into silence and though there was sun the silence darkened around him, loosened the hold of light and shape on things.

## 20

We travelled to Caerllion unaccompanied. Pencarn frequently did this. He seemed to enjoy travelling alone.

I expected the fortress, when we arrived, to be well defended as usual, but the beili was very quiet. There was only one man on the gate, which was open. Meilyr's house stood empty outside. In the yard a few women worked at their querns and the door of the forge stood open, though there was no smoke. It was mild and dry, the right time for sitting and chatting if there was no work.

One of Hywel's new archers appeared carrying a jug and saw us. He smiled at Pencarn and glanced at me before going to announce our arrival. Hywel came to the door of the hall that stands in the beili — not the one on the mound — and raised his hands, bid us god's welcome. He was wearing one of those padded shirts the French wear under their mail, though he hadn't at that time taken to wearing stockings and shoes. He looked a second time when he noticed me, then gestured us into the hall.

'It's very peaceful here' Pencarn said as we passed. He put his sword and I put my spear against the jamb as we went in.

'Griffri' Hywel said. 'I thought you were at home. Yes. Isn't it?' — turning to Pencarn and smiling but not looking him in the face — 'My father's gone to the old court. Have you come from there, Griff? He's gone with my mother and most of the teulu to hear suits and collect dues.'

'No' I said, about to explain my singing for Pencarn. But Hywel went on.

'They went yesterday. My messenger came with them part of the way. Yes.' He paused and looked at me. 'I'm glad you came, Griffri' he said.

I felt that he would say more, but he didn't. He walked with us into the hall. Inside there were only a few stools, a small, smoky fire recently lit, some blocks of firewood stacked. There were no rushes on the floor. This is a building the French made during their occupation and we had fought for it together. Now Pencarn and I stood like strangers in Hywel's silence. We exchanged a look while the prince's — sorry — lord's son stood in thought. Not that this was anything new. You know he's not a great talker.

We all sat on the stools and for moments nothing was said. Pencarn and I grew a bit uncomfortable but Hywel seemed not to notice. The man who'd held the jug stood in the doorway, his hand resting on the top of a strung bow. His thumb flicked noiselessly at the string.

At last Hywel looked up at us, seemed, as it were, to wake, and smiled startingly.

'A novel kind of harp' I said, looking for any words.

Hywel looked uncertain and I nodded to his archer, the nervy moving of the thumb against the cord. Hywel saw and smiled afresh, rubbed his palm on the padded shirt where it covered his thigh.

'A novel kind of harp to set before visitors' I said.

But he found no words.

'The best sort' Pencarn said, to fill the gap.

Hywel thought — visibly thought, if you can understand that — and then looked at Pencarn without smiling.

'Yes' he said at last. 'The best sort. Very good.' There was a moment that allowed me to notice the smokedrift, feel its sting. 'I'm sorry' he said. 'I'm not being a good host am I? I'll. I'll.' He waved to his onestring harpist. 'Andras. Bring the entertainment we've prepared for our guest.'

Andras pushed himself off the jamb and walked away.

Hywel turned to me and said again, 'I'm glad you've come. For a couple of reasons. You helped me to decide to call my cousin today, sort of. Do you remember? After old Morgan was killed. After you'd been ill. The story you told up in the old hall.'

Story. A story is a thing with cauldrons of regeneration and bees that whisper dreams to sleeping queens. I don't know if I fingered the scar on my neck. How old could he have been? He keeps memory better than any of us, behind his blank eyes. There was no obliging candle to cast shadows on his forehead.

He looked to the small fire, to the door, to Pencarn and stared steadily, not as people look when their mind's on something else, but as if concentrating.

I should have realized. It seemed so obvious when it happened. Anybody watching would have guessed. I can hardly think how I must have looked or what I said when it came.

Hywel glanced up and Andras was back and other men with him. Four or perhaps five. Some of the other archers and young Morgan ap Seisyll. They dragged Pencarn to one of the posts and there was the sound of his shouting and the controlled voices of the others giving instructions to one another. Perhaps I shouted. I don't know. I got to my feet. Very slowly, I thought, though I was trying to move fast. Hands held my elbows. A voice said, 'No' close to my ear and I don't know if I recognized then that it was Rhun, but I didn't struggle.

His back — Owain Pencarn's back — thumped against the post and his arms were pulled behind and hands came from behind the post and caught his ears, his thinning hair and the head made a cracking noise against the wood.

'What have I done?' he said.

But Hywel didn't feel obliged to explain. He held his knife close to the head, which tried to flail away, and the point followed all the movements. When Pencarn was buckled on his knees and fairly still, Hywel dug out the first eye. I heard the prince's son say before the blade entered, 'Keep still or it'll kill you.' Before the screech could come with the second gouging Morgan ap Seisyll passed a length of rope between Pencarn's teeth and this was held tight round the post.

There was silence except for Pencarn's gagged screaming, and Hywel, putting the blade in again, shouted — or, no, said loudly — 'For my brother.'

People, the women from their querns and the children, had gathered at the doorway and a child's voice outside was shouting the news.

Hywel moved away and Pencarn was kicked onto his side. Immediately Hywel ordered him to be seized again and the grip on my elbows was relaxed. Pencarn, crying to god, lay curled, and only started to struggle again when he realized what was happening. He was kicked and hit first this way then that. At last they got him spreadeagled face downward over a large block and tore the clothes off his back. Rhun and his servant came to him with tongs and a sharp blade, and that was how they gelded him.

All the men clamping him were bucked a little but his reflex was quickly smothered. The rope was gone from his mouth. He was shouting 'White Jesus' and 'Mother of god'. This erupted into a pigsqueal and then there were the same words, hardly recognizable in an unrecognizable voice.

The men were moving away, some not looking at their work, others watching without expression as the prince's foster son shifted onto his side in the bloodsquirt.

'Give him the best attention' Hywel said. 'Feed the mess to the dogs.'

He turned and almost walked into me.

I couldn't speak. I don't know how I must have looked.

'Look after him' he said to me, was about to pass but paused and said, 'You never did understand politics, Griffri.'

He walked a little selfconsciously as people watched him and got out of his path. At the door he stopped and picked up Pencarn's sword. His eyes moved in the shape of a cross as he considered it. He looked from it to us and his eyes deadened before he carried it away.

## 21

I've had many conversations with him about all this.

'Why?' I say, in a bare hall before a feast is prepared.

He stands at a large window, looking, perhaps, towards a river rolling on a plain.

'Because a madman told me to fear nothing once' he says. He looks to me. 'Because the hawk should be kept in the barn when there's a fire in the hall to save its eyes. Because you told me of your captivity in the hands of a great dwarf. Because in every age, they say, the king sets the trend. Because my brother's dead. Because Pencarn sent messengers to find a wife.'

He talks a long time, eloquently, recites a thousand proverbs, balances his sentences artfully, modulates his voice to echo in the timbered belly of the hall, pauses, poises to make the silence between words speak, talks of his father.

'He's like the cliff his court's built on' he says. 'A crag. A buttress. The earth under our feet. Our base, our foundation; the hawk, the wolf, the dragon, the oak door of Gwynllwg, timber weathered sapless and rocklike, a very siege engine, the wall of his people, the hero of Coed Grwyne, of Bryn Buga, the subduer, through his might and his power, of castles, the grandson of a king of the true line of Tewdrig Cleftskull. And he's old.'

He smiles and his eyes are dark as the light spills around him from the big window. Sometimes the old lawyer's there and their voices mix, make one voice.

'You see, what interests me is to consolidate our position, to achieve security. To be safe. To. Be. Safe.'

Three syllables each stressed like that, an insistent knocking at the door.

That's my yearning for nice irony, though it was ironic enough even without the saying.

'Safe' I say, all scorn, and the timbered belly melts from the very ridge as if it had been snow, shrinks and peels and runs back off itself, all the sapless, smoky rafters withering, collapsing like an empty sack, straws of thatch falling like spent arrows, and his hands raise, a weak gesture from the elbows, his shoulders hunch and his face is terror and astonishment as the hall unfolds, unweaves itself and runs away into the earth, and in ordinary daylight he's diminished, standing shrunk in the globe of sky, his upholstered shirt gone to a rag, and a light lift of wind rocks him as it ruffles wheat growing by the river.

'Safe' I say again, and his face flows too, half of it melts and droops, sets again like cooled wax. He shimmers, distorts, as the world does on a day of glaring heat, reddens, and I spread my arms and smile and he withers, crumples like a fallen sheet, turns to nothing on the riverbank.


## 22

He's a great prince — sorry — lord, and I take no pleasure in telling you that it was two days later, after I'd taken Pencarn away —

I should say his eyes, or rather the sockets, were poulticed and his torn purse sealed with pitch. Rhun let me take a handcart to get him from there and that was how I took him home most of the way. After that we took him to Llandâf where the bishop sheltered him and sent a letter to Iorwerth condemning his son's action, but worded, I understand, purely in the cold formality of admonition, without force of sentiment or real sense of hurt. Pencarn was very ill a while and almost died.

— But I was saying, it was only two days later, after I'd taken him away — it gives me no pleasure to tell you this, none at all — that the French attacked and captured Caerllion from the prince's son.

It was less than two years after the war in which we'd liberated it. The bishop himself — and these aren't my thoughts but his, though it was commonly believed through the whole country — he himself said that it was god's judgement on Hywel. Mind, it was convenient to see it that way so that, god having quickly rebuked the prince's son, no one needed to feel obliged to call for other punishments. Still, god's punishments are strangely approximate and it was a pity for those old women and a few children and one or two of the lame who'd survived wounding at the great siege, who, unlike Hywel and his men, didn't manage to get away to the old court.

Even so, the whole affair enraged people all across the south, as you must know. Iorwerth, I'm told, though I wasn't there at the time, told Hywel in public that god had judged the son by punishing the father. It was Toothless described this to me. Iorwerth had looked straight at his son and Hywel averted his face. 'But he looked up' Toothless said, 'he looked up again and straight in his father's eye and Hywel started to open his mouth as if he'd speak but he never said anything and it was Iorwerth who looked away in the end. And then the prince came back to his own greatness and told all the people that we must be ready for another war and he sent messengers into Afan and Senghenydd and Uwchcoed and even to Aberteifi.'

Toothless doesn't speak much. You know him. He's almost shy when he speaks to you alone, even now in his old age, when men are so awash with half controlled memories that they tell you stories without any prompting. He'll sit and say nothing. Yet, he spoke words that churned all the ocean for me once. I'll come to that.

Even then, as he told me about the prince and his son quietly and with few words, I could see them, the faces half turning away. Pencarn was with us, listening. His head moved to face Toothless when he came to the rebuke. He said nothing but held his head that way a long time as if he expected more.

# 23

It was then the princes of the south started to gather. They joined behind Iorwerth as they had two years before, expecting, I suppose, the same quick victory and payment. Seisyll came from Gwent Uwchcoed and some of his men too, though the French by then wanted to kill him for killing a kinsman of Arglwydd Brycheiniog. He'd offered galanas, but you know how little grasp the French have of law. So they were hunting him then.

Yes. Now you lean forward. It's coming. I promised I'd be quicker this time.

Seisyll then was in what you might, if you were a bishop, call the flower of his days. Not young, but full of strength and wisdom in spite of his hardships, or because of them. His curly hair was greying. He and his men — among them his son Geffrei, who'd been in Gwladus's womb when I qualified as a poet at Seisyll's court, and his penteulu Ieuan — impressed all the court with their modesty and calmness. When men in Iorwerth's teulu made the inevitable jokes about Pencarn, Seisyll didn't laugh, even though his own son Morgan, Geffrei's halfbrother, had been one of the mutilators.

He and Ieuan visited Pencarn one day, quietly. I sang for them — the song to god that Seisyll liked, though no one concentrated on the song.

'You've been wronged' Seisyll said to Pencarn afterwards. It wasn't merely stating the obvious. Declaring sympathy, for a great man, can be dangerous. 'I know what it's like to lose a patrimony.'

And after, Seisyll said to me, 'If it was before me for judgement there'd be full payment. Six cows for each eye and the same for each testicle. This isn't my country.'

You see the fairness of the man. Though I think Hywel might still have thought such an arrangement a bargain.

When foreign messengers came to the court Seisyll and Ieuan went away. Once this Ieuan stayed and pretended to be my brother when a messenger came from the bishop. He'd been in Brewys's prison with Seisyll and was with him at the killing of Brewys's kinsman.

'We will go back and be accepted' he said to me. 'By strength, or by the king's friendship with Arglwydd Rhys. As sure as we'll reinhabit Britain one day.'

He looked straight at me then. He was a very thin man without much moustache. Like a lot of good soldiers he was nothing to look at, though he kept his hair trimmed properly and his teeth clean.

I thought of the moon and a planet and an owl in the trees. Poets shall judge who is of heart. The keeper of memory meaded to forget-fulness. *Do you think we'll ever*.

He stared, Ieuan, signalling he'd be examined to his core, to the roots of his eyes, and every part of him affirmed his certainty. He wore no armour, carried only a small knife. Only the sick need great shells around themselves. His eyes were blue as air. *Do you think we'll We. We will go back.*

Where was I?

Yes. In fact, Seisyll's people around his court went more or less free then, I understand. There was chafing at the edges but his people had their own core where the prince and his men were relatively safe. And if it'd come to another war to win back what we'd lost by negligence, then Seisyll would have openly challenged Brewys in Gwent Uwch-coed.

Well, you know it never came to that. Rhys's justiciarship proved itself worth something. You know about his summer meeting with the king. Rhys himself came to us and you know all those princes rode with him, all the ones who'd gathered behind Iorwerth to threaten as big a war as when old Ricert ap Gilbert was killed years and years ago. When the hay was gathered and war was in its season, Rhys led them all to meet the king, about the end of July, on the feast of Iago'r Apostol, I think, in the council at Caerloyw. You know all that. I've never seen so many scrolls and seals and woven chains.

I didn't go. Iorwerth left Hywel at the old court and told me to stay with Pencarn. I was glad to be with my family a little —

Look, I won't waste time on this. I should delay and tease you on, but life isn't a story, any more than it's a list. I have trouble applying solid technique to real matters.

I don't know what magic Rhys worked on the king but — you know — the castle was restored to us. One of Lleucu's sons who went as a servant to old Toothless told me how the English peeped from their

houses in Caerloyw at our people and stared at our clothes and hair-
cuts, kept their children inside. And that's as much as I learned about
diplomacy — that and Ieuan — who went too, and openly — telling
me about the bowing and endless spouting of Latin courtesies and
gorgeous acolytes shimmering like fish behind the paunchy priestkil-
ler, and then he shook his head and stared into the rushes and said,
'Bloody rubbish.'

Some people said that the king was getting old and tired, others
that he was wise.

Anyway, before the first leaf fell, Hywel walked through the great
gate at Caerllion, wearing a sword with a damaged hilt.


## 24

To the roots of his eyes.

Hywel will look away when you look at him, and even if he does re-
turn your look he's blankeyed, filmed over as people are sometimes
in death.

Ieuan that time, that time of affirming, stays in my mind an uncon-
trolled memory, as if you could look into the backs of his eyes, as if
they were shaped inwards like dishes.

I came to be with him, Ieuan — and Seisyll and Geffrei that Christ-
mas on Iorwerth's instructions. Iorwerth had heard that Seisyll was
to be respected by the French. Their way of saying it was that he
wasn't to be 'punished'. A messenger came from Randwlff de Poyr
speaking for the king to tell us this and went on to Abergafenni itself
with the news.

Our restoration to Caerllion the second time had been a subdued
affair. The silence between Hywel and his father made a darkness in
the court and the first feast and the singing were strained. It was then,
I think, Iorwerth started to drag one foot, the same side as the fallen
side of his face. The quiet of winter became silence and had a strange
appropriateness. I was relieved not to be going home, where Pencarn
was lodged with my family. Cristin asked me once if he was going to
stay with us for good. We'd all thought for a while that he was dying

of his wounds but Lleucu's daughters healed him with herbs and ointments and he drank water only from Cadog's spring. But his darkness touched my people worse than the dark at Caerllion. His presence was like grief and I couldn't bear the innocent cruelty of the children towards him.

Out of those closed places, then, I escaped.

I was singing to Iorwerth on a quiet evening and he sat not listening, rubbing one side of his face and picking at some invisible splinter on the board in front of him.

Something happened. I saw my hands on the strings, heard a stick crack in the fire, and for a moment there were no words. The indifference of the few people there intruded into the song and the hands plucked at a dissonance.

Hywel, who sat with Morgan ap Seisyll and some of his men, glanced up and made a small movement of the head. Some spirit in me pushed my fingers to the right chord and I found the word I'd, for the first time since I'd qualified as a poet, forgotten. I sang to hold out the silence, but it was always still there.

Later Iorwerth came to me and told me to take the message on to Seisyll, though the king's messenger had already gone.

I went home first, to Cristin, and she said nothing but looked at Pencarn and then at the floor. I would have taken my eldest son to sing with me. Perhaps she remembered my stories of myself and Gwrgant. Anyway, that she refused. She wanted him to help her, she said, and though I felt he was of an age to come with me I didn't argue, thank god.

## 25

This is how it was.

I travelled with Seisyll ap Dyfnwal and Ieuan ap Seisyll ap Rhiryd and Geffrei the prince's son and all of Seisyll's chief men to Brewys's castle at Abergafenni to be received and recognized, accepted as men not outside the king's law, and Seisyll took all this as a partial restitution of his — our — dignity. The Frenchman was acknowledging that he'd have to treat with a prince at least on equal terms. So, after long negotiations, Seisyll was buoyant, armed with the expectation of old hurts being healed and with the fact that he owed his allegiance to his great brotherinlaw whom the bounteous king loved above even his own lords and through whose intercession the same bounteous king had restored my master, Seisyll's kinsman, to his own country. So Seisyll saw a time when his father's country would be restored to him and we could be ourselves again.

All shit.

In a story there'd be only the event but in life every moment has its particularities. It was mild. One of those December days that fake spring. Overcast but not raining, the great river full and turbulent, red with the mud of that country. I remember young Geffrei, walking ahead of me, carrying a yellowshafted spear. He was the only one of us who wore shoes. I felt the harshness of the stony places hurt my feet as we approached the castle. From the west it's a high wooden place, the palisade at the top of a high, steep bank.

We were hailed like old friends when we approached the gate and one of the slaves who served there spoke Welsh and greeted us in the right way, extending his arms and calling god's welcome on us. He had bad teeth, I noticed, and no hair at the top of his forehead. I knew, or thought I knew, that this was merely making us something like the same under the one king who butchered bishops, whose people had ruined Ireland, the only free country left in the world. I knew, or thought I knew, that the upshot would be for Geffrei to grow a French beard and chain himself up in his own uncertainties. Even so, the moment had elation in it, like that first restoring of Caerllion after the war. The triumphal strutting. And my best cloak on me that had been Seisyll's gift years before, though the shoulders under it weren't so square by that time. And past the curious foreigners who lived in the town and in through the gate to the familiar, the awful place. Another mound. Another hall. Another pen of animals waiting.

Brewys waited to greet us alongside Randwlff, still in his dark and scalloped robe. Brewys's wife, the witch Matil, wasn't there, nor their children.

I don't remember ever having seen Brewys before this. He was — is — a tall man, young then, thin, though with the incipient paunch common to his people. He was wearing a long white garment tied at

*221*

the waist. It was absolutely plain and he wore no cloak, though I could see at the neck that under his shift he wore one of those padded vests.

One by one the dignitaries were introduced to him by Seisyll's translator — a Cistercian come to think of it, a young man with skill in languages who knew both French and Latin almost as well as Welsh. Brewys glanced each of us up and down as we came to him, particularly at our feet. They think it's odd for an uchelwr not to wear shoes. He looked twice at Geffrei's feet but his expression didn't change.

When I came in front of him I saw a thin young face, corpsepale, with palish brown hair. He clasped his hands, hand to wrist, before him and his fingers were pale and thin, like the bones of a fish. Though he hunted and was a soldier these trades seemed to have made no mark on him. His hair was long and parted in the centre, his moustache scarcely there at all. The beard was a light down, an elongated smudge that made his face even longer and thinner. He looked from my feet to my face. The eyes were dead in his head and rather sunken. I thought that he needed sleep. I noticed his eyes taking in the bagged harp on my shoulder and he looked to the monk, who spoke to him in French. I heard my name and Iorwerth's in all the barking and Brewys looked at me again.

'Iorwes?'

The monk spoke again. The lord unhooked the hand that clasped the wrist, nodded and gestured.

'What will you sing?' the monk said to me.

'A song to god' I said. 'Seisyll's favourite.' I remembered the absurd formalities and added, 'No less a one needs praise on such a great day.'

The monk translated. Brewys nodded like a bishop pretending interest in some minor suit and I thought he almost smiled. But he looked straight at me again and there was no smile.

There were horses nearby. I remember their snorting. When I looked round I saw a groom tending to one of them, looking at us curiously. Though I'd thought it was mild, the horse's breath formed on the air.

It would be suitable to a story to have us now enter the escaping-tower on the mound, but we didn't. We were shown into a long hall in the beili. Brewys and Randwlff watched us as we stacked our spears and bows against the jamb on our way in.

The room was smoky with some green stuff just thrown on the fire and in the haze I could see the long tables.

'Where are the cloths?' Geffrei said.

It was odd that the boards had no cloths.

'Perhaps the spirit of compromise is going further than we thought' I said. 'They've started copying us.'

I gave my harp to Ieuan so that he could present it to me in the usual way for the song and when we'd sat each in his place according to rank, Seisyll and Brewys each spoke. There'd been weeks of messengers shuttling between these two weaving the fabric of this moment. Now it was here, it was stilted, as if none of us knew quite what we intended.

I thought suddenly of old Morgan speaking one Christmas of the possibilities of peace. Smoke and darkness in the silences. To sing in this. *King of the world deliverer of men.* I went over my lines, that were turning into mere words in my head, like senseless pebbles in a sack. *King of all princes, Christ's origin.* Seisyll was speaking. 'Before god I acknowledge fealty, through the Arglwydd Rhys, to his maj et cetera blah' and the monk bending to Brewys and Randwlff, translating, the murmur of his voice, a constructed growling, an undercurrent, a dissonance with Seisyll's talking. *I sang for a prince and he gave me mead* 'and henceforward' *Forgiver of all men who know but the asking.* Pebbles in a sack. Somebody speaking when you're drunk. A feeling there's meaning but no understanding. You know that? A face close to yours speaking urgently, but no sense. Listen, now. Listen to the words. The fish in the lakes in Gwynedd. The translator making discords. *I sang for a lord* chunkataplunk *and he gave me* plunkatathunk *and he gave me and he gave me* senseless pebbles in a sack. Brewys's eyes on me. I remember him watching me as Seisyll spoke. *King of the world, deliverer of all men* 'our future' *gave me bolts of silk. Bolts of silk.* Yes. Unweaving. I saw through the smoke the hall unweave itself, the straws of thatch raining and Brewys rising in his white gown with his arms spread. The ridge of the rooftree like his parted hair. Pale skin like fishbone. *I sang for a lord and he gave me a fishbone.* Barking. *Only one lord is the giver of all things.* The articulated barking and then the monk hailing us with his translation. *Only one lord is the giver of fishbone.* 'My friends, we, the people of this place' *I've garnered sins in sport and in battle* 'we must achieve a new sense of reality' chunkataplunk *I've praised frail lords in frailer singing* plunkata 'and I am optimistic that we shall discover very shortly' thunk plunkata *easier pebble the silk fish who bolt them* 'where the real energy and commitment that will determine' thunk *Easier praising the great lord who made them*. Yes. Plunkatathunk. 'the future governance of our region' *Forgiver of all men who know but the asking* 'may truly be said to reside.' *Forgiver of all men who know but.*

And then Ieuan pulling at my sleeve. Close faces speaking urgently but no sense coming from them. Ieuan close and the monk.

Gwrgant had told me of this fear that paralyses half a man and told me there's nothing to do but hold on and survive it. I'd stopped for Iorwerth, forgotten the words, and he'd sent me away.

'Now' Ieuan said, offering me the harp.

'He's called for you' the monk said. 'Go slow. He wants me to translate. Almighty Christ, I hope it's simple, poet. Is it?'

'I don't know.'

'Christ's nails. Go slow. Nice and clear now.'

I was stumbling to the hearth and my harp was in my hands. Why was there no food? And there'd been no prayer. I was the prayer. My song. My fingers were thick and strange, fleshy stalks unrelated to me. No delicate boniness. Frail fish in frailer singing. I had the sensation that I was standing on a steep slope so that all my weight was thrown one way if I was to keep my feet. So I hunched one shoulder and leant against the imagined slope. Brewys looked, through the static smokehaze, appallingly young, and I thought that to him I was an old man, greyed, with a full moustache, stooped and skewed under an old cloak that had been magnificent.

So I stood until from somewhere a stool appeared and I was able to get my harp in position and begin work.

As the fleshy stalks assembled themselves on the strings I saw Brewys lean towards Randwlff as they whispered. The waxy wood of the king's man's face showed surprise at something Brewys said.

Hold on and survive it. I'd forgotten the words and Iorwerth had sent me away. Just remember the words.

The monk leant forward to Brewys as I started, ready to translate.

> King of the world, deliverer of men
> I ask you now for absolution

My fingers were moving to the right places unwilled and I listened to my voice. It was too slow. Wait. That was what he wanted. Slow. The growl of translation bubbled under the song. How could the growling be anything? In Brewys's eyes I couldn't distinguish between the pupil and the iris. This thin slow voice was me. I listened and the words were opaque sounds, pebbles in a sack. The two voices, one thin and rhythmic the other rumbling and rhythmless and the plinking of the harp jangled. I felt that I was acting my part, as if this was how it should sound and look, the posture and the flourish of hands, a display for baffled but polite foreigners. To god supposedly, but arselicking at its most advanced.

I've praised frail lords in frailer singing

Pretending honesty about ourselves to soap a couple of important men. Then

Forgiver of all men who know but the fishbone

The consternation in the monk's face, any other time, would have been funny. His mouth shut and he stared at me. I merely played a few phrases without words and redid the line

Forgiver of all men who know but the asking

Briefly relief passed in his face and he resumed the growling. Brewys's eyes then seemed to harden. He stared as if from miles away, drowned in the smoke. He murmured to Randwlff who rose and went to the door, talked with a servant.

The growl and the thin sounds. And from outside, horses snorting and stamping and the hoofbeats going.

Seisyll loved that song for its brevity. It was longer than usual that day. They did it as soon as I'd finished.

Instead of the poem hanging in the air around us there was smoke and puzzlement. To me anyway. To Brewys, somehow, I suppose it'd spoken. Believe me, monk, this is how it was and I think the song must have spoken to him. The eyes that hardened spoke back, acknowledged some contact.

I don't know where the men in mail came from. Suddenly they were there, standing close at the backs of the seated men. I saw Brewys, his eyes dull again, give a nod, the slightest nod, hardly a movement. I don't know if that was before they came or not. There was the sense of knowing what was happening but that gap in which you observe the slowness of your own reactions. The soldiers with rehearsed accuracy murdered all the Welsh. Some of them, us, had time to stand and there was shouting, the idiotically banal shouting of things like 'Don't kill me.' Few people manage to be original at such times. I saw Geffrei standing, struggling, held by two men, and the third, because of this, botching his job with the knife so that the boy took a long time to die. Randwlff and Brewys were gone from their places and they carried swords, Randwlff an axe too. I was pressing to the floor and through the tumbled stools and boards I saw Ieuan curled with his arms doubled over his head and two men heaving swords and axes hacked at him. Clean sharp gashes opened in the knuckles of his back. I was kicked and buffeted and rolled and I saw two ironheads over me. They were very young. I could see how young and hairless they were in spite of the haze, the broad flanges covering their noses. I was hit and blood was coming from my mouth. They kicked me and dragged me and I slithered on some wetness on the floor. The rooftree, noise, slid over and I was dragged to my feet. Impatient voices were shouting at me. They hit me around the head and at last I realized they were only slapping me. When I saw that, I lowered my hands. They each took an arm. Seisyll I mean. I saw Seisyll. A man took each of his arms and he was slammed face down on the board, arms spread like this, and another pulled at his hair so that he was stretched, his face to the wood, and there was an axe. It split the back of his neck, though not right through and I saw it rise again.

All that was very quick. I was pushed, dragged, hit out of the hall, never saw it fall the second time.

Outside, clean air hurt my throat with its coldness. The two young men were pulling at my arms, not spreadeagling me, just shaking me. There was laughter and singing. The other soldiers in the hall were singing. Some came out, wiping blades on the December grass. Some — three — came towards us with smirched weapons and one of them argued with the men who held my arms, gesturing to me. One of the men who held me spoke angrily. I heard the name Gwilym.

Then the badtoothed slave was in front of me and talking. His face was close and he smiled but at first I couldn't catch his words.

Over his shoulder I saw horses were being saddled, some of the mailed men getting ready to mount. There'd been a burst of hoofbeats. One party had already gone out. Laughing. He laughed at me. The horses moved. Or no. I was moved, being dragged again, the slave keeping pace with me.

'You lucky old shitsmasher' he said.

My cloak was torn from me. An arm was milling. One of them milled his free hand to wrap my cloak around his forearm.

'Lucky.'

My tunic was torn too and hands searched me, but I had nothing. 'Lucky. Look, don't shake like that. Look at your poor legs. Tell them not to do that. God loves your legs and your arse and your ballocks. And your hide. There. He spares you, see. The lord spares you. Shows himself as generous as any Welshman. Good for him. You must have impressed him.'

We were at the outer wall on its south western side, above where the cleared plain was to the river and a piece of the wall was opening. A man holding the gate open.

'You can sing another one to god tonight and every night. I was going to say you could write it down'

— I was held in the jaw of the gate, felt them bracing to push me out —'but I can see you've already done that on your legs. Unusual shade of brown ink that.'

And I was out, sliding and tumbling down the near vertical bank, and one of the soldiers jumped down after me, laughing and elated. He hit me across the buttocks with the flat of his sword and he raised it again but the others shouted to him and he stopped.

I went on tumbling till I reached the plain and ran away.

## 26

Believe me.

Oppressors can oppress the more by being merciful on a whim. What's produced is a destroying sense of release and complicity. How many times have I told this story now? So that I can't remember whether I remember the event or remember the remembering.

I ran across the treeless plain. There are the rotting bases of the huge trees they felled there to make killing grounds outside the castle wall. I stumbled on them and kept running, reached the riverbank and didn't stop, just kicked out into the rolling red of it. My breath went with the shock of cold but I think I went on making the movements of running even as I turned on the surface of the water. I couldn't have been in long or I would have drowned. The current snatched me away like a leaf and I had no control over where I went. Then I was rammed into the thin trunks of a tree that normally would have been on dry land, and I was wading, running again, on dead leaves. Through trees across the river, I watched the castle as I ran. Above the high splintery stockade blunt dark shapes were swaying on poles.

I ran aimlessly until exhaustion hit me to the ground. I lay listening to my own breath heaving, knew the cold numbing my arms and legs. Still, to lie there looking at the lead sky was miraculous. After a long time I felt I woke, though I don't think I'd been asleep, realized that I'd lain just being, without any thought.

There was noise. Hooves somewhere. I was up and ran again, then walked when I heard no more, but looked around me all the time, sometimes turned full circle on my heels as I walked, approached the turning backs of the larger trees nervously. At every slight noise I started. A blackbird in the brambles could make me run. I hid and walked and hid and walked.

Whether or not I deliberately made for Seisyll's court I don't know. At last I was walking through the thick wood on the shoulder of land above the great river and at my left hand fading up into the grey of low cloud were the cliffs I'd looked at when I'd first sung the song to god for Seisyll. Smoke.

Presently I came to the first clearing and the first house of Seisyll's free people.

I stayed in the fringes of the woodland. The air was smoky and the roof of the small house was burnt, though most of its walls were standing. Quite near me, an old woman was huddled down against a tree. I hailed her but, though she must have heard me, she didn't move. I approached and touched her shoulder and she started, made a short breathy scream, repeated and repeated, and held her hands up stiff like this beside her face. She scrambled, ran out into the clearing towards a row of bundles on the ground near her ruined house, then turned and ran back towards me, saw me, veered in panic into the trees to my left.

Suddenly I saw myself, my face and body bruised, blood around my mouth, my tunic ripped and sodden so that I was almost naked, corpsewhite with cold.

I ran after her calling that it was all right. When I caught her she went on screaming a long time while I shook her and shouted who I was. At last tiredness made us quiet and we crumpled gasping among the wet leaves.

While we drew breath I looked at her again. She wasn't so old as I'd thought at first. Though her hair — her wife's headdress had come away — though her hair was grizzled mostly, it was streaked reddish and had been lovely. When she looked at me now I saw recognition come to her, a shocked recognition through my bruises.

I heard a crackling from far away. Fire. And shouting and hooves again. It was coming dark but I could see the smoke, three bowshots westward, where Seisyll's court stood in the trees.

'I know you' she said.

When it grew dark we'd perhaps see the glare. But it couldn't last long. The world was too wintersodden for good burning. Only the undersides of thatch would take properly.

'How long ago?' I said.

She said nothing. Couldn't speak of what had happened to her. Tumbles of smoking thatch in the gloom and the row of bundles near it. I guessed from their shapes and sizes. Her sister. Her husband. A grown up daughter. And others. Smaller ones. Stiffarmed and dead as logs.

229

She looked too and I saw the wave break on her, her mouth and her eyes crumpling into slits, and incoherent prayer and screaming and her head folding down into the leaves. There was fire in the distance and cold that made me shake so hard I couldn't get to my feet. You'd see this as a picture of hell. I felt nothing so theological as that. I saw the knuckles of the woman's spine showing through her clothes where she hutched down and I saw the blades chop clean notches in Ieuan's back, the smeared axe raised from the board and I felt I'd choke with a sense of the meanness of things. The wave broke on me too.

How long we both snivelled I don't know. We clung together with strange ferocity as if we tried to make our bodies interpenetrate. She was firm and strong, though of small build. Certainly younger than I'd first thought. When I kissed her her breath was sweet and her teeth strong. There were aches and hurts and I tongued my teeth and found that one of them was gone, tensed my belly muscles. After we stopped crying we pulsed against one another like that a long time.

I was cold and still shuddering. At some time she pulled herself away from me. It wasn't quite dark. She went to the clearing and I half raised myself to watch.

She gathered things, had a sack. I saw her approach the bundles, crouch looking at them, still as deer can stand. Then she moved again, bent and worked at one of the bundles.

The thing lolled and sagged as its clothes were removed.

She came back to me, breathing heavily.

'Come on' she said. 'They'll come back. I know a place.'

She threw a blanket on me and handed me faggots of wood tied together.

I half got up.

'The night' I said. 'It'll be dark.'

She looked surprised a moment. 'What?' she said. 'No. It's morning. You slept. Come on.'

## 27

Listen. I've never told anybody this part of my story before. There'll be no intervening of other tellings.

I followed her shouldered sack into the trees. Her head was covered again and her body pulling one way to balance her burden. I felt better for the blanket and when we stopped to rest and she took some cheese from the sack I ate it all. She took nothing herself.

We walked again a long time. I think I talked. Told her.

At last we came to a treechoked valley. Somewhere far to our left must have been Brewys's castle. I looked for Pen y Fal but the air was thick with drizzle. Below us and to our right this steep valley stetched. There were massed bare trees and the valley steepening into a rocky gorge further along, the whole going uphill from left to right into a massif that climbed into cloud.

The old woman looked at me, asked me if I was all right. I think I nodded.

'A journey's further if you haven't travelled it before' she said, and we walked on. 'Will they come after you?'

'I don't know.'

Pause.

'Why did they let you go?'

'They let me. I don't know why.'

'You must go to the princes. Tell —'

She turned and looked at me as she said that and something made her stop. She looked down and walked on.

'There's a cave down here' she said. 'If you have to hide.'

We slid over leaves and split rock to the belly of the gorge. There was a narrow river, fast and clear, forcing among the stones, and constant spray in the air. It was like dusk in the narrow place under the cloud.

We crossed the little river on stepping stones and followed its course upward towards the mountains, so that the water was on our right. There was a place of cliffs that overhung the water. She went ahead along a ledge under these rocks and turned a corner out of sight.

There was the onrush of water and the huge black legs of trees above on the cliffs. I almost shouted and rushed to catch her up, scrambled round the rock corner, and she wasn't there.

I looked round a moment then pressed my back against the rock, looked up the cracked face of the gorge. Yellow grassclumps oozed droplets of water and there were the black legs and jointed nets of twigs across the clouds. There was nothing but trees extending up and away from me. High up somewhere near the moors, deer. Closer, the boar, the wolf. Only that and the river running past me to the great river that swirled by Brewys's fortress where blunt shapes rotted on poles along the palisade. Where I should have been.

I stared down at the boiling white water. It roared louder and I stared and stared. And when I looked from it to the rocks, they melted and flowed, stretched and eddied and distended like the boil of water and then when I almost called out, they began to flow back, to relock themselves in their original forms. Then I heard the rock speak.

'Poet.'

And the old woman's head came out of the face of the rocks.

'Here' she said. 'Poet.'

She came out of the tight folds of stone where the cavemouth was hidden and gestured me forward.

The roar wasn't so loud and all the rocks were refixed. Still, it was hard to follow her when she went back into the cave. I touched the rock where I'd seen it soften and churn but it felt only like rock and I followed her.

We didn't go in far. She was merely showing the place.

The peculiarity of that cave is that its walls are made of ledges of stone. It's just big enough for one person to stand up in and a stream runs on the floor. You stand on two of these ledges that stick in from either side just above the water and you can rest each hand on two more ledges that come close together at the level of your middle. It's as if cut in the shape of a man or woman, a slot to draw you down into the earth.

The old woman with the sack edged on and I stopped. She stopped too and turned and looked fearfully around her sack. She was old again. The redness of her hair was gone and there was only grey and her face was crazed like dry mud in the half light, the colour of dark ash.

'Where are you taking me?' I said.

She turned fully.

'Nowhere' she said. 'It's safe here. Nobody'd find you. Further in the ledges are wide enough to lie on, and dry enough.'

The irises of her eyes seemed paler than the whites as she looked up at me.

I realized at last that she wanted me to go out and I turned and walked back.

The gorge that had been in gloom came back a burst of light and roaring water.

I felt my way along the cliff again, gingerly, the way you do if you've laid a hand on a stone and touched a slug unexpectedly and are afraid to do the same a second time.

'This way' she said.

She led me up a steep bank of earth through mud and dead leaves into immense trees. Nude keels and contorting spines of grey beech, greyer than her skin, and then further, into denser places where the scrub and trees choked, over a crest and to a hollow and up another rise where there were oaks.

We came to a place where we were high above the white river, though the mountain still stretched upward. There was no sound of water here, though the air in the leafless trees could have been a far sea. A huge oak had fallen and skewed in the earth. Its crown lay in the tops of others further down the slope and its ridged trunk was wedged in another tree's fork so that their barks had grown into one another.

'Here' she said. She walked towards the torn roots of this tree. 'It's still got leaves come spring. Is the wood dry?'

I'd been carrying the bundles so long I'd forgotten them. Holding the blanket at my neck with one hand I felt the firewood with the other, looked at it as if I knew what I was doing. I looked up and there was the fallen tree and the churned earth and she was gone.

I looked at the place where she'd stood. There was a squashed place in the mud and leaves that might have been the last place the ball of her foot had touched. I thought the mud might flex and writhe of itself as the rock had, so looked away into the branches. There was almost no movement in the air, but an arm of the half felled oak twisted and bowed a little, as if some unseen weight had settled on it.

The priest's horse. Cadell, that time, when he left the court his horse's tail arched like that.

Drizzle and the greyness overhead smudged darker here and there. Then I heard the earth speak.

'Poet.'

And the old woman's head came out of the earth, from behind the splayed fingers of the torn roots.

'Here' she said. 'Come on. Is it dry enough?' She had the held back impatience of a tired mother.

I went to the edge of the gape of earth, looked down at her. She extended a hand.

'Come on' she said.

When I think of how we were, soaked, and me near naked but for a blanket and a torn rag, and shivering, filthy and blood caked on my chin, and she standing in the hole in the earth calling me down, it's laughable in my memory, like the monk's look of consternation. But her grey face was cracked in the gloom and she stood in silence and I was afraid.

She coaxed like a mother and after a long time I edged down and there was a dry place and a poorly made hurdle laid flat. She was old and I could see the ridges of her fingernails but there was no one else and I pressed myself against her.

She fetched me water in a jug, though I don't know where from, and there was more cheese and a piece of dry meat.

It was getting colder. I looked at the plate of torn roots as we huddled together. The shreds of root were clogged with lumps of dryish mud that hung like the dags on a sheep.

'This is a safe place' she said.

I had a hand at her face. It didn't feel so withered, smoother than my own skin. My finger moved onto her lips and there was no coarse hair. My finger went in to her teeth and they were firm and even. Small. Sweet breath. I tongued my own teeth again, found the gap where they'd kicked one out. It was out entire, root and all, not broken. The sign of an old man, to lose a whole tooth so easily.

I don't remember sleeping but I suppose I must have. I remember finding myself there on the hurdle, stiff and old and more numb and my breath steamed and the cold air hurt my throat, my torn gum. The mud dags and all the earth was drenched in frost, but there was crackling and the sweetness and bitterness of woodsmoke.

I turned on the hurdle and shook some of the powdering of frost out of the blanket. All the colour was shrunk out of the world. And then, the flaring red and yellow of her fire. Some logs were stacked near it to dry. A new branch was on the fire, furrowed oak, the frost still on its moss.

The woman squatted near it, her head covered. Beside her on a stone were half a dozen arrows, a knife, and a new bow made of elm. Her hands worked, plaiting some unyielding wands. She was making a quiver. Her hands moved with strange skill. I don't know what magic she'd contrived to light the fire.

'Hello' she said, when she saw I was awake.

It was that dusk still and I didn't know whether it was morning or evening.

'We can live by this' she said, nodding to the arrows and her work.

Her face was young this time. For a moment I thought it was another woman. Her arms, where her gown fell away, were young and strong.

I dragged my blanket to the fire and huddled over the flames. You know how it is. You feel nothing until your palms are on the flame and burning. After a long time my feet and hands had enough feeling in them to ache.

'We can live by this' she said again. 'Hunting.'

I looked up to the branch that had curved under some weight. It was frostwhitened and straighter now. She was pausing in her work when I looked down but turned quickly back to it.

'I'll go back' she said. 'Give it a while. What about you? Where'll you go?'

The log that had had frozen moss on it was charred and had writhed into an arch.

'Will you go back to Iorwerth?'

The ridges in the log glowed in the deepest places with wounds that were red or paling in shifts of air. Behind me there was the wounded earth gaping like a mouth.

'How do you know this place?' I said.

The miraculous fingers paused in their work.

'It's my own country' she said.

I looked up quickly at the branch but caught sight of nothing.

'What is it?' she said.

235

I looked at her and thought she knew well enough.

She put a hand on my shoulder.

'Here' she said. 'You're shivering.'

She pulled a woollen shirt from her sack. It was rough and there was dried blood on it but I put it on and huddled in the blanket. Though I was stiff and bruised I found I had no worse injury.

Her country. I looked at the earth away from where it was blackened by the fire.

'I naven't travelled like you' she said. 'I don't know other places. My family have always lived here. I used to come here when I was a child. Come and see.'

She pulled me to my feet and led me under the low fallen trunk of the tree.

'Here' she said.

In a hollow where the feathered oakleaves lay stiff with frost, an imperfect circle of stones was placed. A few flat stones were carefully arranged like seats inside, though they were very small.

And the wave broke on her again. She lay in the frozen circle and beat the leaves, crying out.

I shivered and went back to the fire.

I listened to her crying a long time. I looked at the place just outside the scorch of fire. At last she came back to the fire and went on working.

'They used to play there' she said.


## 28

I don't know how many days we were there. I slept a lot, was often awake at night, scared of the sounds of animals. On the nights when the cold was worst hard stars and the track of Caer Gwydion looked up from under the net of branches. I tried to sing in my head

> Tonight on the hill I saw
> Arthur in his battlecar

An old song I never finished.

> Culhwch knocking at his gate
> Indeg stretched across the night
> Caer Gwydion spilt like semen
> Across the dish of heaven,
> And all the angels sang a mass
> To Christ's fathom stretched in Cygnus.

She and I outstretched on the hurdle. It was that time round the Nativity when the sun shrivels, even when it shows is glazed and pale like a dead eye, and it barely clears the mountains all day. From waking to sleeping there's hardly time to milk a cow or to eat and it's always dusk when it isn't night.

She came and went, sometimes bringing food. A hare, once, that we roasted. I never knew whether it was time to wake or sleep. She spoke to me a lot. I remember my head craned up on the hurdle and her looking across and talking but I don't remember much of what she said. Perhaps I never heard the words. When it was overcast the clouds peeled over the trees sucking and contorting into faces and caves. I lay in the gaping mouth of earth and heard her voice. When she came and touched my blanket, to straighten it or tuck it to my sides, I thought she'd lift me, ram my head into the mud where the roots had unconnected. I cried out once and she moved back from me suddenly and I saw the bent branch spring as if something had jumped from it. She was older in that moment, and her nails were long and clawed.

Mostly she was young and her voice was gentle. Sometimes her face appeared over me and hid the endless tearing and shredding of cloud.

One day she came to me out of the gloom and sat next to me. I was feeding the fire with dead logs I'd gathered. I'd started to do that. She sat close and I felt her hip against mine.

'You're better' she said.

I tongued the place where my tooth had been.

'Will you go back?' she said.

'Where to?'

'To your lord in the south.'

I couldn't think. I tried to imagine Iorwerth and the court but it was hard to remember faces. I thought of sharp eyes and a sharp nose but chubby cheeks. Eyes more alive than spring and then the dead eyes in the hare. Holding my young child above my head and feeling my arms weren't my own. Peeling away a leaf stuck to my heel.

'Will you?' she said.

I didn't answer, then said, 'What'll you do?'

She looked at the fire. 'You're better' she said. 'Another day and I'll go back.'

I tried to think where back was for her. Tumbled posts. The row of bundles. Eyes frozen and hands crabbed on air. *Hear my confession, Father.*

And he laughed and told me when he sang I'd hear his.

'What will it be like?' she said.

I shrugged. 'Either there'll be — nothing, or the French'll be installed.'

'Would they kill Gwladus too?'

'I don't know.'

But she was Rhys's sister. I tried to think. Rhys who restored Iorwerth's patrimony with a word to his friend the king. But Geffrei butchered in his stupid shoes. The yellow spear carefully positioned at the door. Yes.

'Probably' I said.

But I was alive, feeding the fire, my feet burning and my back numb. I should be rotting on a pole, staring across the plain where Brewys had felled trees, huge wounded plates of oak, to make a killing ground.

I looked up from the fire and I saw that she thought about this too.

'I don't know' I said.

'What?'

'I don't know why they let me go.'

A pause.

'I ran away' she said. 'I ran and hid in the trees and watched them do it.'

She talked but I couldn't listen. I thought I should be dead, for the man sitting down in the meadow, for the young man in the forge with Pencarn and Ithel. I should be in other flames, other frost. Instead unjointed memories. Daisies and a splash of blood. Iorwerth close, his eyes alive, a bloody arrow brandished in my face.

I think I lolled against the woman and her arm was round me and we rocked. It ought to be Christmas but there was only us and the trees, the meanness of a few people cut to pieces in a yard.

'Sh' she said.

I put my hand on her forehead. It was quite smooth. Nothing grew there but the delicate line of hair, grizzled or reddish. Saint. Angel.

'Griffri' she said.

*I know you* she'd said. I looked at her, tongued the gap in my teeth again. My name.

'How do you know me?' I said.

'You told me. You're the poet' she said.

'Yes. My name.'

'I said. You told me. You *are* known' she said. 'I've heard you sing. Before I was married I served in the court.'

'Seisyll's?'

'Of course. *The* court.'

She clung like desperation, as I did. But I looked at her again. Her hair. The face at its youngest. Almost young. Wise and grieving. Me brokenmouthed like an old ewe. If I hadn't been starved there'd have been a paunch. She'd seen me with my hair neatly trimmed, heard me sing, seen me in my best cloak.

She half laughed through her crying, sat forward and pressed a hand up to her nose, giggled and cried. Something.

'I served you mead once' she said. 'You and your father. You were ever so —' she paused and laughed '— ever so sophisticated. And you both got.' She had to stop because it was the kind of laughter that takes possession of you and breaks everything you put in its way. 'And you both got.' She had to stop again and I was giggling too by this time. Our backs on the frozen dirt and withered leaves and our feet nearly in the flames. I looked at her as we laughed. The straws of grey and red. Something familiar. 'You both got totally pissed.' Our laughing shrieked through the dead trees. We gasped as if we'd suffocate. She tried to go on talking but every word was hilarious. 'First you were full of your skin and then you had a skinful.' And again the shriek. 'You had some sort of fight with him.' And the shriek again. It was hysterical. I'd fought my father in Seisyll's beili. 'Only you were both too pissed for the punches to connect.' And again. 'We scraped you off the yard like dry shit.' Again. 'And you were grinning and your eyes were glazed like this.' She tried to stop and give me the stare but couldn't and she fell against me.

Slowly it went. It had broken on us and washed and drained away,

239

foaming, leaving us spent for a while.

She lay looking away and we were silent a long time. Her cheek, her neck, looked young. No withered flews. I cuffed a hand at the straws of red and grey. Me and Gwrgant drunk in the yard. Her saying something to me as he lay fallen in the rushes of the hall. Griffri ap Gwrgant. So she did and didn't know me. She'd gone and I'd followed, some name I called, a callow joke.

'What's your name?' I said.

The head rolled, came closer to me as it did so.

'Sigfa' she said.

Not the name I'd given her. No. It would have been asking too much. A name I'd never heard. Poet, she called me. Griffri. I was a brokenmouthed sheep who'd somehow avoided the knife.

The poet's hand was stroking her hair. Hardly grey at all.

'I remember you' he said. 'I could have loved you once.'

Did he really say that? I know he meant it, felt it like a crushing knowledge, that he'd wanted this woman, or wanted the name he'd put on her, and he'd slept while she rode away.

Then the old urgency and we rolled, two starved people, on the frozen leaves, and discovered one another's broken mouth. We got onto the hurdle and covered ourselves with the blanket, the sack under us. This is either a boastsong or a confession. I'm not sure which. She smelt of smoke and her skin was very smooth and young. In the need to press together we found the lifted clothes not enough and I almost tore her gown.

'No wait' she said. 'We'll need them.'

But later she tried to tear mine, that bloody woollen tunic that had been on one of her family, and she chewed my slack belly, tongued the mud out of my navel as if we were eighteen. Her miraculous glove that must, I suppose, have yielded way to many children was firm and moist. And when our trunks pressed together there was huge consolation. What can I call it? Some healing. Connecting. Not simple, but like the connecting of a tree with earth. Her hardened feet were raised and my bruised knees and toes were hurting on the plaits of the hurdle. It started to unweave as I pushed and we slid shut on one another. The true communion.

Her head was to the gape of earth where the roots had been and the sack slid under her so that her head was wedged against the mud. Like old lovers we went through all the chronicle of pleasure almost unknowingly. First —. Well, confession would be boastsong for certain if I detailed everything.

We slid round so she was on top of me. Far away there was a crow's voice. And she was over me with the light splaying round her head, her body young, the dugs not heavy or fallen. Then my head in the mud and a dark rim above me. The gape of earth. Beyond her the bent branch. I think it was a large crow perched on it. I think it was a crow.

It was dusk, I think, the light going, though it still seemed bright around her head. The fire, in the pale winter light, was reddening. It crackled and flared in gusts of wind.

Almighty Christ. We were almost burying ourselves in mud and I sat up, pressed against her. Her skin was wattled with cold and I felt it shudder under my cold hands. Tight together as we were she opened her eyes and I saw my own ghost in her pupils. *We ought to be dead* I thought. The pupils were an odd kind of slot and her nails dug into me. Against my palms the wattles grew hot, contorted and boiled into erupting horny skin and ringlets of fur and the claws dug into me and I grabbed at the back of her hair so her chin went up, her mouth open. The light was gone from her head and there were obscure heavings in the bone. Her chin and mouth grew forward, the nose flattened along it and then the appalling screech like a raven opening its throat and the black thing exploded from the branch, flapped out like a wet black sheet and went. The screech held unnaturally. The breasts had gone and coarse fur covered its ribs. A sweetish smell. Its claws bit through the muscles of my shoulders. A sweetish smell like corpses. The mud pressed against my head. The thing was driving me into the earth, taking me where I ought to have been.

You understand me, monk, that I was clamped as in a smith's tongs, being pushed into the fanned ashes. Perhaps it was the dead shriek in the living trees that made me hold on, the sight of its pointed black tongue. I held its throat. Its snout, muzzle, whatever it was, stayed upward, opened and I dug my fingers in, shook, screamed. Some places on it were firm and at others my fingers went in as into rotten fruit. I felt the talons go dead in my shoulders, retract a little, and it rolled from me and I beat its head against the mud, went on choking the tangle of rotted pipes where its neck had been until there was no tension in the thing. As soon as I knew it was dead a shuddering passed through me and I let it go, shook it off like slugs off the fingertips, and sprang back. I felt very hungry.

## 29

I gathered wood for the fire and built it up and stacked some to dry. I don't know whether I did that the same day. Perhaps it was the next day, or weeks later. I did that many times. Then I stripped the corpse. It had clothes and I was cold. It was blackened and indistinct in the gloom. I didn't look hard and kept away from the gape at the roots. The torn ends of the roots reached out like fingers. I tore the rags and bound my feet with them, pulled the sack out from under the thing, that was already dried and stiff as a branch, took the blanket and huddled to the fire, closed my eyes and warmed myself in the smoke.

Then daylight, oddly white, the light coming up at me from the earth, from everywhere. The slow feathers falling and the earth, the fallen trunk whitening, the blackened branch on the shattered hurdle in the gape, whitening. The voices of crows deadened and I felt where the cold feathers settled on my hair and shoulders, settled and calmly melted to nothing on my knuckles where I bunched the blanket at my chest. Then the pale eye of the sun showing obscurely through the whirl of dark flecks and being overwhelmed, fading to smirched grey under the net of branches.

I went to the corpse and it had become a woman again. Very old. No red in the hair. Snow fell on the flews, fell into the emptied sockets of the eyes, settled on the collapsed dugs, and didn't melt.

Voices.

Two unrushed young voices approaching, muffled by the snow. I climbed onto the fallen trunk and scrambled along into the fork of the standing tree, clung to the upright trunk. There was a snuffling and an animal smell. A stink of something hot and living.

Two quite small boys came over a rise towards me. They carried hazel switches and drove half a dozen pigs before them. They looked down to their feet as they talked, passed under the archway of the fallen oak beneath me. As they emerged and went on down the slope and away from me, I heard them clearly.

'Looks like a good one tomorrow.'

'About bloody time, too.'

The pigs hurried on with quick steps. I saw the knuckles moving in their backs. The noise receded and the smell began to fade. Through the trees I saw one of the switches swing and it looked oddly straight and shaped, flattened and grey like a blade. Where they'd passed there were slurrings in the snow but new feathers hid them quickly. As I watched, the pocks and slurs smoothed themselves, disappeared.

An owl called, though it was softened daylight. I held to the trunk. Though the fire was far and I was cold, I didn't want to move. There was the fire and the whitened heap of wood, the bow and few arrows, the gape and the branch, and, the other side of my tree, the small circle of stones disappearing under snow. Standing in the middle of it was a short bench.

Another voice.

Somebody laughing. Over the rise a man came, smiling and walking casually, wearing his bow across his shoulders and carrying a stick. He switched it at the snow and laughed, glanced up.

I shrank behind the trunk but I knew he'd seen me. A slight movement of my head and I saw him, the bow taut, feet rooting through snow, the iron arrowhead brushing the knuckles of his left hand. And along the shaft the eye watched me. I dodged back.

'Griffri' he said, 'Why did you kill me?'

I said, 'It wasn't me. Ask Toothless. I missed. Believe me.'

The tip of an arrow burst through the bark, touched my chest.

'It fell short, honest.'

'You should have come with her to us.'

The owl again.

Another man came over the ridge. A boy. Or a very young man, and a soldier with him. The soldier was Ithel. They held hands. They stand under the tree and look up.

'Griffri. they say, 'why did you kill us?'

They smile. Or Ithel smiles and the young man seems to from the red moon of blood in his neck.

'You should have come with her to us' the young man says. He speaks French, but I can understand him. He smiles upward, sleeping in the forge.

And every moment someone comes. A young man quacking like a duck, his torso almost split in two by a wound starting at the root of his neck.

'You should have come with her to us.'

On the bench, a small man with his cloak furled on his legs, a bowl of milk clutched in his hand.

A young man with a cloth on his face. Tall, and in a good cloak. He fingers the cloth away like this and Owain ab Iorwerth smiles. The curled redgold. The gashes in his white face open with the flexing.

'I never saw the Arglwydd Rhys' he says. 'Never married. Never held a son above my head. Never heard you sing those names you promised me. But what's that? Come with us, Griffri.'

Far up the hill a girl stands holding a small bundle. She smiles and turns away.

Then, over the rise, Ieuan, Seisyll, Dyddgu, Geffrei. A man limping, clutching at his lower leg, wearing a helmet and upholstered vest.

'Griffri' he says in French, 'why did you kill me?'

'I didn't.'

'Yes.'

'I missed.'

'You tried. I died of the wound. A glorious death. But what's that? Come with us.'

And now no snow and I'm standing on earth. Hammering rain freezing my forehead, sluicing mud under the fallen tree, melting the dirt off the old woman, and they're still there. Mud loosens in the gape, rolls and trickles from the mat of rootfingers. Some of them stir, push, work at the wet earth and a hand comes and then an arm and some of the fingers are mudclogged hair. A shoulder levers and works loose and Athrwys clambers from the mud, pulls at other roots, draws out Abram, Ynyr, Eneas with the stump of arrow in his neck. They pull at more hands. Another man, all mud. His face graven in the cheeks. He's naked and hacked and I think he's Iorwerth. No, wait. Morgan. He's got a knife and he cuts the bowstring that holds his mouth shut, rubs his stiff jaw and smiles.

'Griffri' he says, indicates the mud ironically. 'My grandfather was a king. But what's — ? Well, stop this rigmarole. Griffri, come with us. See.'

He gestures to the gape and the rain stops. Cloud clears, makes a break of rich blue, then dulls and frost comes on everything, on the old woman, on all the dead standing watching me. It thaws and there's pale winter sun low in the. He gestures to the gape and they all reach, grasp, drag out another rootman. A youngish man with dark hair and cleanshaven, not muddy like the rest. He smiles, extends a hand. I take, it, kneel and press the palm onto my crown.

*Hear my boastsong, father.*

*Sometimes no song is best, my son.*

I look up and against the branchtangle and low sun he still smiles. Owlsound. Watersound. The thawed ice moving. His head split by an appalling\ wound.

'No no no no no' he says. 'Not that.'

The wound heals itself.

'This.'

Still smiling he gestures to the black vertical wound in his slightly paunched belly.

'Too late now' he says. 'But let's not get sentimental. After all, it's only death.'

And all the dead mutter assent.

'Gwrgant, why did they let me go?'

'I've often wondered about that.'

Seisyll says, 'He means the French.'

'Oh them.' The smiling man nods. 'Yes. How did he look, Seisyll, your murderer? And what did you sing, Cadri? Yes. The song to god. And buggered it up I suppose. Out of tune in the treble? Know your lines? How did Brewys look at you when they told him about your song? Jupiter does what the hell he likes. Sparing's a kind of oppression. People who untune the world need the hugest consolations. He probably loves his children and his dogs, cries at sad songs and loves the shapes of hills. Murder makes men sentimental. The song to god at the Nativity. You're so predictable, Griffrad. But then, so was he, though with the extra tang of irony. You should note that, Gradri. On the high altar of his shit cathedral he made his great oblation with the blood of men.'

'He looked dead himself. White and wasted as a corpse.'

'You should see yourself. Oh yes, he suffers too. So here you are, a bargain for his soul.'

He looks round at the gap he came out of. The rotted woman, her loosed jaw fallen on her chest.

'I see you already improve on his example, in your minor way. So you caught up with her at last. And this. Making your own offering here, in the true church.'

'I recognized what she was. I knew her.'

He smiles. 'Did you? And Brewys saw in you a holy man. You recognized reflections in two mirrors. That's all.' The smile goes and the hand stirs, brushes on my forehead. 'But I'd have done no different in spite of this. You tried to sing in those places.'

He stares and the light around his head turns to bruises under the branchtangle. The bruises open, peel away from a red sun like a wound and there's the cleaving in his head. No branches. The open mountaintop. Wind drags his hair across his face and he spreads his arms, looks down at me.

'Come with us now' he says, half turns, gestures towards the gape of earth.

I turn away and run, stumble through the trees towards the horses and the people.

I stumble against a man. He smiles, has no teeth.

'Let me take some of it' he says.

His shoulders are crooked and he wears a good cloak and half of his face is burnt. I push past.

In a hollow there's rich sunlight and the air's warm. Huge flowers splash white under the trees. A boy comes towards me and the light's behind him, green light through the leaves. There's bread in his hand. The hand hangs at his thigh. He comes close watching me without expression. Brown eyes. Dark hair but pale skin. I think he might have offered anyway but I snatch the yellow bread and cuff him away. He collapses into feathery oakleaves. I gorge on the bread. And there, in the circle of stones, the mud in my mouth, clagged on the back of my throat, and only the gapped bare trees and late daylight.

# 30

The true communion, did I say? Well, what truth is is problematical. I don't know how I lived that winter, but I know a time came when I, as it were, woke, and by the length of the day and the way the light hung in the trees and by a warmth in things, I knew that it was spring.

I walked with the bow and the few arrows up to the higher places, towards the open mountains. I don't know if I had any idea which way I was going. I started to see. From up there, the filigree of coming leaves. The colour of the dirt. I'd looked at it by the fire and clogged on the roots but I hadn't seen. It wasn't the red earth of the great river that runs past Brewys's castle but the yellowbrown earth of the northern part of Gwynllwg.

Think of the rowan. It's leaves are narrow and long like small javelin heads and cluster in pairs along green stalks. If you bring a leaf down you look at the dark green of the upper side. But underneath it's pale, the veins exact and clean as a girl's hair.

I lay for a long time and looked up at these leaves. The sunlight on them made them paler still. On a near twig I saw all the fineness of the tiny threads that wove the leaf. Nothing in a book was so intricately done. A small greybrown bird sleek as a little otter moved gently on a branch and flew a little way to another silently. He gleaned insects with his sharp beak, undulated as he moved. Then more. A household of these birds making some low, soft noise as they flowed among the leaves. I swear I'd never seen these birds before. All things I saw now washed and soothed my eyes. The leaves and the otterbirds. I thought the tree should tear up its roots, the birds scream. But they didn't.

I've nearly finished. This would be a good place. Leave him under the tree.

You've heard something of what happened after I limped back to the court, seven years ago. Instead of the cloak, I had a muddy blanket round my head. And when I stood there skewed and white and

247

unwound it from me I think they expected to see a corpse, and some thought they did.

I was amazed that things went on. Tribute cattle were still driven, dogs scratched themselves in the yard, and though they'd all heard and were shocked and there were refugees in the country, I thought people didn't understand.

I had to talk to Ior — no, to Hywel — a long time, though I think I hardly made sense. Why did they let you go? A bargain for his soul. A ghost told me, and I had to fight a.

When Christmas came I was called to Rhys's great feast in his stone castle in the west. Can you imagine it? Two soldiers went with me and I was supposed to sing for the chair, but I couldn't. Rhys spoke to me in a room apart, with some soldiers. A long time and the same questions. A bargain for his. His face was close to mine, looking, expecting a good answer. His unfamiliar western accent. I don't know how much sense I made. He glanced from me to the men around him, sat back. It was then he gave me the bonehandled knife, had its blade sprinkled with holy water. A droplet ran along it and gathered the candlelight at its point. So I was to lead the men who extracted galanas for the murder of his brotherinlaw and the abduction of his sister.

You know this. I was with Morgan ap Seisyll at Merthyr Dingat when we killed Randwlff de Poyr who was Siryf Henffordd, and a dozen of his best men. We beat him with spears into the mud of the ditch and I stuck Rhys's knife into his neck, here, just below the ear. Not much blood came out. I think he was already dead. And I was with Morgan ap Seisyll when he went to destroy the fortress at Abergafenni last summer. They tell me it's not rebuilt yet. Brewys escaped and I'm too old now for all that, though Morgan I dare say, will try again. And this has been the crowning honour of my old age, to receive Rhys's commission in these matters.

That's the official version. I had to do all this to avoid execution. And I've felt nothing. What I've told you is enough for that to be clear, but after Toothless —

Did I mention that earlier? After my return and I before I went to Rhys's feast I sat one evening with Toothless at the old court. He'd lost his hair by then, as well as his teeth. We sat among the rushes with a jug of mead. He's a shy man, happy to sit a long time with no words. I'd just heard that I was to go to Rhys at Christmas. He'd acquired his belly, too, by then. Toothless, I mean. He sat behind it uncomfortably.

'You all right?' he said at last.

'Fine.'

'Old age eh.'

'Yes.'

'It's a bastard.'

A pull at the jug.

'Hm.'

'Like life.'

'Indeed.'

'That's a bastard too.'

We went on in this profound vein for some time.

'It's hard' I said.

'Yes' he said. 'Hard. That's for bloody sure.'

Another pull at the jug.

'Well' he said. 'And will you go?'

'What?'

'To Rhys at Christmas. Will you go?'

'What choice have I got?'

He nodded acknowledgement of this piece of insight.

'True.'

He paused a long time, pursed his lips and eyed the jug.

'So' he said. 'And what really did happen?'

I looked at the jug and then at the hairless head, the toothless mouth, the downcast eyes that avoided me.

'What?'

'Oh' he said. 'You know. What happened, then?'

'It was like I said.'

'Indeed.' He looked up.

'It was.'

He stared, then his eyes dropped again.

'Think Rhys'll have that?' he said.

'It's the truth.'

'You might not've lasted till Christmas if Rhys's messenger hadn't come.'

'Why not?'

He looked closely at me, half smiling. 'Don't you know?' He looked down. Pursed. Another pull. 'Anyway, as you say, there's no choice. That's the way of things. They've got too much and we haven't got any. Like Brewys. Look at the choices he could make and look at what he went and did.' He sniffed. 'We all have to do things we don't like. Know what I hate doing?'

He waited and I had to say,

'What?'

'I had to drown a cat once. I didn't like that. Kittens are easy. The cat scratched the baby's face and my wife insisted. Slippery buggers, not like kittens. They're not interested in being dead.'

I thought of the woman who'd hidden in the trees. The stiff bundles of her children. All my refusals at the gape. Toothless talked. About his skill in arms, about how difficult it was to drown a cat, about not having any choice.

'Then again' he said, 'you have to see it in its place. I suppose my wife was right. A big he. Black and white. Piss came out of him like a battering ram at a gate. Still. No choice.' He looked at the jug again, the rushes. 'Like the time we killed Eneas. I didn't like that either.'

He looked up and saw something in my face.

'What?' I said.

'You were still a boy, weren't you?' He struggled to remember. 'I wasn't very old myself. It was bloody hard. I waited. Let him shoot first.

'Him?'

'Iorwerth. Caught him in the back. Then I let go as he was going down and it went in the neck. I —'

But he never told me what he was, or if he did I didn't hear. I'd thought that nothing mattered. That nothing could be worse than what I knew. Toothless wasn't talking. Stared at me.

'You did know?' he said.

I couldn't answer. I thought of Gwrgant looking up, resting a hand on the quiver hung from the saddle. A good man. An intelligent soldier. The dark hair in wet ringlets and a thread of black blood against the tallow of the skin. Threads of white smoke standing in the air, the jolted candles snuffed. And before that, two men across the corpse. *I'm afraid you are too much like me.*

'Don't tell Iorwerth I said anything' Toothless said. 'Poor old bugger. Dragging his foot around. Pretending he's all right. He knows it's god's answer to him.'

'Why did you do it?' I said.

He looked up from the raised jug. Again the half believing half smile.

'Well we had to get Morgan to — .' He stopped, shook his head. 'Never mind.' Took a pull. 'Look, I did it because I had no choice. Go on. Don't act so surprised.'


## 31


Since Seisyll's death there've been no new songs. When Hywel's daughter, Gwenllian, was born I couldn't sing. I had to leave it for that bombastic northerner, Llywarch ap Llywelyn. He did a good job, though Hywel's new love of peace — as the latest method of hanging on to his land — must have rankled.

Even for my own children I haven't sung. Cristin, when I came back, was uncertain of me a long time, and I couldn't touch her. I thought of Eneas. Iorwerth looking away. Gwrgant with his hand on the quiver. Iorwerth commanding a poem.

'Cristin' I said. 'Once you came back to me. Now I've come back to you.'

I'd stood crooked by a fallen tree and she'd mistaken me.

'When did I come back to you?'

I reminded her. How Angharad had sent her, told her what was in Cristin's own mind when old Morgan was giving law once at the old court.

'Your memory' she said. 'Yes. Angharad sent me.'

I remembered. We walked. She didn't want to go to the house. Into the untamed woodland. She insisted. Gwrgant and the priest with the sick cow. The looped trunk. We lay there. And then some uncertainty. She spoke. A story of brothers, but she didn't finish it. The arrow across my neck. And then the corpses like driftwood.

She saw me thinking of these things and she turned and walked away.

Like driftwood. And during my illness a great tribute of cattle was driven away. Into Senghenydd. Morgan hacked, the bowstring round his jaw, drawn to the border to talk of my release. Iorwerth hitting Hywel over Owain's gashed corpse. *I'm afraid you are too much like me.* Yes.

Cristin was the only person ever to ask me directly if I had a hand in Seisyll's death.

'You know I didn't' I said.

Her face is thinner now, the colour leaving her hair.

I said, 'And what do you know about Gwrgant's death?'

She looked at me a long time.

'You always knew' she said. 'It was his and her idea. That's why she sent me to you. But I did want to come back, though perhaps not like that. I didn't have much choice. Anyway, it made us safe. I only did it on condition you weren't hurt.'

'You led me into the trees to be taken.'

'And released.'

Released. Sometimes god releases me. How we know ourselves. Her eyes are less alive. Have you seen? The true church. Even there we know nothing. We don't know one another or ourselves.

I thought of the white corpses stretched out, the thrush gathering dead grass for a nest. The two crouched soldiers with spears. The same two I'd seen with Iorwerth and Toothless once, going to hunt and do a little business at the border.

She opened her palms, shrugged. 'Can you imagine what Iorwerth might have done to you if I hadn't been close to Angharad? I wanted us to be safe. My family —'

She stopped.

Yes. A few cattle, the meadow, a regular share of the virgin fees.

But she was right.

We continue. One day the children will look after us. I think when Iorwerth dies, which can't be long now, my share of the virgin fee will stop. Would I like a son to be pencerdd? It'd be worth it for the pay.

That's all.

## 32

Now you know me better than I know myself.

Was I brisker this time? An hour's sleep to us, anyway, before the Night Office. You look unsettled. Better to have left me under the tree, eh? The protecting rowan. But my talk with Cristin didn't hurt as much as you might suppose. It was after I walked from the tree that I saw my last ghost — though not a ghost. I'll end with a meeting between two of the dead.

After I got up, full of seeing and the otterbirds, I walked out onto an immense high moor of heatherclad peat. As I walked in the spring sun I had the sensation that this place was without boundaries, that I could walk forever and there'd be only the springy plants.

After a long time I looked down from a high place on the moor and in front of me there were mountains. The moor dropped and then became a series of ridges rising to become mountains running south, away from me, fanned like huge fingers poised on some chord.

I've said before, I don't know if I knew where I was walking to. The valleys between the ridges were treed, part green with the early leaves, the paler greens of spring.

I followed the course of a stream down, then got onto the root of a ridge, followed it as it lifted and broadened, up, out of the trees again, to make a wide, heathery back. I looked to left and right across valleys to the neighbouring ridges and as I walked the shapes followed a familiar line. I stopped, looked to my right. There were deer above the trees on the far slope of the valley. Over my shoulder, northward and far away, beyond the moor I'd walked across, there was a mountain with two peaks. I looked south but couldn't see the ocean, only the endless ridges.

I went down the slope, off the ridge, came in sight of the edge of the woodland. The heather gave way to better pasture. Goats, and further down, a few thin cows. A curve of pasture angled southward, steepening to the course of a stream.

The hafod looked shrunk, recently rebuilt at the edge of the trees, but not well put together. Smoke was filtering through the thatch. There were no people outside. I approached, put the bow and rough quiver by the jamb, called a greeting and, stooping, stepped in through the open door.

There was smoke and the smell of cheese, stew, wormwood. Withered herbs were hung in bunches here and there. There was a small fire and on a stone near it the pot of stew. An old woman squatted nearby, her elbows on her knees and one hand at her cheek. She was looking at me but in the half light I couldn't see her face clearly. She extended her hands briefly.

'God's welcome, visitor.'

With the economy of exhausted old age she gestured for me to sit. There was a silence. She was observing the etiquette of not asking where I'd come from or where I was going, which was just as well as I didn't know.

'This is a lovely place' I sàid, 'this valley below us. What's the river that runs in it called?'

'It's called the Gwedog' she said. 'The others are down the bottom. They'll be up shortly. So.' Her face turned to me. The oldest face I've ever seen, hanging away from the skull like a loose mask, the eyelids dragged down, gaping red at the lower edges. The hand at her face was knobbed with arthritis. 'Eat' she said.

She put a little stew in a bowl, and slowly, as if her back was stiff, reached some cheese from a bag hung from a timber.

'Not much water' she said. 'I used to fetch the water but I can't any more.' And when I'd finished and wiped my fingers on the blanket, 'You were hungry.'

'I've travelled a long way. I serve Iorwerth ab Owain.'

'Still alive is he? My husband — peace to his dust — fought for old Owain.'

She gave me more stew but I couldn't eat it.

'Is it your children who're coming up?' I said.

'Grandchildren mostly. Most of my children are dead.' She was matter of fact about it, had lived through her grief. 'I wish god'd let me follow them. Iorwerth ab Owain. I lost a son to Owain too. My youngest.'

'How was that?' I said.

'Oh he was taken to become a poet.' And she explained.

'What happened to him?' I said.

She shrugged. 'He died there.'

'When?'

'Years and years ago. My son Heilyn — peace to his dust too — Heilyn went to visit him with some man who called. I forget. Off they went. I was ill. Heilyn thought news of him would do me good. When they got there he was dead. Some illness. Still only a child. I always thought it'd happen. God never forgave Owain Wan's family for the time his father fought with the French. That's what my mother told me. Poor Heilyn didn't know how to tell me. Men are no good at talking about anything real. So that was him and Berddig gone.'

Stew and cheese were sticking to my teeth. I thought of the water from Cadog's spring, slopping and glittering in the pails. Lleucu young. A beautiful young woman. The figures coming out of the billow of trees. Gifts for Non and Mair. A good trip and perhaps a girl at Seisyll's court. How had Gwrgant done it? A quiet talk with Heilyn as they travelled, when the soldier lagged or went ahead. Heilyn, perhaps, haggled. Then settled for a horse. Bought. He'd sung no song for Cadi. Couldn't face. Tried to make a space in me for himself.

'Berddig in battle' the old woman said. 'Well, of wounds, so they say. I never saw him. They never brought him back.'

'He must have been a brave man' I said. 'Poets sing about men like that.'

She snorted.

'He was a bloody fool' she said, 'and he was running away. Mallt. Peace to her dust. He couldn't face me after Mallt got.' The knobbed hand came across the grey face. 'What's it to you.'

It was said like that. Not a question.

The hand moved away, the face cleared, as if all that was wiped from her. She was quiet and looked more closely at me.

'You live there?' she said. 'At the prince's court? You might have known the little boy. He'd be about your age, I'd say, if he'd lived. Or no. A bit younger, I'd think. Do you remember him?'

'No' I said.

*255*

# *Glossary*

| | |
|---|---|
| Adda | Adam |
| Annwn | The underworld |
| arglwydd | lord |
| bardd teulu | poet to the war band |
| beili | courtyard (French origin) |
| Cacr Gwydion | The Milky Way |
| dadolwch | reconciliation, a poem of reconciliation |
| distain | steward at a lord's court |
| galanas | death feud or death fee |
| hafod | summer dwelling |
| iarll | earl |
| Mair | Mary |
| marwnad | death poem, elegy |
| pencerdd | chief poet |
| penteulu | war band chief |
| plygain | early morning service at Christmas |
| prydydd | poet |
| taeog (pl. taeogion) | approximate equivalent of serf |
| teulu | war band (in medieval times only. In modern Welsh teulu means family) |
| uchelwr | nobleman |

# People in the Story

| | |
|---|---|
| Griffri ap Berddig | the narrator |
| Gwrgant ap Rhys* | a poet |
| Non | Gwrgant's wife |
| Mair ferch Gwrgant | their daughter |
| Cadwallon ap Gwrgant | their son |
| Morgan ab Owain Wan* | prince of Gwynllwg |
| Rhagnell | his wife |
| Owain ap Morgan (Pencarn)* | their son |
| Iorwerth ab Owain Wan* | Morgan's brother |
| Angharad ferch Uchdryd* | Iorwerth's wife |
| Owain ab Iorwerth* | their son |
| Hywel ab Iorwerth* | his brother |
| Cristin | Angharad's maid |
| Seisyll ap Dyfnwal* | prince of Gwent Uwchcoed |
| Ieuan ap Seisyll ap Rhiryd* | penteulu to Seisyll |
| Dyddgu ferch Owain Wan* | Seisyll's wife, Morgan's sister |
| Morgan ap Seisyll* | their son |
| Gwladus* | Seisyll's second wife |
| Geffrei* | son of Seisyll and Gwladus |
| Ifor Fychan ap Meurig* | prince of Senghenydd |
| Rhys Ddu | his storyteller |
| Dafi | soldier to Ifor |
| Selyf | soldier to Ifor |
| Nicol* | Bishop of Llandâf |
| Cadell | a priest |
| Heilyn | Griffri's brother |
| Meilyr* | a madman |
| Rhun | a blacksmith |
| Abram | |
| Athrwys | |
| Eneas | soldiers to Morgan and |
| Toothless | Iorwerth |
| Ynyr | |

Ithel                  soldier to Pencarn
Andras                 archer to Hywel ab Iorwerth
Llecu                  servant to Gwrgant
Gwilym Brewys*         Arglwydd Brycheiniog
Randwlf de Poyr*
Sigfa
An old woman